Portraits From Ayodhya

Scharada Dubey has been a college lecturer, a radio announcer and a producer of video features for television. As Scharada Bail, she has penned several children's books, including travelogues such as *Footloose on the West Coast* and *Malwa On My Mind*, and biographical volumes like *Icons of Social Change* and *Growing Up*. Scharada set up the Sahriday Samiti in Faizabad, Uttar Pradesh, to work for the resolution of man-animal conflicts, which led to the title, *Monkeys in My Backyard* (Scholastic, 2011). Scharada now lives and works in Lucknow.

Portraits From Ayodhya

Living India's Contradictions

SCHARADA DUBEY

TRANQUEBAR PRESS
An imprint of westland ltd
61, II Floor, Silverline Building, Alapakkam Main Road, Maduravoyal, Chennai 600095
93, I Floor, Sham Lal Road, Daryaganj, New Delhi 110002

First published in India in TRANQUEBAR by westland ltd 2012

Copyright © Scharada Dubey 2012

Scharada Dubey asserts the moral right to be identified as the author of this work.

10 9 8 7 6 5 4 3 2 1

ISBN: 978-93-81626-21-4

Typeset in Aldine401 BT by SÜRYA, New Delhi

To
Him who resides at Hanuman Garhi
and in the hearts of all pilgrims who approach Ayodhya.

And to Gopal Krishna:
the reason I came here.

Contents

CONTENTS

Acknowledgements

A book of this nature is intrinsically tied up with many people who lend support, encouragement, provide information or insights, and highlight any mistakes or oversights that come to their notice. *Portraits from Ayodhya* could not have become what it has without the cooperation of all the twenty-five subjects profiled in this book, and I am grateful to each one for the time, thoughts and hospitality they offered me.

Kanishka Gupta of Writer's Side helped immensely in propelling this idea forward and putting me on the Tranquebar list! He has also kept me anchored and focussed all through the writing, and special thanks go to him.

From Faizabad and Ayodhya, thanks are also due to Shitla Singh, Suman Gupta and Amarnath Verma of the Faizabad-based newspaper *Jan Morcha*, senior journalist K.P. Singh, Dr Anil Singh from the Department of Hindi at Saket Inter-College, Avinash Kumar of the Ayodhya Shodh Sansthan, Ram Prakash Tripathi of *Dainik Jagran*, Om Prakash Pande, indefatigable guide of Ayodhya, Comrades Dinesh Singh and Vinod Singh, Dr Ramakant Pandey of Sriram Hospital, Ayodhya, and his lovely wife, Poonam, who offered me sweet sisterhood. Among the sadhus, thanks should also go to Jagadguru Purushottamacharya of the Sugriva Qila temple of Ayodhya, who was kind enough to explain some points about the Ramanuj and Ramanand traditions to me, for which I am extremely grateful. My sincere thanks to the Ayodhya Shodh Sansthan at Tulsi Smarak Bhavan, Ayodhya and the ever-friendly help provided by its manager, Avinashji.

ACKNOWLEDGEMENTS

Ravish Kumar of NDTV, whose 'Ravish ki Report' had done such a thorough exploration of today's Ayodhya on television, and Dr Purushottam Agarwal of JNU, who made the kind offer to read some chapters also must be thanked.

Thanks are due to my friends, for cheering me on in Facebook posts, to my mother-in-law, Krishna Devi Verma, who sustained and nourished me throughout the process of interviews and writing, and most of all, to my children, Shivani and Shishir Bail, who have been with me on this from the inception, have accompanied me on some interviews, and have given me the gift of unstinting belief and support.

Finally, to my editors, Dharini Bhaskar and Renuka Chatterjee, for their patience, persistence and all-encompassing kindness.

I hope the book does justice to the immense goodwill I have received from all the above, and from dozens of unnamed people in Faizabad and Ayodhya.

SCHARADA DUBEY
December 2011

Foreword

In an iconic photograph dating back to 1999, that captures the spirit of Ayodhya like few words can, a group of people is shown standing by the steps of the Faizabad district courtrooms. In the centre is the mercurial Paramhans Ramchandra Das. Beside him stands his friend and legal opponent, Hashim Ansari. By Paramhans's side stands Zafaryab Jilani, the lawyer who has represented the Sunni Wakf Board for years. A smiling mahant Bhaskar Das of the Nirmohi Akhara stands in front of the first three. The picture captures a priceless moment – when the whole group was sharing a smile over some small matter, even as they engaged in a decades-old litigation battle against one another. In Ayodhya, such contradictions exist without causing any comment. Truth lies in paradox.

The property dispute in Ayodhya, in which all these individuals were involved for years, lies at the heart of the events that have convulsed our nation from the mid-1980s. But it cannot be said to be the cause of these events. It was the manner in which this dispute was picked up and projected to the country, as a clash between two faiths, that unleashed hate and bloodshed and repeatedly tested the resolve of a secular democracy.

This book is not an attempt at tracing the steps of the movement for a Rama temple, so 'Ayodhya' became synonymous with a troubled India. There have been several excellent studies of this, the most notable of which are *Creating a Nationality: The Ramjanmabhumi Movement and Fear of the Self* by Ashis Nandy, Shikha Trivedy, Shail Mayaram and Achyut Yagnik (Oxford India,

2005) and the documentary film, *Raam ke Naam*, made by Anand Patwardhan in 1992. Apart from these, there are valuable accounts of the build-up to the temple movement in Ayodhya itself, in the work of Peter Van der Veer, a scholar from the University of Utrecht, who lived here and observed firsthand the initial meetings organized to drum up support for the temple in 1984.

If I had any reason to write this book at all, it was to look at what has happened to Ayodhya and its people so many years after their lives were overtaken by 'the Ayodhya issue'. But since looking at their individual portraits is an incomplete experience without having a grasp of the background of events from recent Ayodhya history, I have chosen to provide a chronology of events surrounding the Babri Masjid-Rama Janmabhoomi case, the developments that affected the lives of each of the twenty-five people profiled in this book.

The land in the Babri Masjid-Rama Janmabhoomi area came under dispute in 1885, when the first suit was filed claiming rights over it. This was done by the Nirmohi Akhara, who cite traditional rights over this land, going back several centuries to when *akharas* were first set up to protect the Hindu faith. Coincidentally, this was also the year the Indian National Congress was born.

Under this suit, Mahant Raghubar Das' application to build a temple on land adjoining the disputed structure was rejected by the Faizabad Deputy Commissioner. An aggrieved Das then filed a title suit in a Faizabad court against the Secretary of State for India, seeking permission to build a temple on the *chabutara* or raised platform in the outer courtyard of the disputed structure.

Dismissing the suit, the then Faizabad magistrate announced, given that the alleged demolition of an original Rama temple by Mir Baqi had occurred over three hundred and fifty years ago, in

1528, it was 'too late now' to remedy the grievance. 'Maintain the status quo. Any innovation may cause more harm than any benefit,' the court had said.

However the case was revived in 1950, due to the events of the intervening night of 22-23 December 1949, when the idols of Rama, Lakshman, Bharat and Shatrughan, depicted as children, were placed inside the Babri Masjid by a group of persons. An FIR was lodged alleging that fifty to sixty people had broken the locks of the structure and installed a Rama idol and several other Hindu idols and articles of worship.

Following the filing of this police complaint, the structure was attached six days later, and placed in the custody of receiver Priya Dutt Ram, appointed by the Faizabad additional city magistrate. A scheme of management was drawn up by the magistrate; the receiver was to ensure that the idol was worshipped through a *pujari*. People in Ayodhya became accustomed to this form of worship, and it went on peacefully.

In 1950, the matter was revived in the courts through a clutch of suits that continue to be heard to date, in 2011. The first case was filed on 16 January 1950 by Hindu Mahasabha member, Gopal Singh Visharad, and Paramhans Ramchandra Das, mahant of the Digambar Akhada in Ayodhya. Both had filed a civil suit in the Faizabad court against some district officials and Muslims. They sought an injunction against the removal of the idols and demanded permission for uninterrupted *puja* and *darshan*. An interim court order in these cases ruled that the idols should remain in place. In that same year, lawyer Umesh Chandra Pandey appealed that the gates be unlocked and free entry allowed for puja and darshan. However, this appeal was not a part of the title suit over the land.

On 26 April 1955, the Faizabad court confirmed their interim order, letting the idols remain in place for regulated puja and darshan. On 17 December 1959, the Nirmohi Akhara and its mahant filed a suit against the court receiver and UP government seeking delivery of the property to itself. This was the third title suit for the land and a revival of the demand that mahant Raghubar Das had made in 1885.

The next milestone in the tortured legal history of the 2.77 acres of land in Ayodhya is the filing of a suit on 18 December 1961 by the Sunni Central Wakf Board. The Board sought the declaration of the structure as a mosque, the handover of the plot to itself, and the removal of the idols and other articles of worship. This was the fourth suit. On 6 January 1964, all the four suits relating to the land were combined.

While this was the legal history of the dispute, as a part of everyday life people had now become accustomed to worshipping the idols on a small and peaceful scale at the Babri Masjid-Rama Janmabhoomi site. One sadhu who conducted an *akhand kirtan*, the unbroken chanting of Rama's name near the site, received offerings in cash and kind from the pilgrims who arrived there. The place was only one of many temples in Ayodhya and did not receive visitors on the scale of Hanuman Garhi, Kanak Bhavan or even Nageshwar Nath.

This is how things remained till 1984, when the Vishwa Hindu Parishad (VHP) began its campaign to build a Rama temple at the site.

On 1 February 1986, the District Judge at Faizabad accepted lawyer Umesh Pandey's thirty-six-year-old plea to allow for a darshan and puja at the Janmabhoomi site and directed the Uttar Pradesh government to open the locks of the grille behind which the idols had been placed. The popular perception is that although this was a decision by the court, it was seen to have the backing of the then Prime Minister Rajiv Gandhi. In this same year, the VHP formed the Rama Janmabhoomi Nyas, a trust set up to oversee the construction of a temple for Rama at his birthplace in Ayodhya.

Rattled by the formation of this trust, prominent Muslim leaders in turn formed the Babri Masjid Action Committee in February 1986. Following this, the Sunni Central Wakf Board challenged the 1 February order of the Faizabad magistrate on 12 May 1986. Meanwhile, out of court, the VHP had begun mobilizing people across the country in large numbers to lend their support to a proposed temple at Ayodhya. In their appeal, one that was emotionally loaded, they exhorted people to come forward and offer *kar-seva* (actual physical labour) at the temple site. The calendar of the VHP campaign and its confrontations with the government at the centre and in Uttar Pradesh during the term of Mulayam Singh Yadav have been detailed in Chapter 17 of this book.

On 16 December 1987, the Uttar Pradesh government sought to transfer all the Ayodhya title suits from the Faizabad court to the Allahabad High Court. The matter had now become too important a national issue for it to be left at the district court level. However, the number of litigants in the various title suits was set to increase once again when a fifth title suit was filed in July 1989 by retired high court judge, Deoki Nandan Agrawal, on behalf of Rama Lalla Virajman (the deity of young Rama, installed at the site), making Rama himself a party to the case.

By this time, waves of kar-sevaks from different parts of the country had begun to arrive in Ayodhya, in response to the VHP, the BJP and other Sangh Parivar outfits. Because of such arrivals and the public meetings being held in Ayodhya, on 14 August

1989, the High Court restrained political parties from disturbing the status quo at the disputed structure.

On 25 October 1989 the High Court allowed the Uttar Pradesh government to take possession of land around the structure but later, on an appeal from Muslim groups, set aside the acquisition of the 2.77 acres adjacent to the disputed structure. It prohibited any permanent construction. Following this order, the Uttar Pradesh government was left with 42.09 acres around the disputed site in its possession, with only 2.77 acres having been surrendered after the appeal from the Muslim groups. These 2.77 acres effectively became the core of the Babri Masjid-Rama Janmabhoomi dispute. The government in office at that time was the Congress, led by N.D. Tiwari. This was followed by Mulayam Singh Yadav taking over the reins of office with BJP support in December 1989.

Meanwhile, on 10 November 1989, the Congress government at the centre allowed *shilanyas* or a foundation-stone laying ceremony to be performed by the VHP outside the 2.77 acres. With this, effectively, the foundation for a Rama temple had been laid at the threshold of the disputed site.

The Bharatiya Janata Party's relationship with Mulayam Singh Yadav rapidly soured due to his staunch opposition to the temple movement and insistence on maintaining law and order by controlling the large crowds of kar-sevaks arriving in Ayodhya. The culmination of this was seen on 30 October 1990, and 2 November 1990, when the police fired on kar-sevaks in Ayodhya resulting in the deaths of a few people. The rest of Mulayam Singh's short term witnessed political crises, ending with him handing over the reins to the BJP's Kalyan Singh by January 1991.

On 20 March 1992, Chief Minister Kalyan Singh transferred

the 42.09 acres around the disputed site in possession of the Uttar Pradesh government to a private trust, the Rama Janmabhoomi Nyas. The VHP and RSS were trustees of the Nyas.

The lead characters of the Rama Janmabhoomi Nyas and the ideologues of the VHP and BJP were now engaged in a cat and mouse game with the government of P.V. Narasimha Rao at the centre. On 27 November 1992, the Supreme Court permitted symbolic kar-seva at the shilanyas site at the Uttar Pradesh government's assurance that there would not be a law and order problem, and no harm would come to the existing structure. Meanwhile, hearings in the title suit continued; the court was to pass an order on 4 December 1992, which was postponed to 11 December 1992, which would have given further clarity on how and up to which point kar-sevaks and worshippers could approach the disputed structure.

Before such orders could be passed, however, on 6 December 1992, the structure of the Babri Masjid was demolished by mobs of kar-sevaks. When the structure of the masjid came down, the Hindu idols that had been kept there in December 1949 briefly disappeared from public view. Chaos reigned at the site following this, and security forces were able to capture the site back only by the morning of 7 December, by which time the idols had been 'reinstalled'. There is a lot of conjecture in this book about what happened to the idols when the debris of the masjid was falling, and several possible scenarios have emerged in conversations with different subjects.

With the idols now housed in a tent surrounded by the flattened remains of the disputed structure, on 1 January 1993, the High Court ordered a meaningful darshan for devotees on a plea by the VHP. Just over a year later, on 7 January 1993, the Centre acquired the entire disputed land through an Act, and got the president to ask for the Supreme Court's opinion on whether there was an ancient Hindu temple at the site. At this time, the government promised to do everything to implement the court's opinion.

On 24 October 1994, the Supreme Court in a majority decision declined to consider this presidential reference and returned the case to the Lucknow bench of Allahabad High Court.

Another wave of kar-sevaks were returning home to Gujarat in February 2002, when the train in which they were travelling caught fire at the Godhra station. This triggered one of the worst riots in independent India, in Gujarat, and led to the widespread destruction of Muslim homes and property and the death of Muslim citizens. The horrors of these riots doubtless weighed on the minds of the judges hearing the plaints in the different Ayodhya title suits. The High Court on 13-14 March 2002 banned all religious activity, symbolic or actual, at the site. Further, it asked for excavations to be undertaken by the Archaeological Society of India in 2003 to determine whether a Hindu temple of antiquity had existed beneath the structure of the Babri Masjid.

Meanwhile, after the BJP had come to power at the centre with Atal Bihari Vajpayee as the prime minister on two different occasions, and conditions for a Rama temple to be built at the disputed site had still not materialized, the movement gradually lost steam. The struggles of the BJP to stay afloat in coalition politics and their craven surrender to terrorists in the Kandahar hijacking case in 1999 also dented their credibility – their tough, nationalist image. The Ayodhya case continued to be heard in the courts and the status quo remained the same in Ayodhya. The only noteworthy developments were the barricading of the entire complex, and a terrorist attack by suspected LeT terrorists on

5 July 2005. Each twist in the Ayodhya story rocked the nation, with the citizens dreading a return to the disturbed times of the 1990s.

When a division bench of the Allahabad High Court was to pronounce judgement in the Ayodhya title suits on 30 September 2010, state and central government agencies prepared for the day on a war footing. In Uttar Pradesh, very strict policing could be observed across the state, with Ayodhya awash in a sea of blue and khaki uniforms. Life came to a standstill several days before the judgement. The judges indeed had a tough task before them. Some of the issues they had to decide on were:

Was the demolished structure a mosque as claimed by Muslim organizations? If it was a mosque, then when was it built and by whom—the Mughal emperor Babar or his Awadh governor, Mir Baqi Tashqandi?

Was it built at the site of a Hindu temple after demolishing the latter?

And had Muslims prayed there from time immemorial? Had they been in possession of the property openly and continuously from 1528 (when the mosque was allegedly built), and with the knowledge of the defendants and Hindus in general?

Alternatively, was the plot indeed Ram's birthplace?

Had Hindus worshipped the site from time immemorial? And had they earned the right to pray there through adverse and continuous possession?

Were the Rama chabutara as well as the *bhandar* and Sita *rasoi* (structures installed by Hindus over the years) demolished along with the main structure?

Had the idols and other objects of worship been placed in the structure on the night of 22-23 December 1949, or had they been there before that?

Can no mosque come into existence on the plot, in lieu of Islamic tenets (because idols have been placed there)?

Can the structure legally be a mosque since it doesn't have minarets? And is hemmed in by a graveyard from three sides?

Can the structure, after the demolition, still be called a mosque? And can Muslims use the open ground at the site as a mosque to offer prayers following the demolition of the structure?

Is the land adjoining the structure, to the east, north and south, housing an ancient graveyard and a mosque?

And is the structure 'landlocked', and wholly inaccessible except by passing through the Hindu places of worship around it?

What relief, if any, are all the plaintiffs entitled to?

In the judgement they delivered on 30 September 2010, the judges of the Lucknow bench of the Allahabad High Court were clearly aware of the immense repercussions of their pronouncements. This seems to have weighed so heavily on them that they ended up dividing the land among three parties – something none of the plaintiffs had expected or wanted.

The Court accepted that the land under the fallen central dome of the masjid was the Rama Janmasthan. The disputed Ayodhya land was to be distributed into three parts – one to the Wakf Board, another to Rama Lalla, and the third to Nirmohi Akhara. Thus, in actual terms, one third of the land would go to Muslims and two thirds to Hindus. The title suits of the Sunni Wakf Board and Nirmohi Akhara were rejected.

This book was written following this extraordinary judgement, when all the parties in the various title suits were in the process of appealing against the judgement.

The rest of the story – the story of these people, and those who remain hidden away from the public eye – lies in the chapters ahead.

Introduction

The town of Ayodhya, small as it is, needs – not one – but twenty-five such books written, in order to begin to do justice to its history and character. I have attempted only one volume of oral history, concentrating on the people who are still active and living in Ayodhya in 2011, out of a belief that these accounts will bring readers some important insights that go beyond the headlines about Ayodhya.

When compelling personal circumstances brought me here to Ayodhya in 2008, after a lifetime in the big cities of Mumbai and Chennai, the stark contrast between India and 'Bharat', that I had been used to as a media-created cliché, suddenly took on a new meaning. Nothing in the big cities prepares you for life in the smaller towns, whether it is being stuck in a traffic jam of tractors and Vikram tempos, seeing open gutters (as against giant, silent, invisible underground sewers), or having one's notions of political correctness thrown out of the window.

Ayodhya exemplifies the ill-developed smaller towns of India in every way, and yet has a unique character of its own, chiefly because it has been the site of the flowering of many faiths. While the Hindu claim on the town's history has been in the news for all the wrong reasons since 1984, Ayodhya can equally be claimed as a holy site by Buddhists, Jains and Sufi Muslims. In 'Ayodhya's Forgotten Muslim Past',* Yoginder Sikand writes:

---

*Sikand, Yoginder, 'Ayodhya's Forgotten Past', in *Countercurrents.org* (5 August 2006) <http://www.countercurrents.org/comm-sikand050806. htm> [accessed 7 April 2011].

The Buddhist claim is not unfounded. According to Buddhist tradition, Ayodhya, then known as Saket or Kosala, was a major city in the kingdom of Shuddhodhana, father of the Buddha. The fifth century Chinese traveller Fa-Hien visited Ayodhya and mentioned a tooth-stick of the Buddha in the town that grew to a length of seven cubits, which, despite being destroyed by the Brahmins, managed to grow again. Two centuries later, another Chinese Buddhist traveller, Hsuien Tsang, came to Ayodhya, where he noted some three thousand Buddhist monks, with only a small number of the town's other inhabitants adhering to other faiths. At this time, Ayodhya had some one hundred Buddhist monasteries and ten large Buddhist temples. The Hindutva argument that Ayodhya has always been a Hindu holy city is, as this evidence clearly suggests, patently untenable.

In the Hindutva imagination, the relation between Muslims and Ayodhya is characterized by continuous large-scale destruction and bloodshed. Serious historians have forcefully challenged this image, and have pointed to the fact that the spread of Islam and the emergence of Muslim communities in the area owed principally not to violent invaders but, rather, to the missionary work of Sufi saints. Considerably before the emergence of Ayodhya as the centre of the cult of Rama, it appears that several Sufis had settled in the town and its vicinity. With their message of love and compassion, based on an ethical monotheism, they attracted a large number of followers, particularly among the 'low' castes, victims of the Brahminical caste system. In other words, Ayodhya's association with Islam and Muslims dates to a period much before the construction of the Babri Masjid in the sixteenth century.

As many local Muslims themselves believe, Ayodhya is a particularly blessed town. They consider it to be the *khurd makkah* or the 'small Mecca', because of the large number of Muslim holy personages who are believed to be buried therein. These include, or so local tradition has it, two prophets, Sheesh, son of Adam, and Noah, or Nuh. In addition, there are said to be more than eighty Sufi shrines or dargahs in Ayodhya. Interestingly, most of these shrines attract both Muslim as well as Hindu devotees.

A number of Sufis made Ayodhya their centre for spiritual teaching and instruction from as early as the twelfth century. One of the first of these was one Qazi Qidwatuddin Awadhi, who came to Ayodhya from Central Asia. He is said to have been a disciple of 'Usman Haruni, the spiritual preceptor of India's most famous Sufi saint, Khwaja Moinuddin Chishti of Ajmer. Another great Muslim mystic of Ayodhya of pre-Mughal times was Shaikh Jamal Gujjari, of the Firdaussiya Sufi silsilah. According to a popular local story, the Shaikh would regularly go out of his house carrying a large pot of rice on his head, as the men of the Gujjar milkmen caste did, which he would distribute among the poor and the destitute of Ayodhya. This is how he earned the title of 'Gujjari'. His spiritual preceptor, Musa 'Ashiqan, who also lies buried in Ayodhya, would liken his distributing food among the poor to sharing the love of God with all mankind.

Ayodhya also seems to have been home to a number of spiritual successors of the renowned fourteenth century Sufi of Delhi, Khwaja Nizamuddin Auliya. The most important of these was the famous Sufi Shaikh Nasiruddin Chiragh-i Dilli, who lies buried in what is today New Delhi. Shaikh Nasiruddin was born in Ayodhya, where he learnt the Qur'an from one Shaikh Shamsuddin Yahya Awadhi. At the age of forty, he left Ayodhya for Delhi to live with Khwaja Nizamuddin Auliya. Yet, he would often return to Ayodhya to visit his relatives and make disciples who, in turn, emerged as great Sufis themselves. These included people such as Shaikh Zainuddin 'Ali Awadhi, Shaikh Fatehullah Awadhi and 'Allama Kamaluddin Awadhi. Other *khulafa* or spiritual deputies of Khwaja Nizamuddin Auliya from Ayodhya included Shaikh Jamaluddin Awadhi, Qazi Muhiuddin Kashani, Maulana Qawamuddin Awadhi and Shaikh 'Alauddin Nilli.

From my personal wanderings in today's Ayodhya, I noticed that the town had residential neighbourhoods like Raiganj, the 'sadhu' belt stretching from the Digambar Akhara to Pramod Van and Vasudev Ghat, and the temples and *matts* close to the Sarayu riverbank such as the Lakshman Qila and Asharfi Bhavan, besides the neighbourhoods in the tortured periphery of the Rama Janmabhoomi that feel the effects of the barricading and police presence the most, such as Tedhi Bazaar, Ramkot (the heart of Ayodhya), Begum Pura, Vashisht Kund and Brahm Kund. According to Shitla Singh of the Faizabad newspaper, *Jan Morcha*, and the activist, Yugal Kishor Sharan Shastri, while there are only two temples of real antiquity in Ayodhya – the Dantdawan Kund and the Chandra Hari Kund temples – there are hundreds of little shrines and bigger temples all over. Indeed, the only sound you hear in some of the smaller lanes, as evening sets in, is the ringing of temple bells and the hum of *aartis*.

I also noticed that there are three types of Hindu places of worship – temples run by private families or trusts, caste-based temples, and ashrams set up around charismatic guru figures of relatively more modern origins. Private trusts like the famous Kanak Behari temple and the Janaki Mahal have been bitterly criticized by one man I spoke to as 'a means for people from other cities to park their funds. Their deities inside are golden and floors are marble, and outside people still live in ill-lit shacks next to overflowing gutters.' The caste-based temples came into existence after 1857 to assist pilgrims from their respective castes during their Ayodhya sojourn, and protect the caste identity. There are the Nau (barber) Mandir, Badhai (carpenter) or Vishwakarma Mandir, the Sant Raidas Mandir for dalits, the Halwai Mandir for the Gupta pilgrims, the Dhobi (washerman) Mandir and the Chitragupt Mandir for Srivastava pilgrims, among others.

Of the newer ashrams built around charismatic guru figures is the Ramayanam Ashram, which propagates the teachings of Pandit Ram Kinkar Upadhyaya, through his disciple and Ramkatha expert, Mandakini. Such places draw younger devotees and even offer more modern forms of devotion. On 1 November 2010, the *jayanti* (birth anniversary celebration) of Guru Ram Kinkar was brought in at this Ayodhya ashram with a birthday cake and conical hats, sweets, trumpets and balloons. Hinduism is adapting to globalization and succeeding, at such places.

As to the contradictions that the people of Ayodhya illustrate with the way they live their lives, the book will provide ample examples of the renunciate versus householder dichotomy. Whose moral code should be upheld in society? While sadhus have traditionally had the upper hand in Ayodhya, conditions are changing as the very demographic profile of the town demands a more ordinary, less ascetic and rigid view of rules and requirements.

Caste is another contradiction that is thrown up by Ayodhya's living examples in this book. While the prevalent tradition among Ayodhya's sadhus is Ramanandi, there are also some Ramanuji matts. The Ramanuji tradition continues to have Brahmins in the posts of *mahants*, while the Ramanandi tradition has done away with caste among sadhus, even though it persists in hidden forms. Between the two traditions, there has been a tussle of proving theological superiority through the encounters of Ramanuji Raghuvar Prasad and Ramanandi Bhagavadacharya in the early decades of the twentieth century.

There was also a revolt by Ramanandi sadhus against the Ramanujis around the ritual baths of the Kumbh *melas*. Before this revolt in the 1920s, the Ramanujis used to be considered *bhitariyas* or those who stayed indoors. They thus performed cooking and house-cleaning duties at the camps of the Mahakumbh. The Ramanandi sadhus were the *bahariyas* or outsiders, who would sweep the premises and carry the Ramanuji Mahamandaleswars in their palanquins to the Ganga to bathe. The revolt and its resolution have left the question of caste looming in the background of Ayodhya's sadhuhood.

In writing this book, I have attempted to bring readers a sense of Ayodhya's struggle to remain connected with its historical and religious roots while claiming its place in modern, democratic India. As everyone who has been following the Ayodhya story knows, the inhabitants of this territory have had their concerns being pushed aside. Their views have been misrepresented by leaders, all of whom come with their own agendas; they camp on these shores and thunder all sorts of dire threats. 'If there is one big tragedy that Ayodhya faces today, it is the lack of a single good leader who can articulate its needs on the national stage,' says Tarunjeet Varma, the last individual profiled in this book. The years following the retreat of the Acharya Giriraj Kishores and the Ashok Singhals from Ayodhya have unfortunately not thrown up anybody to fill the vacuum.

Since this is a book of oral history, I have concentrated on the accounts of the profiled personalities. I have included their unique points of view. On initiating this project, I ensured that I did not begin with any thesis of my own. My own responses however, have been described wherever I felt they were appropriate and important for the reader. If these appear like taking liberties with the accounts at any point, I apologize. However, I think the omission of my emerging opinions would lead to gaps in the overall narrative.

I hope *Portraits From Ayodhya* goes a small way towards enriching the understanding of the place and her people.

PART I

MAVERICKS
AND MADMEN

Swimming against the tide in a town of temples and sadhus, priests and pilgrims in Ayodhya is not a task for the faint-hearted. To endure the ridicule, contempt, anger and indifference of a religious establishment reinforced by social and cultural sanctions, it is necessary to have an exceptionally thick skin, apart from huge reserves of courage and cleverness.

Who are the individuals who live in Ayodhya, yet challenge its prevailing norms and power structures? From where do they draw sustenance for their ongoing struggles?

Consider these examples of dissidence and individual resistance.

1

Vineet Maurya
Buddha's Displaced Disciple

Pair jab ladkhadate hain, dande ka sahara lete hain,
Dimag jab dagmagate hain, panda ka sahara lete hain.

(When feet stumble, they take the help of a walking stick.
When minds go astray, they seek the help of a 'panda' or Hindu
priest.)

—Anon

An active, slim and muscular figure cycling furiously to his
next appointment is how Vineet Maurya appears daily to
fellow residents of Ayodhya. In fact, he is often on his cycle,

covering the distance of six kilometres between Ayodhya and Faizabad, and another four kilometres up to the district court where his family has been engaged in a long litigation to recover the compensation due to them for land acquired by the government in 1989.

At the time of Vineet's birth in Ayodhya, on 1 September 1972, his family was prosperous, engaged in agriculture, with eleven acres of fertile land right next to the area that is known as Rama Janmabhoomi. His father, Shyam Lal Maurya, was an employee of the Uttar Pradesh government, and his mother, Ram Dulari, worked hard in the vegetable fields as well as in the kitchen to feed a large circle of immediate and extended family.

The Mauryas are a pious and peaceful vegetarian community consisting essentially of gardeners. The acres that his family owned were used to grow seasonal vegetables like pumpkin and bottle-gourd, cauliflower, tomatoes, bitter-gourd and brinjal, besides the ubiquitous potato, Uttar Pradesh's staple fare, and the bright yellow marigold flowers used for pujas in Ayodhya's temples.

'Since we were better off than a lot of our relatives in the smaller villages of India, we always had boys coming and staying at our home to study and appear for exams. We had a big house; there were always plenty of vegetables! When I was going to the government school at Ayodhya, I remember the cousins who came and lived at our place for a few months, then left to go elsewhere or return to their homes. Ayodhya was a larger town than the places they came from, but my home carried the ambience of a village,' says Vineet.

Since his family was steeped in religion – it could not be avoided in Rama's birthplace – there was never a shortage of religious reading material around the house. As a child, Vineet was given the *Shiv*

Purana to read in story form – a collection of tales in praise of Shiva. However, far from becoming convinced about the greatness of Shiva, Vineet actually found the gods 'immoral and corrupt'; they didn't appeal to his sense of what was to be respected or worshipped.

This contrary sentiment was perhaps the precursor to Vineet's move towards a different interpretation of life and reality – the one offered by Buddhism. 'In 1983, when I was in the sixth standard, I began hearing of and being influenced by Buddhist teachings. Whatever I read or heard at that time increased my liking for Buddhist practice,' he says.

Even as Vineet grappled with matters of faith, he was simultaneously forced to tackle questions about income and livelihood. The reason was, in 1989, the Uttar Pradesh government embarked on an ambitious project called the Rama Katha Park. It proposed to depict the life of Rama in pictorial form. A large tract of open, arable land was required, and it was found, rather appropriately, around the Rama Janmabhoomi area. The government went ahead and acquired it. In the process, it eased out the farming families that lived there, including Vineet's, for a compensatory amount that had not been released till August 2011.*

------

*The delay was due to a conflict in the estimated value. While the government had deposited cash at the rate of fifteen rupees per square foot of land with the then district magistrate, a Special Land Acquisition officer valued it at only two rupees and forty paise per square foot. When the Mauryas approached a District Judge to have the deposited funds released, they found they had entered the bewildering maze of the Indian administrative and judicial system. Their original plea is still being decided upon.

Understandably, losing the land that had represented their main source of income and family prosperity caused a tremendous change in the quality of life of the Mauryas. For Vineet, by then a spirited seventeen-year-old, the change in status quo meant facing some bitter truths. When the family land had been intact, the choice of vocation for Vineet had been fairly obvious. He could either become a government servant like his father, or a farmer like the rest of his household.* With the land gone, such comfortable choices were denied entirely to Vineet.

The loss was, for Vineet, the final proof that the religion that his family had been following, the dominant faith expressed in the structured and organized systems in Ayodhya, was responsible for their being consigned to poverty and obscurity. After all, they were being displaced and deprived for *Rama katha,* the story of Rama. And this was despite the family's attempts at building temples, praying to idols.

'The thing is, if you ask the original residents of Ayodhya, many will remember that even before 1949, there was a gang of five people who used to go around establishing temples in place of Muslim graveyards. My father was one of the five. The others were Ram Ashray Yadav and Ram Mangal Das of Gokul Bhavan, Ramchandra Yadav, and another gentleman whom I now remember only as Guptaji, who later left Ayodhya and went to live in a nearby village. These people would dig up old graves, level the

---

*Vineet's elder brother is, in fact, even today a government employee who works to maintain the plants and gardens in the sprawling, thickly barricaded Rama Janmabhoomi complex. The irony of his being a paid employee to safeguard trees and bushes on what was once his family's property is not lost on the Mauryas.

land and establish idols on it. This was easy for them to do when such spots were at the edges of their farmlands. In fact, my father had established one such temple by installing a Shivalinga that he had received as a gift from a debtor on top of Kuber Tila inside the Janmabhoomi complex. Such installations were quite common. The one that made the biggest news was the 1949 installation inside the masjid, but that one had a different gang behind it. Legitimacy was provided to that installation by a *chalisa* which begins, "*Bhay pragat kripala*" (the merciful one appeared), identical to the lines in the *Ramcharitmanas* of Tulsidas, which used to herald the birth of Rama. Only, this is a modern, post-1949 poem written and sold in a collection of aarti songs. My father and his friends had been involved with the same kind of installations, but on a smaller scale.'

In 1989, after the acquisition of land, an angry Vineet began asking his family why the god they had worshipped and served for so many years had let them down in such a manner. His questions fed into another wave sweeping over Uttar Pradesh in the late eighties – the rise of an iconoclastic Kanshi Ram and the emergence of Ambedkarite Buddhism as the religion of choice for dalits and the most backward classes. Vineet's family felt stirred by such questions and could see around them other examples of formerly Hindu families embracing Buddhism and overturning, with one stroke, or so it then seemed, the caste system and the many burdensome ritualistic practices.

A major turning point came in 1990, when Bhante Dhamm Tejankar Deep Mahathera of Bareilly, who had mentored Vineet and nurtured his interest in Buddhism, filed the first case for the Buddhist faith, claiming it to be a part of Ayodhya's legacy. 'Bharatiya Baudh Darshan Saar Society versus Paramhans

Ramachandra Das and Others' is a case still being heard today. The contention by the Baudh Darshan Society was that Ayodhya was a Baudh Sthal or a land sacred to Buddhism, developed by Ashoka around the fifth century B.C.E., visited by the merchant, Vishakha, and mentioned by the Chinese pilgrim, Hiuen-Tsang, during his travels in A.D. 639-40. It was when Buddhist vihaaras were flourishing in Ayodhya in the time of Ashoka that a famous Buddhist monk known as Baawri is said to have lived here. The masjid that later came up on this land, known as the Babri Masjid, was derived from the monk's name and referred to what had formerly existed at that very place. The case that Bhante Deep Mahathera had filed therefore opened up a new angle on the land already locked in an interfaith dispute from 1949.

The Maurya family felt empowered and emboldened by this initiative of the Baudh Darshan Society, and it noticeably increased the acceptability of Buddhism for Vineet's parents, as well as other elders more used to traditional ways. By 1990, Ayodhya had already become the destination for the slogan-shouting mobs who would raze the Babri Masjid to the ground two years later. Vineet's family felt removed from these hordes, and felt no solidarity for their cause. They lived in clear view of the disputed structure but had never been disturbed by its presence before their own land had been snatched away. However, their lives would be further encroached upon in the years to come, both by mobs of kar-sevaks and the security cordon thrown around the Janmabhoomi complex by the government, post the destruction of the masjid.

Everyone you speak to in Ayodhya refers now to the masjid as the *dhaancha* or frame, which fell down so easily under attack in December 1992. Some call it 'Janmabhoomi', depending on their own approach and conviction. It is very rare indeed to hear people say 'Babri Masjid' out loud.

For Vineet's family, the dhaancha falling down was the beginning of a nightmare because it led to tall metal angles and barbed-wire fencing of the entire Masjid-Janmabhoomi area. Their home, once so easily accessible from the main road and from all directions, is now surrounded by what locals call the 'barricading', which is a more powerful symbol for Rama Lala (the deity installed in the Rama Janmabhoomi) in this town than any other visual cue.

After the brutal firing on kar-sevaks by the Mulayam Singh administration in 1990, which had been provoked by thousands of people from all over India converging in this small town to begin the process of constructing a temple on the Rama Janmabhoomi, Ayodhya's psyche was left scarred and resentful. Security was understandably extremely tight in 1992, before the final assault on the Babri Masjid. In the days and weeks before 6 December, Vineet's family lived a life under siege. While other families in other parts of town were playing host to kar-sevaks, as a duty performed for Rama, the Mauryas did not feel obliged to do the same. But their movements were under constant scrutiny, and they had to live in very close proximity to armed police and para-military forces. This only completed their disaffection from the faith whose deity was Rama of Ayodhya.

Vineet's family still lives completely surrounded on three sides by the barricading. Even taking pictures of it can be interpreted as a security risk in the wake of a terrorist attack on the Janmabhoomi complex in 2005. Any of the policemen on duty around them 24/7 can challenge you and seize your photo/camera. So I had to take Vineet's picture in front of his door, with the barbed wire just visible in the top right hand corner.

Against the backdrop of the turmoil surrounding the masjid-mandir dispute, Vineet was yet to identify a source of income and survival. 'It was important to prove to my family that I was not a wastrel. I began going out in search of work. For a while, I worked as a daily wager or a coolie. I also sold vegetables in the Ayodhya Sabzi Mandi. The family economy was shattered after 1990. I contributed in whatever way I could.'

Mirroring the social change that was sweeping over large parts of Uttar Pradesh, Vineet's family adopted Buddhist practices in 1993, when the youngest of his three sisters was married with Buddhist marriage vows. Now with his family backing his faith, Vineet was able to study and practise Vipassana. He remembers these years as a time of great struggle to improve himself with the most meagre of resources. Ayodhya was feeling the effects of the Babri demolition in the decade following 1992. The most crippling effects were economic – from armies of kar-sevaks who had to be offered hospitality as guests, to the dwindling tourist traffic of pilgrims and devotees from different parts of the country. In his twenties, Vineet, like many of his fellow townsmen, felt anger, confusion, frustration – all the hallmarks of living in a virtual battle zone.

In 2003, Vineet became a Buddhist monk. Before this official induction, he had gone with some friends on a cycle tour of some of the vihaaras – in places like Lumbini, Sravasti, and Bodh Gaya. The religious journey was after all not only about stern asceticism, but also about fun. Following his adoption of orange robes, local people began referring to Vineet Maurya as 'Bhanteji' and he was given his new Buddhist name of Baawri Tiss Vineet. His mentor, Bhante Mahathera, who named him, was particular about giving him the name of the monk, Baawri, who had once lived very close to Vineet's actual home.

The new Buddhist identity inspired and invigorated Vineet,

and he organized a Diksha programme on Magh Purnima (the February full moon night) in 2005, under the auspices of the Vishwa Baudh Sangh. By now, Ambedkarite Buddhism had become a fact of life for millions of families in Uttar Pradesh, and hundreds took Buddhist vows at this community Diksha. Such activities brought Vineet into the public eye in Ayodhya and people began to perceive him as a figure opposed to traditional Hindu practices.

It was thus that he began associating with another noted dissident of Ayodhya, Yugal Kishor Sharan Shastri, about whom we will learn in another chapter. Shastri had moved away from the Sangh Parivar despite being a sadhu, and was established by 2005 as the spokesperson for the secular cause in Ayodhya. Shastri drew support and inspiration from Asha Parivar, the organization headed by Dr Sandeep Pandey, Magsaysay awardee. This organization has been active in the field of education, women's empowerment and the Right to Information in Lalpur, Uttar Pradesh, besides being a part of the National Alliance of People's Movements (NAPM).

Shastri was, and continues to be, sought out as a speaker and chief guest by all kinds of groups that organize functions that challenge Hindu orthodoxy and identity. There is a reason for this. As a sadhu, a man who is still presiding over a temple in Ayodhya, his speeches against the entrenched ideas of supremacy and identity, represented by caste or religion, have an immediate impact. So Muslims, dalits and many other sects disaffected by the caste-driven nature of Hindu social practices routinely invited Shastri to their programmes.

It was one such momentous occasion, when Vineet accompanied Shastri, that led to the former spending three months in jail and becoming associated with an incident that is forever embedded in the psyche of Ayodhya – the garlanding of a picture of Sri Rama with a festoon of chappals.

On 15 January 2006, the Vishwa Shudra Mahasabha, a group of radical dalits, had organized a function in Lucknow. One of the points on the agenda of this gathering was to denounce the portions of the *Ramcharitmanas* that were offensive to people from some castes. 'Warnings had been issued by this group that if the offending portions were not removed by Geeta Press, Gorakhpur, then Rama's portrait would be garlanded with chappals,' says Vineet. However, on the day of the function, which is described in greater detail in Chapter 3, Shastri and his companions from Ayodhya, which included Vineet Maurya in his orange monk robes, reached the deserted meeting venue to find that the garlanding had already taken place and some activists of the Shudra Mahasabha had been arrested. They went to the police station and identified themselves as part of the Shudra Mahasabha function. This was enough for the police to swing into action.

'First, the police beat us. Actually, completely thrashed us is a better way to describe it. I received a very hard lathi blow on my kneecap which pained acutely for months. We had one lady with us, and she was entirely isolated. My name was noted in the police records as Baawri Shiv Vineet – the police could not understand "Tiss", and replaced it with Shiv. After the sound beating, we were put in jail, and spent three months there. In the entire jail, the police and prisoners were on one side, and we were on the other. That was how much people resented us and turned against us. And we had not even been present when the actual garlanding with chappals happened!'

When the high court finally granted bail to Vineet, Shastri and the rest, and they returned to Ayodhya, they found it very difficult to overcome the locals' revulsion against the crime that had been committed in their absence. To this day, mention Shastri and someone is bound to say, 'Oh him! Yes, he is the strange man who went and garlanded Rama with chappals.' Vineet and Skanda Maurya, son of a journalist called Raj Kishor Maurya, whose story is told later in Chapter 23, found they had hurt their families' feelings as well. As a natural consequence of this incident, both fell out with Shastri. They have remained acquaintances, but are no longer friends.

'I do regret this incident very deeply,' says Vineet. 'We did not know they would actually go ahead and do it. We were not there, and all we had wanted to do was take a stand against some offending *dohas* and *chaupais* in the *Ramcharitmanas*. But I would not say that the time in jail was wholly wasted or bad. After all, any movement for change begins with a jail-sentence. While in prison, there is time to think and plan. Also, your public image changes. People begin to perceive you as someone with a commitment to ideals and a spirit willing to surrender for a cause.'

Following this period, Vineet kept a low profile, only emerging to play an active role in organizing an annual Buddha Jayanti programme in Ayodhya – collecting funds, making speeches and getting more people to attend. It was through cultural programmes and street theatre work that explored themes like untouchability, superstition and religious fraud, through the organization of yoga camps (he learnt yoga as a child from his father, an experienced practitioner), and through study and research that would document 'Saket' (as Ayodhya was known in the Buddhist era), that Vineet rehabilitated himself after the trauma of his imprisonment. He also regained a measure of goodwill among the locals.

Vineet's critics, and there are many, are mainly from his own adopted community of Ambedkarite Buddhists, such as Dr Bhaskar or Gautam Kumar. These earnest and politically conscious men, several years older than Vineet, decry his lack of stability and consistency. They accuse him of half-heartedly abandoning causes midway, of being fond of short-cuts and adopting the ways of sensationalists. But whatever be their analysis of Vineet's character, it remains a fact that they are more comfortably off as government employees with a secure income. They do not have to struggle with an endless *jugaadu* or a makeshift tapestry of survival as Vineet has done. Nor do they have to hang on by the skin of their teeth to the Buddhism that today makes Vineet an outsider in his birthplace. Vineet's personality is very clearly that of the-son-of-the-soil, and he knows people from every walk of life in Ayodhya.

In 2002, Vineet had contested municipal elections against Asad Ahmad, the son of Haji Mehmood, a saw-mill owner who came into prominence after his house was damaged by rampaging kar-sevaks around the time of the demolition. Although Vineet lost, he is still recognized as somebody with social and political ambitions. Since 2007-08, he has been actively trying to get the Department of Tourism of the Uttar Pradesh government to promote Ayodhya as a Buddhist destination in order to attract the international tourists who flock to Varanasi and Sarnath, Kushinagar and Sravasti, but completely bypass Ayodhya. 'All we get in Ayodhya are rural pilgrims who come to bathe in the Sarayu and do *parikrama* several times a year during the different melas. These people come on foot or in overcrowded tempos. The *melahru* (mela-going) *janta* can never represent great money or gains for Ayodhya. Unless we attract dollars, we are going to remain a town where people are still satisfied with earning Rs 100 or Rs 150 a day as wage labour,' he says.

What depresses Vineet is the lack of change so many years into the twenty-first century. 'The original inhabitants of Ayodhya are very poor. There are eight degree colleges, but only one of them is affiliated with the Awadh University. The rest are affiliated with the Sampoornanand Sanskrit University. The irony is that after all this, not one person speaks proper Sanskrit in Ayodhya! Neither is there a single factory or industry. Groaning municipal facilities can be gauged from the fact that head-loads of waste are still carried away here. There is no desire in Ayodhya's people to change anything. All they want is mere *daal-roti* (basic survival) and nothing else. The majority of the lower castes are still taught that they are suffering the wrongs of a previous birth.'

In December 2007, Vineet went to Chennai for the release of M. Karunanidhi's book on the Sethu Samudram. He was invited there by the Periyar Foundation. He met very articulate intellectuals, including the poet, Meena Kandasamy. 'It felt like heaven,' he now says. 'It was so clean, so much more developed, and dalits there are a lot more aware of their rights. Marina Beach is simply unforgettable!'

For the immediate future, winning the land-related case and receiving the money due to the family as compensation is important for Vineet and his kin. He has created a niche business for himself by selling Ambedkarite literature from various publishing houses at important community gatherings, workshops and seminars. 'What makes me happy is that I have been able to carve out my own identity with *mehnat* and *imandari* (honesty and hard work),' he says. 'Today, younger people want things a lot more easily, they are unused to hardship.'

Aside from promoting Ayodhya as a place of Buddhist significance, what are the other items on Vineet's wishlist for

Ayodhya? 'I wish for a world-class university of the calibre of Takshila or Nalanda to be built in Ayodhya on the sixty-seven acres,' he says, referring to the site of the mandir-masjid dispute, a piece of which once belonged to his family.

For this pragmatic son of a farmer, a glorious past can never make up for a poor and impoverished present.

2

Swami Hari Dayal Mishra
Saturn's Own Soothsayer

Karo na in se bair, hoga bura nateeja,
Mujhko hai sandeh, ki netra khul jaye na teeja.

(Don't make him an enemy, the result will be disaster.
I have a doubt – what will happen if his third eye opens?)

—Anon

The ramshackle buildings in a lane near the towering Hanuman Garhi temple in Ayodhya, placed in a compound housing a flock of geese, several cows, and an equal number of dogs, don't look too different from other structures around them. As if to distinguish them, 'Shani Dham' is written on a board hung on the bamboo frame gate. This is the office and temple of Hari Dayal Mishra, a reclining figure in saffron robes on a *takhat* or wooden plank-bed, who has a stream of daily visitors and clients. Swami Hari Dayal Mishra is an astrologer and *tantrik*, referred to by the sadhu community in Ayodhya as *'jyotishiji'*. Everyone you ask has heard of him, and yet, he is a comparatively recent resident in Ayodhya, having arrived here only in 1992. People turn guarded, and look at you curiously. 'You have business with jyotishiji/ Hari Dayal Shastri?' they ask, trying to figure out the nature of such business. After meeting with a dozen such responses, it is clear that the swami inspires a certain uneasy awe and fear, quite unusual for a single individual who is not backed by a powerful temple or institution.

Hari Dayal Mishra is perfectly at home with his many animal friends, whom he feeds and tends to as his pets. Monkeys, who abound in Ayodhya, swing by in large troupes in the compound, adding to the Garden of Eden effect. The swami lives in another building close to where he usually sits, with his family of wife and three sons. He is not a renunciate, but a householder sadhu. In the shadow of Hanuman's temple, he is a proclaimed worshipper of Shani, or Saturn. Not directly involved in the Rama Janmabhoomi-Babri Masjid tangle, he still attends meetings between the main players and sadhu community to figure out what should be done next. Some of the key figures in the whole dispute regularly visit him and seek his opinion. How did he become a parallel power centre in Ayodhya? Like many other stories in these parts, it all starts from Bihar.

Hari Dayal Mishra was born on 16 October 1940 in a village near Ismailpur station in Bihar's Gaya district. He was the great-grandson of a very famous vaid (ayurvedic physician), also a wrestler, who lived by the principle, '*Aage shaastra, peechhe shastra* (before one, the scriptures/learning; behind one, weapons/might).' Hari Dayal showed an uncommon intelligence and disregard for authority and tradition from the days of his childhood.

His fiery great-grandfather was invited to settle in the village where they lived by the nawabs, who then controlled all the land. He laid down the conditions to come and stay. 'I will not eat, defecate, live or sleep on anyone else's land!' This proud declaration resulted in him being given 150 acres of land. He made a fortune as a vaid and landlord, and had many Bhumihar followers. Hari Dayal's father followed this lineage on a smaller scale as a homeopath, although he continued to be a rich landowner.

Dismayed by the fact that he had a son who seemed averse to the very idea of academics, Hari Dayal's father engaged for him a tutor named Brahm Dev Mishra, who offered to teach his student in exchange for meals, a place to stay, and Rs 55 a month. 'He used to teach me in a very natural way,' recalls Hari Dayal, for whom this was the very first introduction to alphabets and vowels. This home tuition was good enough to get him admitted straight into grade four at the village school. Then, he studied so effortlessly that he got a scholarship from the very next year, grade five. By the next year, he had begun helping the teachers teach other children!

That Hari Dayal was bright and quick to learn attracted the attention of his grand-uncle, Ram Rekha, then a very famous astrologer and tantrik. The rich grand-uncle did not have any children, and was always surrounded by a coterie of yes-men who applauded his every word. Once, when Hari Dayal was staying at Ram Rekha's home, he summoned the adolescent and taunted him, 'Are you going to study only English lessons? If you really want to be learned, study the Puranas!'

The teenager retreated, and was found a day or two later deeply engrossed in a thick volume. Noticing his absorption, the grand-uncle questioned, 'What are you reading?' 'The Garuda Purana,' replied the boy, making his grand-uncle and other relatives blanch. This text is normally reserved for reading after a death has occurred.

Another encounter between the astrologer and his grand-nephew followed. 'You know the difference between your home and mine?' Ram Rekha asked Hari Dayal. 'Here, we believe in the motto, *'Kaal kare so aaj kar* (don't postpone for tomorrow what you can do today).' In your part of the family, it is just the opposite!'

That afternoon, the boy went out and bought a coffin cloth, which he laid at his grand-uncle's feet. 'What's this?' asked Ram Rekha. 'Your shroud, Sir,' replied his unrepentant nephew. 'I thought I would do today what I may have been putting off for the future!'

It was from such battles that Hari Dayal's father became convinced that his son would succeed his astrologer grand-uncle. However, he still tried to make him an ayurvedic doctor, sending him off to Patna to study for five years to finally graduate as a qualified practitioner of ayurvedic medicine.

The boy himself had still not formed a complete idea of what he wanted to do as an adult. As a child, he had not formed any definite idea of God. In fact, he was more of an atheist. The turning point came one day when, along with his grand-uncle and others, he happened to witness a funeral procession. A young boy had died of a snake bite. As the procession was passing, Ram Rekha enquired, 'Whose wedding is this?' The shocked mourners laid down the dead body and told him what had happened, but he was unconvinced. He performed some tantric rituals over the body using special mantras. A snake appeared, as if from nowhere, and bit the boy again. Miraculously, this time, the boy revived. Hari Dayal, watching his grand-uncle perform this feat, was powerfully affected. It was from this point that he decided, with absolute determination, that he would become a tantrik. He became the student and apprentice of the grand-uncle he had provoked so boldly in his childhood and adolescence.

Hari Dayal's own turn to revive somebody from a snake bite came after his wedding date had been fixed. Just a day or two before the wedding, on the day that a ceremony called *mandva* is usually performed to set up the wedding *mandap*, he was sitting by the south-eastern edge of his village, Daboor. Suddenly, an Ambassador car came along the road to the village and stopped beside him. 'Where can we find Hari Dayal Mishra, Ram Rekha's nephew?' asked the group inside the car.

'I am Hari Dayal,' he said. 'What do you want?'

'Our son has died of snake bite. Please come and revive him!' pleaded one of the men in the car, falling at his feet.

Not stopping to inform any of his family members, who were engrossed in preparations for his wedding, Hari Dayal got into the car and left with the grieving party. He managed to revive the boy within twenty-four hours. 'They offered me money, but I did not feel I could take it,' he reminisces. 'Meanwhile, since I had gone missing, my brother got married to the girl who I was supposed to have married. I realized my family must have been very upset with me, and I took off for the Kamakhya temple in Assam, where I stayed for twelve long years, studying tantric practices in earnest. When I returned home to my village one day, I found that all of them were preparing to eat the lunch made for my *shradh* (feast for the dead). Since I had not been heard of for twelve years, it was assumed that I had passed away.'

No one recognized Hari Dayal when he unexpectedly turned up for this occasion. He had grown a long beard and long hair, and looked like any wandering sadhu. Calmly, he sat down to eat at his own shradh along with all the rest of the invitees. It was when his father came to enquire after each one, and looked his son squarely in the face, that he recognized his offspring. He was so enraged at his son's effrontery – that he had dared to join a feast commemorating his own death – that he slapped him. Hari Dayal lay sprawled across the ground and suffered a cut on his lower lip. He still carries the scar.

Following this, Hari Dayal went off to Nepal for two years, where he further delved into tantric studies and was an astrologer at the royal court. In the early 1970s, he returned to Gaya district and set up a school named Vidya Niketan. However, his career as a swami/godman/astrologer was set to take off in a big way, and he did not stay long in Gaya, leaving shortly thereafter for Varanasi, where he had a friend, M.L. Pandey who worked for All India Radio.

In 1971, Hari Dayal Mishra was living in Varanasi, where the Station Director of AIR, one Mr Sahgal, gave him the opportunity of conducting a weekly puja at his home every Wednesday. It was on one such Wednesday that a distraught man came to the Sahgals' house; his man-servant had run away with his daughter and a large amount of jewellery. He wanted the swami who was doing his puja to help him find his girl. Hari Dayal was told the circumstances and pronounced thereafter, 'They have gone to Delhi. Search for the couple there.'

'Please come with us!' requested the father, and Hari Dayal agreed. When they reached Delhi, they found and caught the runaway couple at the station itself, as the latter were preparing to board another train. The family considered this to be an amazing example of clairvoyance and marvelled at the swami's powers. He was given eleven thousand rupees.

Another lucky break for Hari Dayal came when he reached the AIR station at Delhi to meet his friend, Shyam Pal Singh, who worked there. At that exact time, a group of AIR employees were just setting out to meet him, having heard of his powers of prophecy. When they ran into him, they considered it most auspicious, and thus began a phase when he was in hot demand as an astrologer and spiritual guide among people who worked in All India Radio and Doordarshan.

It was through these expanding circles of followers that Hari Dayal met a man named Munawwar, harried by a haunted house that he had inherited. Hari Dayal took up the challenge of exorcizing the ghost and was successful. Munawwar came to stay peacefully in the haunted house, and Hari Dayal's reputation as a fearless sadhu grew and he acquired more followers. One of these was film actor, Prem Nath, Raj Kapoor's brother-in-law, who was known for his fondness for swamis and mystics. Hari Dayal and Prem Nath became good friends, and the former predicted the phenomenal success of *Bobby*, the Rishi Kapoor-Dimple Kapadia starrer, in which Prem Nath had a prominent role as Bobby's father.

Such prophecies were bound to get him an entry into the glamorous and deeply superstitious world of the Hindi film industry. Soon, Swami Hari Dayal became a sought-after astrologer for some of the big names of Bollywood. He took up residence at the Hotel Horizon in Juhu and began receiving rich and famous clients who came to have their fortunes told. In this period, he was one of the priests who officiated at the ceremonies for Jitendra and

Shobha's wedding on 31 October 1974, and Shweta Bachchan's birth in March 1974.

Away from the world of showbiz, Hari Dayal met and married his wife, Shanti in Assam. The couple has three sons, of whom the eldest, Nitin Mishra, a lawyer at the high court in Lucknow, recalls, 'Our childhood was one of travel and adventure, completely unpredictable and very enjoyable. Papa would either have us staying in big suites at five-star hotels where he was receiving his clients, or travelling with him by road in a car that had a contraption strapped to its roof – a tent large enough to camp anywhere. We had a stove and provisions with us, so we could cook a meal anywhere, and an assistant of my father, Mishraji, used to travel with us too. This man doubled up as a secretary, motor mechanic, odd-jobs man; in fact, he could accomplish anything he was asked to do! We never knew when we would stop at some place for weeks, or when we would leave in a few days – and it was always by road. The three of us in the back seat with our mother got used to this nomadic life, as did she herself. The car, a much-modified Fiat, with its attached gadgets, was quite a sight, and Papa did not hesitate to change its appearance at will! I remember, once, after a trip somewhere, as we went up to our hotel room, my father instructed Mishraji to paint the vehicle while we were sleeping! When we came downstairs to go out again, our car was a different colour!'

Nitin's mother smiles and continues the story. 'It was evening then, and the car had been coloured with aluminium paint, so it glittered, and we thought it looked great! Only when the sun came out the next morning could we see the actual effects of the disastrous paint job. There were blotches and patches all over.'

'But Papa was undeterred,' says Nitin. 'The hotel guys said,

"Swamiji, why are you having it painted like this? Painting a car is a precise skill, spray painting is necessary, etc. etc.!" And Papa just went ahead and instructed Mishraji to paint it another colour!'

'That car and its journeys are simply unforgettable for us,' says Jatin, the youngest son. 'I remember looking out of the back window once and seeing a tyre rolling by itself alongside our car on the highway. "Hey, look, there's somebody's tyre!" I said, and in another second, our car lurched to the side and came to a stop. That tyre was one of ours!'

'We had plenty of accidents, but never got hurt,' continues Nitin. 'Papa was concerned about us not being able to go to school in a sustained manner because of constant travel. So he would engage tutors who came and taught us in our rooms at the hotels, and this is how we continued for quite a few years. In fact, it is only after we reached Ayodhya and stayed on, that our education assumed formal shape. We went to school and college.'

Before reaching Ayodhya, however, Swami Hari Dayal would negotiate the corridors of power in New Delhi. In 1976, Hari Dayal Mishra was in Assam, where he met supercop K.P.S Gill, and foretold his subsequent assignment in Punjab. 'Stay away from women whose names begin with the letter "R"!' he claims to have also told him. The indecent behaviour charges that IAS officer, Rupan Deol Bajaj, slapped on Gill in 1988 seem to have borne out this particular piece of advice.

Indira Gandhi arrived in Assam in 1976 to attend a session of the Youth Congress in Dishpur, where Swami Hari Dayal met her. An affable Mrs Gandhi gave him a ride in her car where she talked to him about her political prospects. She was then so offended with his forecast of a defeat for her in the 1977 elections, that she summarily had him ejected on a mountain road, from where he had to walk a good twelve kilometres to his destination.

Perhaps inevitably then, Hari Dayal found a friend in Prime Minister Charan Singh after he had taken office. Their friendship began with Hari Dayal meeting Charan Singh's brother and predicting his rise to ministership, and his brother's ascension to the prime minister's seat. Swamiji began to enjoy the status of being a special advisor to the prime minister, and was the one who advised him to move from his 5, Race Course Road address to 12, Tughlaq Road.

In this period, Sanjay Gandhi's *kundali* was shown to him and he predicted that Mrs Gandhi's younger son would be around for just a few more weeks. This sensational disclosure made it to the front page of the *Navbharat Times* on 1 June 1980, but there was no reason for anyone to take it seriously. How could Sanjay, then young and healthy, who had emerged as such a powerful personality during the Emergency, suddenly leave the world? Swamiji's prophecy may not have startled those who had heard it when he first made it public, but it certainly shocked the public when, on 23 June, the rising son of Mrs Gandhi tragically died in a private plane crash.

Reporters and media persons now thronged around Swami Hari Dayal. On 26 June 1980, the Delhi edition of *The Indian Express* carried a report titled 'Astrologer had seen it', in which the Sanjay Gandhi story was repeated. Going a step further, Swami Hari Dayal predicted Mrs Indira Gandhi's demise within another four years. He also performed a public *havan* praying for her health.

When Swami Hari Dayal arrived in Ayodhya in June 1992, six short months before the demolition of the Babri Masjid, he was bringing his wife Shanti and sons Nitin, Sachin and Jatin to a town completely dominated by sadhus. The religious establishment of powerful mahants, controlling different temples and having large groups of loyal supporters at their beck and call, kept ordinary householders and their families in a state of timidity. They were afraid to raise their voice against the smallest injustice.

'It was a time when even getting into an argument with milkmen who came to your house to deliver milk was fraught with risk. These men would ask you challengingly, "Do you want to stay around Hanuman Garhi or not? If you want to live here, just remember, this place is ruled by sadhus, not *grihastha* men who are tied to their wives' *pallus*!"'recalls Shanti Mishra. 'Women were not seen walking about these streets after dark. There were plenty of stories swirling about of girls and young boys who had been snatched off the road and taken to some ashram or temple. Who knows what truth there was in those stories, but they served to create an atmosphere of terror.'

For the first few months after their arrival, Swami Hari Dayal and his family stayed at the Janaki Mahal Trust, a private trust with a temple and many rooms available for pilgrims to stay in on their Ayodhya visits. The natural destination for more prosperous visitors to this temple town, Janaki Mahal was a hub of activity for the VHP in the years leading up to the demolition of the Babri Masjid. This daily contact with members of the VHP and Sangh Parivar was the basis for Swami Hari Dayal's short honeymoon with the VHP.

During this period, two famous predictions brought jyotishiji a huge following within VHP ranks. The first was at a meeting on 24 June 1992, at which VHP leaders asked Swami Hari Dayal to make a prediction about when the Rama temple would be built. In this meeting, he predicted the fall of the existing structure in December 1992. Another sensational forecast was made concerning

Vinay Katiyar. Swami Hari Dayal predicted that his opponent, Kusum Mishra, would make a statement in Katiyar's favour on a Saturday, which duly happened. The lady had earlier accused Katiyar of rape.

His fans within the VHP notwithstanding, Swami Hari Dayal slowly became disenchanted with the policies of the VHP and the Sangh Parivar and began to provoke them on several fronts. 'They brought down the structure in 1992, but in 1993, when the presidential elections were held, the VHP supported a Christian candidate against S.D. Sharma,' he says. 'I do not like the double standards they practice. They preach Hindu pride and purity, but do just the opposite. For instance, when Advani took his *rath yatra* in 1990, the driver of his so-called rath was Mohammed Shamim, a Muslim. And this man was greeted with aartis everywhere he went. This irritated me. Why spread such hatred against Muslims, when, if it comes to a job and providing employment, you give it to the community you tarnish? The VHP leaders violated Hindu principles in their personal lives as well – Advani's niece married a Muslim, whose home he visited, where he ate and drank – even the minor social norms that Hindus observe, of not eating or drinking in their daughter's *sasuraal*, were not observed.'

On a more serious note, Swami Hari Dayal observes, 'The VHP and Sangh Parivar have really played with the sentiments of Hindus for their own advantage. Twenty crore bricks were collected for the Rama temple, and for each one, pujas had been performed in people's homes. Even if you value each brick at one rupee, the total amount collected would have been a staggering sum. But the bricks just vanished! No disclosures have been made about where they are kept and how they will be used. These people only used the Rama movement to collect huge funds and amass personal fortunes.' In his efforts to make the VHP account for the money it had collected from the public, Swami Hari Dayal became one of the petitioners in a case filed by his close friend, 'Baba Dharamdas and Others versus Ashok Singhal and Others' in 2003, which is still being heard today in the district court at Faizabad.

After the initial months in Ayodhya which the Mishra family spent in Janaki Mahal, they moved to their present home in Nazar Bagh, a locality that is next to the Hanuman Garhi temple. The compound where they live is just behind the rooms and temple of the Samajwadi Sant Sabha, a group of sadhus attached to the Samajwadi Party, led by Bhavnath Das, a mahant from Hanuman Garhi. Soon after their arrival, this proximity led to one of the encounters that made people in Ayodhya feel that jyotishiji was not a character to be trifled with.

Because of Hari Dayal's extreme fondness for animals, he accumulated a couple of cows and several dogs in his new home in Ayodhya. These roam around freely in the compound, venturing out into the street too whenever they wish. Late one night, when the swami was away in Delhi, a young woman visitor to the Samajwadi Sant Sabha rooms was bitten by one of his dogs. Enraged, a group of young sadhus picked up *lathis* and chased the dog to the Mishra home at the back, and began following him inside.

'I was sleeping. In fact, we were all sleeping. It was around 1.30 a.m.,' says Nitin Mishra. 'Suddenly, I woke up to the sound of loud voices arguing. It sounded as if some men were fighting with my mother, so I came out. Apparently, our dog had bitten a female visitor and a mob had come to seek vengeance, kill it. "Hand us the dog or we will enter the house and drag it away ourselves!"

they began telling my mother, and she was arguing with them.' He pauses and recounts the scene. 'Seeing a group of men with long beards, brandishing stout sticks screaming for the dog's blood, was most unnerving. I was in grade nine, and secretly wished we could hand over the mutt and buy peace! But how could I let my mother down?'

'There was no question of handing over the dog,' says his mother with her customary quiet firmness. 'But Nitin was brave – he told the men to get off our porch and speak from the courtyard outside, and they listened.'

When they were forced to retire in a little while without the dog, the sadhus were most disgruntled. They found another little dog wandering on the street in the night and killed it, leaving it outside the Mishra compound, in a move calculated to send across a message. Seeing a poor creature killed in this needless fashion was distressing, and Shanti Mishra narrated the whole sequence of events to her husband on his return. He promptly filed an FIR and had the group of young Samajwadi sadhus arrested, among them, Bhavnath Das' favourite *chela*. When this man's bail application came up, swamiji opposed it saying that the man was from Nepal and he could not be given bail till his original address in Nepal had been verified. The man spent a few more weeks languishing in jail. Finally, Bhavnath Das came and offered swamiji a kind of truce, which has remained in place ever since.

Social relations in Ayodhya are, to a large extent, dependent on people's perception of how powerful you are. Not only did Hari Dayal Mishra receive powerful visitors, but he also developed a reputation over the next few years of having many people summarily arrested and clapped in jail. Accustomed to reading the Indian Penal Code in his leisure moments, the way we would read newspapers or novels, he says, 'When I came to Ayodhya, the law of Hanuman Garhi ruled supreme. Sadhus considered themselves to be superior to *grihasthas*. After my arrival in this neighbourhood, a conspiracy was hatched to get rid of me. I was not afraid to clash with the powers that be in Ayodhya. There was a big struggle going on for control of the different matts, and the police were involved in this too on behalf of different parties. I got an inspector put behind bars after taping his voice in an implicating situation. I had fake policemen in *farji* costumes imprisoned in another case. Prem Bhushan of the VHP was giving a talk at Karsevakpuram when he was arrested on another complaint of mine. Krishna Sahi, a big con woman, had swallowed a whole lot of property in Gola Ghat area, and had many sadhus imprisoned. I had her sent off from Ayodhya and she has not returned to date – there are eight or nine warrants against her.'

These years of going on the rampage against the religious establishment in various ways finally culminated for Hari Dayal Mishra in the organizing of the Danda Poojan in Ayodhya in 2003, a programme designed to needle and infuriate the VHP – till then famous for their Shila Poojan in the build-up to the Rama temple. 'That was one hell of a programme,' recalls lawyer, Deendayal Sharma, a friend of Nitin's who had worked as a volunteer for the event. 'The concept was that no outsider who creates trouble will be tolerated in Ayodhya. If he arrives to whip up controversies, he will be hit and chased away with *dandas*. We had managed to gather a big crowd – there was free food at the event. But there was a bigger stampede for the special dandas being handed out at the event, which were actually baseball bats! People went crazy about those dandas. In fact, they have become a big part of life in Ayodhya. To this day, if there is some big neighbourhood fight, somebody is certain to take out one of those dandas!'

The sudden organization of such headline-grabbing programmes is a trait that has persisted to this day. In the fortnight following the Lucknow High Court's judgement on the title suit in the Rama Janmabhoomi case, delivered on 30 September 2010, several statements and initiatives were unfolding in Ayodhya. Swami Hari Dayal Mishra decided to approach it in his own way by organizing a pledge taken with the river Sarayu as the witness. The pledge was taken by some sadhus and mahants like Khunkhun Dasji, Awadh Ram Dasji of the Jamvant Qila, Raghunath Dasji, Hari Dayalji, Naga Santosh Das of Hanuman Garhi, Man Mahesh Das of the Naik Mandir, Hashim Ansari and Sufi Muslim leaders from Kheda, Gujarat – Zahid Ali, Syed Mehdi Hassan and Murtaza Mehdi – who poured water and milk into the waters of the river and made a commitment of startling simplicity and significance: 'We shall work to keep religion free of politics.' Explaining the concept behind the ceremony to newsmen, Hari Dayal Mishra said that Rama Rajya was a state where no one slept hungry or in need. But the dispute over the Rama temple had affected Ayodhya economically, pushing *pandas* (the priests who are glorified guides), boatmen and other such vulnerable sections dependent on tourist traffic into severe poverty. 'Today, before the Sarayu that has witnessed bloodshed and violence in the name of religion, we pledge that we will keep politics and politicians away from religion!' The *mali-panda-nau* (flower-seller, guide, barber) community, accustomed to operating along the banks of the Sarayu, applauded this event wholeheartedly. Hausla Prasad Pande and Ram Nath Pande, Nanku Prasad Pande and Gharib Das Nishad shared their enthusiasm with me.

'What is the great Gyandas doing for us, sitting in his temple? He rules the roost and does not care about our survival. We need more sadhus like Jyotishiji, who understand our plight,' they said. 'People who play politics in the name of religion are evil and must be exposed!' It was very clear that we were in a post-judgement, post-Rama-temple-movement world in a steady state of decline.

'Ayodhya is the easiest place for a person of criminal antecedents to grow a long beard and melt into the community of sadhus,' says Hari Dayal Mishra. 'Every matt and temple should keep a register showing where their sadhus have come from, much like the RTO tracks vehicles from other states. But this is never done, so is it any wonder that we have the kind of criminals in our midst who are interested only in grabbing land and chasing women, all in God's name?' Disillusioned with what he has seen since he came to live here, the swami has penned a wickedly satirical poem lampooning all the major heads of Ayodhya's institutions, including the late Paramhans Ramachandra Das, and many others still alive and active today.

As he lies on the takhat in his courtyard, surrounded by his feathered and four-legged friends, it is clear that the swami is only planning his next major move, unfazed by the possibility of any opposition he may encounter. Behind him is the temple he has set up, housing Surya – the sun god, and his dreaded descendants – sons Shani and Yama, and daughter Bhadra. Like all these dark deities, the swami too is crossed only at one's own peril.

3

Yugal Kishor Sharan Shastri

Secularism's Sentinel

Lashen jiski neenv mein, khooni har deewaar
Wah mandir he rama tum mat karna sweekaar!

(Whose very foundation is laid on corpses, and every wall spattered with blood,
Please, dear Rama, don't accept such a temple!)

—Lakshmi Shankar Vajpeyi

In the small town that is Ayodhya, with a population of 75,000 in the 2001 census, it is inevitable that people know one another. They may not be on intimate terms, but most are aware of each other's names and professions, sometimes even addresses: 'Oh, so and so from that *mohalla*,' they will exclaim in recognition when you mention somebody by name.

Within such a setting, it is difficult to find someone who has attained the kind of notoriety that Yugal Kishor Sharan Shastri has. To the man on the street, he is someone who has been a brazen party to an unforgivable crime – garlanding the picture of Sri Rama with chappals. To more sophisticated minds such as Phalahari Baba's, he is someone who searches for recognition through sensational acts. To violent critics such as Gopal Krishna, founder of the Faizabad-based Movement for Rights, he is a prime representative of Ayodhya's *parjeevi* (parasitic) culture, where people try to achieve fame and earn money with absolutely no effort or merit, and without creating anything new.

And yet, with so much weighing against him on the scale of local public opinion, it is an undeniable fact that Shastri is the man to seek if one is searching for a 'secular' voice in Ayodhya. Along with other notables, like editor Shitla Singh and Suman Gupta of *Jan Morcha*, Shastri has soldiered on for the cause of secularism for the last decade or longer. He is a much sought-after name on the national and international circuit when it comes to seminars on communal harmony. Despite having lived along the margins as the mahant of a small temple on Parikrama Marg – that encircles Ayodhya and Faizabad – he has derived tremendous mileage from brand 'Ayodhya' among academics and activists, students and professors.

Shastri's journey to Ayodhya began with his birth into a Yadav family in a Yadav-dominated village in the Motihari district of Bihar sometime in 1954. The sheer number of Yadavs here led to the village being known as *Khirhar,* or those who steal milk, a direct allusion to the pastoral God, Krishna. 'It was a dark night around the time of the big floods that year,' he recalls. 'My mother remembered it as *anhariya raat* in *Krishna paksh* (probably the night just before a new moon in one of the monsoon months). At the time of my birth, the family was prosperous enough to have a cow and buffalo, most important for the milk-supplying community of the Yadavs.'

Motihari is one of the districts in Bihar adjoining Nepal, and Yugal Kishor's paternal grandfather came from Nepal, as did his maternal grandmother and mother. Yugal Kishor's parents had two sons and two daughters, and his father wanted to educate both his sons. Yugal Kishor began going to the village school, but used to cry so much as an eight-year-old that his mother thought he was possessed.

It was decided to rid him of the evil spirits that had taken hold of him through a ceremony called *Anchala Prakritaniya Naach*, a dance performed on a piece of cloth before the village goddess, Saaton Beheni Jagdamba. A ram was also supposed to be offered as a sacrifice during this ceremony. Unfortunately, this ram had been the kid of a house goat very dear to Yugal Kishor, and when he found out about the sacrifice, he was very sad indeed. Preparations for the ceremony had been completed for the next day, but, unknown to his family or anyone else, the eight-year-old boy got up and dug up the *bedi*, the basin that had been set into the ground at the place for the offering. In the dead of night, he immersed it in the village pond.

The astonished villagers were puzzled by the loss of the bedi the next morning, but decided to go ahead with the sacrifice anyway. But at the actual moment of offering, Yugal Kishor cried so much that his parents quarrelled over the whole thing and the ritual sacrifice was cancelled. The ram was later surreptitiously sent off with the butcher and a bribe of twenty-five paise was given to the child.

When Yugal Kishor was ten, there was a drought in Bihar that lasted four long years. The cow and buffalo were sold off, and food became a scarcity. Used to staying hungry many evenings, the boy cooled his hot and hungry stomach by hugging the smooth trunk of a guava tree in their courtyard. 'We would eat *masoor ka bhabhda*,' he recalls, 'an oil-free *chila* or pancake made with masoor dal, flour and salt. There would be half a kilo of dal for six people to eat, accompanied by watered down *khichdi*. I attended school wearing only underwear – there was no money for clothes. Even the price of land had dropped in the drought. I was so maddened by hunger that I would sometimes snatch my sister's share, then I would later cry, feeling sorry for what I had done, while she just looked at me. Even today, after all these years, when we meet and remember those difficult days, the tears flow.'

The Yadav boy was already testing caste prejudices in his village because of his friendship with *Teli* boys from an untouchable caste. 'I loved eating soaked raw rice, but my mother forbade me from eating it with my Teli friends, saying that my face would turn black if I did. I ate with my friend, Dev Nandan Saha, then touched him and ran home to look at my face in the mirror – would I be found out by my black face? I saw that I was still the same. I had proved to myself that there was no truth in all the taboos around untouchability, so I collected a group of boys around me and told them all, "What the *siyaan* (elders) have been telling us all these days is wrong!" Soon, other boys started eating and drinking with the Telis and a village of five thousand people started freeing itself from caste taboos.'

Yugal Kishor's other memories from his Bihar village are of going to a madarsa for two years. Thirty per cent of the people in his village were Muslims. As a child, he did not distinguish between people on the basis of caste or religion. In his imagination, there were two types of people, vegetarians and non-vegetarians. He himself had once had a pet cat who killed mice and lovingly left these as offerings on his chest at night. He would cook these mice on a cowdung fire, skin them and eat them like the famous Bihari *chokha*. However, on seeing a goat getting slaughtered one day, with all its hackles raised, crying in terror, he gave up meat forever.

Like so many others before and after him, in 1968, driven by poverty and hunger, Yugal Kishor Yadav left Bihar. He was accompanying Ram Balak Das, also known as Janak Das Phalahari, to become a sadhu in Ayodhya. Even as he left, he had to give the clothes he was wearing to a *bania* in lieu of money due to the latter. He arrived in Ayodhya wearing just a *gamchha* or thin cotton towel around his waist. When he had stopped eating meat, he had started wearing the tulsi beads around his neck, known as a *kanthi* – one of the outer signs of being a sadhu.

For the first two years after his arrival, Yugal Kishor attached himself to Mani Ram Chhavani, the sprawling and powerful temple and matt presently presided over by Mahant Nritya Gopal Das. Here, he was given food and a place to sleep, and in return he washed the huge cooking vessels used for *bhandaras* or community feasts, and even took care of the daily cooking for dozens of sadhus. The Valmiki Bhavan, an imposing structure with wall murals illustrating the entire Valmiki Ramayana, was being constructed in Mani Ram Chhavani in those days, and Yugal Kishor worked as a labourer in its construction.

It was in this manner that he came in contact with Shri Ram Manohar Sharan of the Sarayu Kunj Rama Janaki Mandir on the Parikrama route alongside the river Sarayu. Ram Manohar Sharan took the young lad under his wing, gave him a place to stay and encouraged him to study Sanskrit. Yugal Kishor landed up at the Sanskrit Vidyalaya, where the teacher, Ram Bali Dwivedi took one look at the boy from Bihar and advised him to begin studying from *prathama*, the primary level. 'Let me begin at *purva madhyama* (the next level),' begged the boy. 'I promise to go back one grade if I am unable to come first among all the boys in purva madhyama!' To everyone's surprise, Yugal Kishor topped the class with record marks.

Yugal Kishor's life as a young sadhu was producing its own set of complications. The handsome bare-chested youth in a dhoti was noticed by a lady neighbour, who began to get into trouble with her in-laws for ogling at him!

As a boy still in his late teens, he was very fond of sports, so he landed up at the ground of a trust being set up by followers of Swami Bhagavadacharya, a very important figure in modern Ayodhya, near the *sabzi mandi*. Here, he joined other youngsters playing *kabaddi*, staying on to discuss the game. Consequently, he was recruited by Shyamji Maurya into a *shakha* of the RSS.

Yugal Kishor began going out to play regularly and became very active as an organizer and teacher in the RSS. He would leave early in the morning in the biting cold of Magh (early February), wearing the khaki knickers of the RSS, to call people to shakha meetings. One hardworking doctor, Shambhu Singh, whom he went to call in this manner, had to be woken up each time by his wife. She got irritated by this whole sequence of events and Yugal Kishor, and told him not to come and disturb her husband in the mornings. But the next morning, there he was at her door again in the pre-dawn hours. The enraged Mrs Shambhu Singh threw a bucket of cold water all over him! Yugal Kishor narrates the incident with a chuckle.

Yugal Kishor earned his Sangh Shiksha Varg certificate in one year. He spent some time at Varanasi and the Gorakhnath temple at Gorakhpur. In 1981, he became a *pracharak* and was sent to Barabanki, a district neighbouring Ayodhya-Faizabad. A pracharak rules over the flock of supporters of the various Sangh organizations in direct and indirect ways. He discreetly oversees the organizations running under the Sangh's umbrella, such as the classes for moral education, the social-service initiatives, the efforts to expand the base of the Sangh and to draw more supporters from within the community. Ironically, Yugal Kishor, who had faced times of near-starvation during his childhood in drought-hit Bihar, had to face problems relating to food once again because of the meagre resources then available to pracharaks. Pracharaks, after all, were told to carry out their duties in the spirit of sacrifice, not well-fed comfort!

But Yugal Kishor's innings in the RSS was a cause of discomfort in other areas as well. 'The concept of *sanatana-dharma* propagated by the Sangh is impossible without the *varna vyavastha* or caste system,' he says. 'In fact, in the teachings of the Sangh, they call the *Manu Smriti* the first Constitution of India. Within the RSS, they are opposed to untouchability, but not to the caste system.' It became apparent to Yugal Kishor over a period of time that his growth within the Sangh hierarchy was handicapped by the fact that he was a Yadav, not a Brahmin or Thakur.

'Yugal Kishor likes to portray himself as a person from the backward castes who was discriminated against by the Sangh,' says

Srikrishna Madhukar, a dalit news-vendor who has held office in several Sangh outfits, and whom we will know more closely in Chapter 21. 'But the truth is that he was discredited within the Sangh only because he embezzled money when he was entrusted with keeping it for any purpose.' This is a charge made by several people, when Yugal Kishor Shastri's name is mentioned. But Shastri himself is very clear and candid when he asks, 'If I had been a Brahmin, wouldn't they have forgiven many wrongdoings on my part too? The upper castes always oppose a Yadav, are uncomfortable when he rises within the ranks, particularly if he is bright and seems to pose a challenge to them.'

By 1988, Yugal Kishor Shastri had become disillusioned with life within the RSS, and parted ways with them. The spiritual vision of the Rasik Sampradaya, the moving philosophy behind the Sarayu Kunj temple where he lived, proved much more satisfying to him. 'The Rasik Sampradaya is a branch of Ramanandi Vaishnavism, similar to Sufism,' he says. 'It enshrines *shringar ras* or perceiving god as one's beloved, and achieves the transformation of the erotic urge in human beings into something sublime and enduring.'

If Shastri is to be believed, he was also inspired by a thousand-poem work on Gandhi written by Swami Bhagavadacharya, and the Kabir Bijak. These two sources made him feel he should oppose the RSS and Sangh and the Hindutva they espoused within Ayodhya. If his detractors are to be believed, he discovered that being professedly secular would bring him a lot more mileage than staying a mere pracharak, which is why he took up the cause. The truth probably lies somewhere in between. Shastri's is the lone voice that has stayed consistent to secularism for many years. And yet, it is also true that he has repeatedly made sensational announcements, or taken part in programmes with suspect political agendas, merely to make waves and achieve a kind of fame.

In the years following the demolition of the Babri Masjid, the VHP became a discredited, even a hated and reviled force in Ayodhya. The community of sadhus and mahants of various matts, who had flirted with the VHP for many years, and whose support was indispensable for the formation of the Rama Janmabhoomi Nyas, gradually began to distance themselves from the VHP and the Sangh. The sadhus perceived the VHP as having let down those who had supported them in the movement for a Rama temple. When it became apparent that even with a BJP-led NDA government at the centre the building of the temple was nowhere in sight – the BJP was learning the delicate art of coalition politics – millions of people who had staked a lot for the dream of a glorious temple in Ayodhya became bitter and cynical. When Mahant Gyandas, the head of Hanuman Garhi, the most powerful temple in Ayodhya, began to say that the 'BJP has used Sri Rama as a polling agent; they remember him at the time of elections alone!' he was actually mirroring what the men on the streets of Ayodhya had begun to say in different ways.

Without the heady cocktail of the movement for the Rama temple, Ayodhya needed a fresh rallying point and an attempt was made in the first few years of the new millennium to provide it in the form of 'Ayodhya ki Awaz'. It was a group committed to secularism. It put forward the view that Ayodhya had always nurtured peaceful coexistence between the major religions, fostered the famous 'Ganga-Jamuni *tehzeeb*' (a culture of mingling, symbolized by the merging of two great rivers). Its citizens were perfectly committed to maintaining this culture of coexistence, and would not tolerate the presence of outsiders who vitiated the atmosphere, left Ayodhya isolated on the national stage, and robbed it of the 'pilgrims and the paisa they brought'.

Ayodhya ki Awaz had been ushered in by the imprisoning of local firebrands like Gaurav Tiwari (Beeru), Rangesh Achari, Neelmani Achari (Badal) and Gopal Krishna, along with Dr Sandeep Pandey (the 2002 Ramon Magsaysay awardee for Emergent Leadership, and a resident of Lucknow), following a dharna on 15 March 2003 before the Tulsi Chowra temple in Ayodhya. When the five spent their week in jail, they discussed the importance of providing a uniquely Ayodhya-based voice to resist communal forces, and the result of that discussion was Ayodhya ki Awaz. It was registered as a local organization, but the presence of Sandeep Pandey resulted in other personalities like Ram Puniyani and Dr Asghar Ali Engineer from Mumbai, tireless crusaders for the secular cause, and Shabnam Hashmi of ANHAD (Act Now For Harmony And Democracy) from Delhi, becoming gradually associated with the group.

In the post-mandir phase, at first, the events and programmes that this group staged in Ayodhya began to draw a fair number of people. Major players like Mahant Gyandas lent their voice to the secular cause. Ayodhya ki Awaz successfully organized a big community feast on 6 December 2004 called 'Sauhard Bhoj', where Hindus and Muslims ate together. Mahant Gyandas and Hashim Ansari were present. Gyandas is still registered as a member of the governing board. Other successful initiatives of this period have been described in Chapter 20 on Gaurav Tiwari. It was during these times that Mahant Gyandas arranged for the famous *roza-iftaar* gatherings in the premises of the Hanuman Garhi temple. Here, prominent Muslim citizens would break their Ramzan fast with fruits and food provided by the temple.

What was galling for the original group that formed Ayodhya ki Awaz was the way in which Shastri became positioned as its sole inheritor and spokesperson, encouraged and enabled by Sandeep Pandey. In fact, even today, on any of the websites – *Communalism Combat* for instance – Yugal Kishor Sharan Shastri is described as a founder of Ayodhya ki Awaz, although he was neither part of the original dharna that led to its formation, nor a part of the registered founder members. This is one of the factors that lies behind many Ayodhya and Faizabad residents' accusation that Yugal Kishor Sharan Shastri has set up a 'secular shop or business'.

By January 2005, a split occurred in the Ayodhya ki Awaz banner, with Gaurav Tiwari, Rangesh Achari, Shariv Husain and Badal Achari writing a letter to Dr Sandeep Pandey expelling him from the group due to his promotion of Shastri in matters relating to the group. Unfortunately, the original members did not follow up this letter with concrete attempts to keep the Ayodhya ki Awaz banner alive in public memory through meaningful programmes.

Instead, Yugal Kishor Sharan Shastri had become established by late 2005 as the voice behind Ayodhya ki Awaz. He was the person getting pamphlets printed and distributed, getting stickers printed and pasted in public spots, organizing *sadbhavana* (communal harmony) camps and seminars. '*Jisne baanta desh ko, nafrat ka paighaam,/ Us mandir mein bhool kar, mat jana bhagwan* (that which has divided the nation with its message of hate,/ please God, don't step into such a temple even by mistake).' Thus goes one of the many stickers that have been distributed in the last few years by Yugal Kishor Shastri.

Yugal Kishor was assisted in his mission by thinkers like Ram Puniyani and Asghar Ali Engineer, who have contributed immensely to his publications and workshops. In the context of the 30 September 2010 judgement on the Masjid-Janmabhoomi title suit, Shastri brought out two excellent booklets. *Apno se Apni Baat* (In Our Own Words to Our Own People) explains the different strands in the argument favouring a temple in ways that people can understand. It shows how the whole battle that convulsed a nation is about a piece of land, not about faith. The way in which political interests have contributed to social schisms has also been explained very well in *Rama Janmabhoomi banaam Babri Masjid: Mithak evam Tathya* (Rama Janmabhoomi versus Babri Masjid: Myths and Facts). This second booklet has been on sale since the time of the judgement. Another novel method of communication that Shastri has used in recent times has been bulk SMS-ing for communal harmony in the days leading up to the judgement.

'The names that Sandeep Pandey brought in for communal harmony programmes and his immense clout in the NGO and media world was too much for us to stand up against,' says Gaurav Tiwari. 'If the whole country and the world know Yugal Kishor Shastri as the voice of secularism in Ayodhya, it is the might of Sandeep, Asha Parivar and NAPM (National Alliance of People's Movements) that has created this image. But only we locals know the real story, only we see the dwindling, in fact, almost non-existent local audience for many of his so-called *shivir*s (camps).'

When I met Yugal Kishor Shastri for the first time in October 2005, and I wrote a piece based on our meeting for *The New Indian Express*, he was busy getting a pamphlet printed denouncing Mahant Gyandas in the context of one of their local disagreements over the appointment of a mahant. Since I have come to live here in February 2008, I have seen him as an active speaker at communal harmony events outside Faizabad, always holding a pile of pamphlets or stickers or booklets to be sold or distributed. His tireless efforts are evident. However, even I, as a relatively dispassionate observer, have not failed to notice the lack of local support and enthusiasm for his initiatives. In fact, I have my own theory, which is that sadbhavana – the term he uses to promote secularism locally – is like a red rag to a bull as far as the local police are concerned. As recently as October 2009, they had him clapped in jail again for sadbhavana!

'This lack of enthusiasm for sadbhavana coming out of Ayodhya is because it is not, in fact, truly secular. Secular should mean equally respectful of or equidistant from all religions. But Shastri's secularism is shallow. It has actually often been practised as Muslim minorityism. By pandering to Muslims all the time, you make ordinary people believe that being secular is something they can't do convincingly in their own personal lives. *Hum aise secular nahin ho sakte* (we can't be secular in this way)!' says Gopal Krishna. 'It is because this fake type of secularism has been practised for so long in Ayodhya that people have got fed up and do not want to be part of it.'

'For a long time, Yugal Kishor Shastri has been a tool for various interests who like to say that they have got a sadhu from Ayodhya to denounce Hinduism,' says Dr Anil Singh from the Department of Hindi at Saket Degree College. 'His service to secularism would have been much more valuable if he had not been seen as conveniently available to attack Hindusim whenever and wherever he was asked. In fact, Shastri's secularism is in keeping with the whole character of Ayodhya – here things are not what they seem to be. Everything is done for some ulterior motive. The whole culture works to destroy your sensitivity, your dreams.'

In his own defence, Shastri produces a copy of mainstream

Hindi magazine, *Sarita*, whose issue in May 2007 contains his interview stating that the character of Rama needed to be re-evaluated and discussed in the present day. 'At least I have always raised questions about the backward and inhuman facets of religion,' he says.

Apart from secularism, Yugal Kishor Shastri has worked to counter the ideas of caste supremacy that he had faced first-hand during the years he spent in the RSS and Sangh Parivar outfits. From 2003, he joined with dalits, inspired by Swami Bhagavadacharya, who had been a founder-member of the Harijan Sevak Sangh set up by Mahatma Gandhi. During this period, 2003–04, Shastri formed the Bhakti Andolan Manch and demanded that dalits be granted the right to worship or perform pujas within the precincts of the Hanuman Garhi temple. 'We sent a notice to both the district magistrate and the Hanuman Garhi temple, informing them that if they did not initiate such a puja themselves, we would storm the temple with a thousand dalits and conduct it ourselves,' he recalls. 'The DM called me and said it would not be possible under the then government (Mulayam Singh Yadav's). He advised me to withdraw my demand, but I held firm. So, apprehending major trouble, the administration surrounded both my residence at Sarayu Kunj temple and the Hanuman Garhi temple itself, with a huge number of PAC (Provincial Armed Constabulary) soldiers.'

Yugal Kishor did not succeed in his mission of getting dalits to worship at Hanuman Garhi, but he did acquire a following among them by the mere fact that he had raised the demand. Perhaps it was this that led to his involvement with the episode that remains stuck forever in public memory – the garlanding of Sri Rama's portrait with chappals and shoes.

The actual incident is replete with elements from the theatre of the absurd – which really is life in Uttar Pradesh. In January 2006, Shastri had been invited to speak at a function of the Vishwa Shudra Mahasabha in Lucknow. The organization – a group of radical dalits – that had named itself to deliberately counter the grandiose-sounding Vishwa Hindu Parishad, had threatened to garland Sri Rama with footwear if dohas and chaupais offensive to the lower castes were not removed from the *Ramcharitmanas* published by Geeta Press in Gorakhpur.

'We were a little late, when we tried reaching the meeting venue,' remembers Shastri, referring to himself, Vineet and Skanda Maurya and a few more people. 'And when we got there, the place was empty, except for some musicians.' 'Musicians?' I ask, puzzled. 'Yes, musicians who had been engaged to sing some songs at the function. They said that they were waiting because they had not been paid their dues. When we asked them where the rest of the people had gone, they told us that they had been taken away by the police.' Instead of quietly sneaking away, Shastri decided to go and speak up for the dalits at the police station. 'I thought my stature would protect them from further harm,' says Shastri, with almost stunning naivete. Their actual reception by the police is recounted in Chapter 1 on Vineet Maurya. The troubling aspect of this whole incident is that while Shastri is candid enough with me and tells me the real circumstances, he has proudly proclaimed elsewhere (including to Rakesh Kumar, the writer from *Communalism Combat*) that he wasn't afraid to garland Rama with shoes. This two-faced version of the incident has not gone down well with locals.

Another sensational declaration by Yugal Kishor Shastri concerns M. Karunanidhi, the wily leader of the DMK. Shastri had decided to call him 'Shudra Samrat' (Emperor of Dalits) because he had questioned the engineering credentials of Lord Rama. Karunanidhi had also alleged, in 2009, that A. Raja was being accused of corruption in the 2G spectrum allocation because he was a dalit. Since the country has subsequently had a chance to find out more about this former Telecom minister, Shastri's enthusiasm for Karunanidhi's anti-Rama and pro-dalit stance appears excessive. But he says he did it stung by the VHP and Ram Vilas Vedanti's attack on Karunanidhi in 2007 during the war of words on the Sethu Samudram project.

A more effective dalit protest was achieved locally by Shastri and his group in 2007, against an anti-dalit plaque carrying offensive lines from *Ramcharitmanas* at the Tulsi Udyan in Ayodhya. When a meeting was held asking the DM to remove these lines from the park, the offending sign was painted over by a responsive administration almost immediately.

A thorn in the flesh of the VHP, Shastri worked doggedly in 2008 to expose former BJP MP from Pratapgarh, Ram Vilas Vedanti's claim that he had received threats to his life on the phone from SIMI activists. Investigation by the police had then revealed that the phone calls were from his own followers! On the other hand, the Hindutva cadre as well as those whom he displaced in Ayodhya ki Awaz opposed his being awarded the Guru Gobind Singh Award for communal harmony by the Uttar Pradesh government in 2008. In fact, a *fatwa* offering a reward of one lakh rupees for Yugal Kishor Shastri's scalp was announced in 2008 by powerful mahants like Ram Vilas Vedanti, Nritya Gopal Das, and Narayanachari.

Perhaps his most sincere period was when Yugal Kishor Shastri worked with Bhoodan activist, Nirmala Deshpande, from 1988 to

December 1993. This period was marked by efforts to foster communal harmony at the grassroots level though social service and meetings in Ayodhya, as well as travel to other parts of the country, speaking about the ill-effects of the movement for a Rama temple. In fact, Shastri headed the Rachanatmak Samaj that Nirmala Deshpande had formed for social change, which was a group of intellectuals and social workers committed to communal harmony and ending social inequality. Of the two occasions that mark the bloodiest chapter in recent Ayodhya history, Shastri has this to share: 'I had been so bitterly opposed to the VHP, that a month before the events of 30 October 1990, the local administration had sent me to jail. In fact, whatever I knew of the police firing on that day, and on 2 November, I know from Bahraich jail. *Dainik Jagran* had described rivers of blood flowing in Ayodhya. This was a definite exaggeration. But even *Jan Morcha*, Faizabad-Ayodhya's own paper, mentioned that thirteen people had died. There was a tremendous wave of hatred against Mulayam for what he had done. People used to beat tin cans in jail, and curse Mulayam with obscene invectives all through the night. But I had a different take on things. I used to wonder: "Instead of firing on innocents, why didn't Mulayam get Ashok Singhal killed?" If he had taken oath under the Constitution, he should not have let such people go scot free.'

Like everybody else, I question him about the day of the demolition. 'Nirmalaji and forty-two Bhoodan volunteers were staying with me on 6 December 1992,' says Shastri. 'Suman Gupta (a journalist with the local paper, *Jan Morcha*) had earlier been threatened at Janaki Mahal, "You will be killed!" She still went to the site of the demolition, and returned in a terrible state. She had been man-handled, her clothes torn, abused. I had seen the mobs earlier, and was not surprised that they were capable of such violence. The worst was, they came chasing after her right up to my house. I had her hidden safely in an inside room, but I only managed to save her by telling them that she had come running in through the front door, and gone running out through the back entrance, which opens on to Parikrama Marg. Thankfully, they believed me. Seeing their rage and violence on that day really made me think, "Religious fanatics are a lot more cruel than ordinary persons!"' Following the demolition on 6 December, Shastri reminds me that sixteen Muslims were burnt alive in Ayodhya, and 168 houses, including saw-mill owner Haji Mehboob's, were destroyed, but not a single FIR was filed by the local police. 'Instead, on 7 December, they once again arrested me, along with Phalahari Baba and Ramashray Yadav, on charges of conspiring to bring down the Babri Masjid! This was such a ridiculous trumped-up charge because we were the only people within the sadhu community to have kept a distance from the Rama temple movement.' This arbitrary arrest was hotly protested by leading citizens like Shitla Singh and Congressman Nirmal Khatri, as well as by Nirmala Deshpande. 'We were released in half an hour, it is true,' concedes Shastri. 'But what was the use? They did not arrest a single member of the VHP.'

'I have once encountered Shastri standing by the side of the road with a garland, waiting to greet Uma Bharati when she had left the BJP and come on a visit to Ayodhya,' says senior journalist, Krishna Pratap Singh. 'When convenient, he plays his Ahir card (being a Yadav, in order to appeal to Uma Bharati who belongs to a backward caste). He does most things for publicity, not out of inner conviction.' K.P. Singh, senior independent journalist, tells me this in Shastri's presence, but it does not faze the secular mahant of the Sarayu Kunj temple of Ayodhya. Smiling and unmoved, he says, 'The struggle against communalism must always continue in Ayodhya.'

Love him or hate him, it is impossible to ignore Yugal Kishor Sharan Shastri in Ayodhya.

4

Ram Sharan Das
To God, Through the Gutters

Neech tehel grih ke sab karihaun,
Pad pankaj biloki bhav tarihaun.

(I shall willingly perform the lowliest domestic duties, sing praises of the Lord's lotus feet, and cross this sea of suffering.)

—Goswami Tulsidas

Like any small town with an open sewage system, Ayodhya has crisscrossing *naalis* or open gutters that run like dark rivulets along the sides of all its roads and streets, alleys and pathways. These smelly streams, containing waste from thousands of bathrooms and kitchens, get clogged with polythene packets and thermacol plates, plastic and leaves, twigs and fruit peels particularly at uneven levels of the ground or around turns. The overworked municipal workers go about dredging the gutters, collecting the waste in sordid little piles along the roads for removal. As the population of Ayodhya grows, the strength of the staff remains the same as it was many years ago (as we shall see in Chapter 7 on the chairman of the municipality, Mithilesh Pandey).

However, even this skeletal staff gets paid for the service they perform. Standing ankle-deep or knee-deep in the gutters, clearing them by digging with a spade and removing the bottlenecks, unmindful of the injury on his leg where he was bitten by a street dog, is a man who looks well past the retirement age of most government employees. He is, in fact, closer to ninety than sixty. He is no municipal sweeper, but a sadhu from the Basantiya Patti of the powerful Hanuman Garhi temple. Ram Sharan Das follows his own path of service to Sri Rama and Hanuman. For the last sixty years, he has been cleaning the gutters of Ayodhya. He has been doing this for so long that people refer to him as '*naali wale baba*'.

Born in Hirni village of Darbhanga district of Bihar in 1920, Ram Sharan Das came to Ayodhya at the age of fifteen to learn astrology from Chhatru Maharaj Vasudevacharya of the Dant Dhavan Kund. However, he studied for only a few months. In this short time, he learnt enough to cast his own natal chart or kundali. From this, he was surprised to find that he had many planets in the twelfth house.

'I learnt that I would have a lot of trouble in my old age,' he says, musingly. He walks slowly, but unaided. His living quarters consist of a single room, roughly ten by ten square feet in size, which has plain bricks placed to form a floor slightly higher than the level of the ground. 'When it rains, water enters the room because it is at the same level as the street, and dampens my belongings,' he says, gesturing towards the objects that can be counted on the fingers of one hand. A cloth bag, a tin can, a wooden bed that has a few bedclothes on it, and some books inside a steel bowl. His kitchen is across the corridor leading to the inner quarters of other sadhus like him. It is another small room with a small kerosene stove on raised plain bricks. No provisions or vegetables mark it as a place to create sumptuous meals. In fact, Ram Sharan Das says he has stopped eating vegetables because it is too much trouble to make them. 'I make a single large roti for my dinner,' he says. 'At other times, I eat in the temple if there is a bhandara, or where someone offers food.'

My middle-class domesticity makes it difficult for me to see an elderly person in such austere circumstances. So we go to the home of one of Ram Sharan's friends, where we can sit and talk in relative comfort. Ram Sharan Das waves aside my concern for his condition. 'Did you see the Barahdari Bangla Mandir?' he asks me, referring to a temple on the main road, close to his quarters. 'It was founded by Baba Janardan Das. My guru, Shri Keshav Dasji, appointed me mahant here. There was a lot of land around it which belonged to the temple. There is still land belonging to this temple in places as far away as Begusarai and Bishanpur. When I became mahant, I gradually began giving away the land. I say "giving away" because I sold it for very low amounts, sometimes as low as five hundred or a thousand rupees, disregarding common wisdom that went, *"Joru jameen jod ke, aur ghate to aur ke* (hold on tightly to your wife and land. Loosen your grip and you have lost them)."'

'Why did you do that? Wouldn't it have been more comfortable to have a lot of land, temple staff and devotees making cash offerings just like in so many other temples?' I ask him.

'That is one way,' agrees Ram Sharan Das in his slow and deliberate manner. 'But I believe in a different way. *Ekante va nadi teere, athva shunya mandire* (alone by the banks of a river or in an empty temple) is the true place for a sadhu. The more possessions you acquire, the more you have to suffer their complications. On the spiritual path, all the trappings of domesticity are huge obstacles.' Quoting his favourite inspiration, Goswami Tulsidas, Ram Sharan Das points out – *Grih karaj nana janjaala, te ati durgam shail vishaala* (domestic duties have a million complications; they are huge boulder-like obstacles to be overcome).

The man who works among the gutters with his bare hands has enjoyed periods where he has engaged in other occupations. He has worked as a correspondent for the *Pioneer* and *Swatantra Bharat* in Ayodhya. Old-timers recall him as an educated man in a sea of barely-educated sadhus. It is his actions in a previous birth that have led to his present circumstances of penury, he believes.

'When I first came to Ayodhya, there were people of *sattvik vritti* (a good or higher nature) to be found in every village, every religion,' he says. 'Now, even if we were to go searching for such people, all we would find are those hungry for wealth, and ready to do anything to keep it. *Rama rajya* is not so hard to imagine if people stay true to their good nature. After all, it would mean a state where no police is needed. Tulsidas saying, "*Mange hain barid, dehi jal* (when clouds were asked for water, they rained)" with reference to Ayodhya only showed people's inherent closeness to nature at that time. That all-pervading spirituality is completely lacking today.'

The young Ram Sharan Das has been a wrestler who was fond of exercise. When he followed his guru Keshav Das first from Darbhanga to Begusarai and then to Ayodhya, he had already heard about the three big akharas for exercise and wrestling then active in Hanuman Garhi temple. 'Balanandacharya, brother of the Maharaja of Jaipur, became a sadhu. In those days, a man named Bhairon Giri used to kill sadhus, and Balanand wanted to track him down. But he remained a fugitive, somewhat like Osama Bin Laden!' he says. 'During the period when Balanand was training the sadhus to defend themselves, he set up the three *ani-akharas*: the Nirvani, Nirmohi and Digambari Akharas at Hanuman Garhi.' Ram Sharan Das belongs to the Nirvani Akhara.

In the more than six decades that Ram Sharan Das has spent in Ayodhya, one of the personalities from whom he has drawn the most inspiration was K.K. Nayar, the district magistrate of Faizabad-Ayodhya in 1949, when the idols were first placed inside the masjid. 'It is Nayar saab who used to have the heart and guts to do this work,' he says. 'I have seen him sweep the streets and clean the gutters myself. He was very close to the sadhus of Hanuman Garhi. I began doing this work from that time. The irony was that Nayar saab's wife, Shakuntala Nayar, was a member of Parliament. She was elected thrice on a Jan Sangh ticket from Kaiserganj. But she considered her husband to be a wastrel! From among us sadhus, only Abhay Ram Das, Paramhans Ramachandra Das and I were close to Shakuntalaji,' he says.

Ram Sharan Das brings up an interesting angle on the conspiracy that ultimately resulted in the idols being placed in the masjid on the night of 22-23 December 1949. He asks me if I know the present Yogi Adityanath of Gorakhpur. 'Yes, of course, I know of him,' I say. 'His guru's guru, that is, Avaidyanath's guru, came to

Paramhans Dasarath Dasji's ashram at Katra in Ayodhya in 1949,' he says. 'This was an ashram that K.K. Nayar saab used to visit frequently. There was a meeting where Shri Poddar from Geeta Press (Gorakhpur), Shri Guru Dutt Singh (magistrate), and Ram Subhag Das joined Nayar saab and the Gorakhnath mahant. At this meeting, Mahant Digvijaynath instructed, "Go and keep the idols in the masjid!" I was present in this meeting, so I know how seven people were appointed for the functions of cook, caretaker, etc., for the Rama Lalla idols and temple.'

I am not really surprised when a Gorakhnath peeth connection turns up in the conspiracy of placing Hindu idols in the masjid in 1949, in my conversations with Ram Sharan Das. After all, the present head of the temple and matt, BJP MP Yogi Adityanath has aggressively promoted himself as a protector of the Hindu faith ever since he took over the reins of this religious post. I have heard his eloquence in what are clearly 'hate speeches' in the documentary *Saffron War* made by Rajiv Yadav, Shahnawaz Alam and others, a film that underlines the Gorakhnath peeth's connection to several events that have convulsed Indian history. From the accounts of some of the scholars and academics featured in the film, I learnt that the gun that Nathuram Godse used to kill Mahatma Gandhi was supplied by the Gorakhpur temple authorities. If the matt now appears in the context of Ayodhya, as being part of the original conspiracy that was set to pit two communities against each other, it is quite consistent with the subsequent engagement and public posturing of its leaders.

But my dialogue with Ram Sharan Das must navigate our differing perceptions of the Gorakhnath matt and try, instead, to get to whether Ayodhya has suffered as a result of the idols being placed where they were on that night of December 1949. 'Is it right to approach the whole matter of faith and belief in God only through a piece of land?' I cannot help but ask Ram Sharan Das.

Unlike others to whom I have put this question, Ram Sharanji does not show any sign of agitation or aggression. Instead, he answers slowly, 'Muslims are inclined to take over land in a creeping, slow, determined fashion. Graveyards, masjids, meeting places, *tazia* places (places where Shia Muslims keep decorated caskets representing Imam Hussein and others during the period of Muharram), they begin to mark all spots as their own. They worship religion, not God. Since Babar came, Hindus were massacred. First they were reassured that a *parikrama* was being built around Rama Janmabhoomi. But when Hindu devotees came there to pray, they were killed and thrown into a huge pit. This is not just about land, but about restoring our faith and dignity.'

Feeling resigned on being confronted with this classic defence of a Rama temple, I turn the topic to his work of cleaning naalis. 'From a socio-political viewpoint, social reformers like Gandhi have countered municipal negligence and social neglect in their own way,' he says. 'The three-volume biography of Mahatma Gandhi, penned by Bhagavadacharya, has been deeply inspiring for me – *Bharat Parijatakam*, *Bharat Parijata Pahad*, and *Bharat Parijat Saurabh*. In fact, in 1960, I had a memorial built for Bhagavadacharya in Ayodhya. In those days, it cost eighty thousand rupees. Swami Narasimha Das from the Jagannath mandir in Ahmedabad instructed me and helped in this. He gave the money to Bhagwan Das Khaki and I supervised the construction.' Readers may recall this memorial from Chapter 3 on Yugal Kishor Shastri. This is the spot from where he was recruited for an RSS shakha. Also, Bhagavadacharya's work on Gandhi has inspired Shastri too, as he has mentioned.

'First I used to wander a lot and go to distant places and clean naalis. Now I work mainly around Hanuman Garhi,' says Ram Sharan Das. However, he has once been at the receiving end of Mahant Gyandas' temper. 'Because of my work as a journalist, he used to want me to write the press notes and press releases for the temple. Once, when I did not write such a note, he got a lock put on my room door, and I was left homeless for about three months. I would wander about, sleep and eat where I could. If it had not been for Shri R. N. Singh, I.P.S., who was a friend and well-wisher of mine, I would have been out on the street. He had my room opened for me once again.'

Notwithstanding his opinion of Muslims, Ram Sharan Das is a good friend of his contemporary, Hashim Ansari. Indeed, every single person who is asked in Ayodhya has only good things to say about Ansari. 'Hashim Ansari is a very hard-working and honest man,' says Hari Dayal Mishra. 'There are few people as straightforward and good-hearted as him.'

'I have been friends with Hashim Ansari for as long as I can remember,' says Ram Sharan Das. 'We became friends because he had a cycle repair shop in Shringar *hat*, and I had a cycle for the longest time. I tried to keep it in top condition.'

'So where is it now?' I ask.

'I had to sell it after the wound on my leg from the dog bite did not heal for several months,' says the old sadhu. 'It was too painful to cycle then'

Why has this man, who has chosen such a unique path of service to Sri Rama and Hanuman, not accumulated followers and imitators? 'He would have been far greater if he had been able to inspire even five other people to carry on his work,' tartly remarks Krishnavati Maurya, an Ayodhya housewife. 'What words can be used to describe Ram Sharan Dasji?' says Sharad Sharma, head of the media cell of the VHP at Karsevakpuram. 'His sacrifice and service to Ayodhya and Sri Rama are incalculable.'

In spite of such encomiums from the organization that spearheaded the movement for a Rama temple at Ayodhya, Ram Sharan Das has not found any naali-cleaning volunteers to follow him from within the VHP.

'People watch me, but don't join in. They sometimes even abuse and scold me, in fact. Others sing praises, or show exaggerated respect. But even they do not try to emulate my work. It is very difficult for people to join me,' he says, wiping his eyes and the contours of his old and weathered face. 'This work demands that we rise above both caste and class.'

The 'naali wale baba' of Ayodhya is a stark reminder of the contradictions and social conditioning that imprison us.

❧

PART II

ESTABLISHMENT ENTITIES

What place does a spiritual search have within the trappings of power? Who forms the establishment in Ayodhya? While some have followed a well-laid tradition to hold their present positions of religious, ceremonial or municipal authority, others have led a life of such unimpeachable dedication that they have become institutions themselves.

Presenting profiles of some of the foremost citizens of Ayodhya.

5

Bimalendra Pratap Mishra
Raja in Rama's Kingdom

Ramanath jahan raja, so sukh barani ki jayee
Animadik sukh sampada, rahi Awadh par chayee.

(Where Lakshmi's husband is himself the king, how does one describe that happiness? Such indescribable joy remained over Ayodhya.)

—*Ramcharitmanas* by Goswami Tulsidas

Setting out to meet the Raja of Ayodhya, Shri Bimalendra Pratap Mishra, the first thing that strikes you is how a Brahmin came to occupy a throne that belonged to kshatriya kings, Dasharath and Sriram, in times described by the Ramayana. In fact, in the last Lok Sabha elections in 2009, the Raja, also known as 'Pappu Bhaiya' had stood for elections on a BSP ticket, part of Mayawati's attempt to consolidate her support base among Brahmins and those who may have otherwise voted for the BJP.

It's a different matter that the Raja lost the elections and reportedly also a *kothi* in Lucknow costing over ten crores, that he had signed over to the BSP before the elections in order to be given a ticket.

On the street, the Raja's *praja* (subjects) discusses the electoral defeat dispassionately. '*Haar bhi gaye, Ayodhya ki pratishtha bhi mati mein mila diye* (not only did he lose, but he also brought down the prestige of Ayodhya),' says Suresh, a young pujari at one of Ayodhya's many temples. These citizens of an independent India have long learnt to take their royalty with a pinch of salt. In the case of Bimalendra Pratap Mishra, they are rather more liberal than a pinch. This is because this Raja stays cut off and alienated from his fellow Ayodhya-ites.

To get an appointment with the Raja, I speak to him on the phone on several occasions, send him sample chapters of my book by e-mail, and talk to his son, Yatindra Mishra, poet and the moving force behind the Vimla Devi Trust, a cultural organization founded in memory of the Raja's mother. My attempts result in a short meeting with the Raja, wherein I explain the need for a longer interview for the book. 'Perhaps if readers across the country read what people in Ayodhya have gone through, they will be able to see how Ayodhya is like their very own city – full of the challenges and contradictions of modern India,' I say, gushing somewhat. The Raja gives me a long-suffering look, as if I am to be pitied for what I have said. 'Ayodhya is not like any other place,' he says.

'Well, yes, of course, it's absolutely unique, but you know what I mean,' I trail away. Does he know what I mean?

I do my best to draw him in conversation, my attempts faltering against the perfectly civil, but glum and reserved manner that the Raja maintains throughout our encounter.

Our surroundings are elegant. Giant bottle palms in urns extend thin fronds around us; tea is served in fine china, with milk and sugar in separate pots. This is a rarity in Ayodhya, and I savour it. 'Earl Grey?' I enquire, and the Raja waves a hand and says, 'Possibly, yes.' He isn't really interested in these small matters.

A *desi* touch is provided by a sumptuous helping of *gajar halwa* and some *kheer*. I have spent time in so many sadhu quarters, been given tea in *kulhads* and *namkeen* hurriedly bought from the market, that the Raja's offerings are startlingly different by contrast. They are also designed to fob me off.

I commiserate about the election defeat, my remarks again sounding gushing to my own ears. 'Of course, aside from the election, you two must be friends,' I say, referring to the present MP of Faizabad-Ayodhya, Nirmal Khatri of the Congress.

'Yes, we are close friends. In fact, his brother, Rajkumar, is my doubles partner in tennis,' says the Raja. I try, with great difficulty, to avoid the impression I am forming that the Raja is deliberately making me feel like a social outsider. I decide that I shall not make any further notes, or gather any more impressions, till I have had a chance to meet him again. We part on that note, and outside, where Yatindra is sitting reading proofs on a bench next to a fountain with white geese in it, I again remind him of how he is to arrange our next meeting.

Many calls and text messages later, it finally dawns on me that the next meeting is never going to take place.

The Raja of Ayodhya was not always a supremely isolated individual/institution. The last king who enjoyed immense popularity and is still remembered by people in Ayodhya was Dadua Maharaj from a kshatriya clan that hailed from Saiganj and ruled as Ayodhya's royal family. Dadua Maharaj is credited with shaping modern Ayodhya, particularly its network of many temples (*see* Chapter 8), and reclaiming land from Muslim burial grounds. In his time, regal traditions that involved the people, such as festive celebrations and feasts, charity and some measures for the common good, were maintained and brought him goodwill.

Dadua Maharaj was politically razor-sharp. During the tumult of 1857, the British received intelligence reports that he was a hostile king. They therefore made a plan to attack him from the nearby garrison of Gorakhpur. However, when Dadua Maharaj learnt of this plan, he turned the Tulsi Udyan, a park in Ayodhya, into the Victoria Park overnight. Through such minor gestures of appeasement, he was able to win over the British, who consequently rewarded him by having a whole lot of *zamindari* lands included in the kingdom of Ayodhya. Earlier, the king had also arrived at separate understandings with the Nawabs, which had resulted in him receiving lands from them as well. Sahadat Ali Khan, Nawab of Awadh, is in fact said to have bestowed the *riyasat* (honour, large landholding, in effect, kingdom) of Ayodhya on his 'loyal Brahmin soldier Dwijdeo Mishra of the Kasyapa gotra', for quelling revenue rebels in Mehendauna in Eastern Uttar Pradesh. This is how the Mishras claim their royal lineage. In local parlance, Dadua Maharaj is referred to as a kshatriya by most people. Under this king, Ayodhya expanded geographically, while his 'adjustment' with the British also brought political stability.

The only tragedy, if it can be called that, was that the canny king was childless. He therefore adopted his minister's family, and this gentleman's son was accordingly anointed his successor to the throne. This king's name was Raja Jagdambika Pratap Narayan Mishra – and here we have the entry of the brahmins. However, in his lifetime, this king used both Singh (kshatriya) and Mishra (brahmin) suffixes to his name. Continuing the problems relating to heirship, Raja Jagdambika Pratap did not have any sons. He only had a daughter, Vimla Devi, who was the mother of the present king, Bimalendra Pratap.

There are whispers in Ayodhya that the accession of Vimla Devi's son to the throne was not a smooth or easy one because Raja Jagdambika Pratap's brother, Jagdish's progeny, had patriarchal rights, while the present king is in his maternal grandfather's place. The person who is said to have been deprived of his rights is Vimla Devi's cousin, who went by the name of 'Bahadur Mama'. In fact, some claim that the present king has no formal documentation of his legal right to rule, but has just gone ahead by bulldozing his way within the family. However, all this is just conjecture, and no one is willing to reveal the deep divisions that may have existed on the issue of succession. '*Ab yeh navaase hain, yeh to doosre paitrik adhikar walon ko bura laga hi hoga* (now he is the maternal grandson, so his ascension to the throne must have disturbed those with a clear claim through their father),' is the statement one hears, without any real dates or details of any suits or claims filed. Consequently, I don't feel like putting on my running shoes and going in search of Bahadur Mama. Besides, one Vijay Krishna Mishra, who is the maternal uncle of the present king, by virtue of being his mother's cousin, stays in the Raj Sadan at Ayodhya. So there is one maternal uncle being honoured, even if it isn't 'Bahadur Mama'!

What is of more interest than these murmurs of family differences over the throne are the present king's actions in the context of the Indian republic. In recent times, a legend that links Queen Huh, wife of King Suro, who was the founder of the Karak kingdom in Korea, with Ayodhya, came into prominence. Queen Huh was supposedly a princess from Ayodhya, whose father, the then king of Ayodhya, was inspired by a dream in which he received advice to marry his daughter to the Korean king. The marriage took place and the princess from Ayodhya moved to Korea sometime in the middle of the first century AD. There is a plaque inscribed with this story at Queen Huh's monument on the banks of the Sarayu at Ayodhya.

The monument came to light in 2001, when the mayors of Ayodhya and Kim-Hae town of South Korea signed a 'sister city bond' to commemorate their historical ties. There is a three-metre-high stone monument that weighs more than 7,500 kg which was made according to Korean traditions, with stone brought specially from South Korea. The Koreans are so attached to the memory of Queen Huh that they had hosted a delegation from Ayodhya to celebrate their historical association with this town. Two hundred crore rupees were also to be given for the development of Ayodhya by the South Koreans. The money could certainly have been useful for a cash-strapped town whose municipality is denied proper funding even to conduct its annual melas (*see* Chapter 7).

The Raja of Ayodhya went to Korea as the head of the Ayodhya delegation. His detractors claim that, once there, he alleged that Princess Huh was from his family, and that they had once been adherents of Buddhism. However, he backtracked on these claims when challenged by journalists. If one is to go by Yatindra Mishra's interview to *The Financial Express* in 2004,⋆ the actual story is that the Prime Minister of Korea invited his father to play a ceremonial role in commemorating the national link to Ayodhya, because two thousand years ago, a princess of Ayodhya had been sent as a bride to the Khmer prince, Suro. Out of the couple's ten children, nine became Buddhist monks while one built what we know today as Korea. It is his descendants that today form the ten million strong Kim clan. In the same article, Yatindra traces his royal lineage back to three hundred and fifty years, with Sahadat Ali Khan's gift of the Ayodhya *riyasat* to Dwijdeo Mishra, which makes the chances of his being related to a two-thousand-year-old princess rather remote.

Following the discovery of the Ayodhya-Korea link in 2001, every year a group of dignitaries comes from Korea whom the Raja greets and hosts. Whether this has actually resulted in funds being received from Korea for Ayodhya's development was something I could not confirm by talking to him. But there were plenty of disgruntled people muttering remarks like, 'He went on government money! Did he bring anything back, or was it just tourism?'

A dissenting royal family follower said, 'He carried a whole load of gifts for them from here, and received an unprecedented welcome. His brother-in-law (*behenoi*) who accompanied him described the dozens of gifts he received in return too. But the Raja has not kept any of them. He distributed some of them in Korea itself, declared the rest to the government. He did not lower the prestige of Ayodhya by seeming to be a *'bhikhari'* (beggar).'

Leaving aside these local differences of opinion on their Raja, what emerges is that this remains probably the only instance in

---

⋆'Plaint of Ayodhya', 22 August 2004.

recent times when the Raja has been in the public eye for some community-related issue. Many of the subjects of this book, who grew up in Ayodhya, have passed through the portals of Maharaja Inter-College, their alma mater. This institution, ideally placed to groom fine future citizens of Ayodhya, and founded by the royal family, rarely sees the Raja. 'He appears on a few occasions in a purely ceremonial capacity. Otherwise his family members don't concern themselves much with what happens to us students,' says Ajay Dwivedi, a student himself.

The Shankar and Annapurna temples inside the Raj Sadan compound are reputed to have an intrinsic tie with the people of Ayodhya. Old-timers recall how the *jhaanki* (glimpse, tableau) of the Devi used to be a special attraction for the people during all the nine nights of Navaratri, in times past. There is also a Ganesh idol made of coral that is remembered at these palace temples. But the inclusive nature of the temple festivities has seen a gradual change over the years. Now, while midnight pujas with tantriks and cronies by the Raja's son are spoken of by some, others bemoan the low public participation in the palace jhaankis. Apart from their palace temples, the royal family of Ayodhya also has shrines like the Sitaram temple in the Raj Dwar area, the Radha Brijraj temple adjoining the State Bank of India on Ayodhya's main road, and also hold a lot of land in neighbouring Gonda. All their pujaris are paid a salary for their services at these temples, making the whole business of maintenance a costly affair unless it is supported by generous offerings from the public in the form of *chadhaava* (devotional gifts of money). Whether such offerings are forthcoming from a surly and indifferent Ayodhya citizenry today is a matter of some doubt.

The one area where Ayodhya's royal family could be said to be making a regular contribution is in the arena of culture, more specifically, through the Vimla Devi Foundation awards. In my brief meeting with Bimalendra Pratap Mishra, the only time he showed a degree of animation was when he spoke on the subject of the foundation, the Vimla Devi Foundation Nyas, established in early December 1999, that gives awards to eminent personalities with a significant contribution to music and dance. Stressing the fair nature of such awards, Bimalendra Mishra spoke of how the committee that selects awardees is completely independent, and made up of authorities in the field of culture, so that the purity and integrity of the awards is beyond doubt. 'Ashok Vajpeyi, Kunwar Narayan . . .,' the names tripped off the Raja's tongue, and, even the performers at the Vimla Devi Foundation festivals at which the awards are presented make up an impressive list, including Gangubai Hangal, Girija Devi and Shubha Mudgal. In March 2010, the line up was similarly illustrious – rudra veena maestro, Asad Ali Khan; qawwali group, Ahmed Khan Warsi and party; Bharatanatyam dancer, Geeta Chandran and group; Kathak dancer, Prerna Shrimali; and conversations with the lyricist, Gulzar.

In his 2004 interview to the *Financial Express*, Yatindra Mishra says, 'I plunged into local culture, because it seemed obvious that someone needed to get involved. Today we have a deal with Virgin Records of the UK for old archival recordings, whereby royalties go either to the artists themselves or to their survivors. The artists who have passed away include Ustad Amir Khan, Pandit Onkarnath Thakur and Kumar Gandharva. Living artists so far include Girija Devi of Varanasi on whom I wrote a book in Hindi. It got me noticed in the Hindi literary world. And then, Hans Harder, Professor of Indology at Martin Luther King University, Berlin, saw it fit to translate my Ayodhya poems from Hindi to German.' ('Plaint of Ayodhya', Sunday, 22 August 2004.)

The truth lies between the lines. Getting noticed in the Hindi literary world has obviously been an important side-effect. In the same interview, Yatindra goes on to speak of Pagal Das, Ayodhya's own musical legend, a *pakhavaj* artiste credited with the revival of the *mridang* in Hindustani classical music. He makes a passing mention of this musical great, along with the crafts of Ayodhya such as making *khadaon* (wooden sandals used by sadhus) and *sindoor*. But the real regard that the royal family has for the memory of Pagal Das can be learnt from his disciple Vijay Ram Das 'Taalmani', himself a talented mridang, pakhavaj and *tabla* player, and the guardian of the Pagal Das legacy through the institution the maestro founded – the Sri Hanumat Vishwakala Sangeetashram at Ayodhya.

'Ayodhya's musicians and artistes are languishing from a lack of patronage from Ayodhya's royal family,' he says. 'The Raja and Yatindra never encourage us by showcasing our performances here, or anywhere else. In fact, what is most hurting is that after such consistent neglect, they remember us only if some or the other accompanying artistes fail to show up for their "great" performers, the big names. Then they send people to chase us and ask us to play tabla for that evening.' In an incident that is stunning in its reflection of condescension and callousness, Vijay Ram Das recalls an occasion when he played for one of the Vimla Devi Foundation events and the occasion was being archived to be converted to CDs later. While the part of the evening where Shubha Mudgal sang was duly archived, when Vijay Ram Das went to ask for his performance's recording, he was told that it had got corrupted due to some fault in the equipment, and therefore deleted. So much for the Vimla Devi Foundation's efforts at presenting the great Pagal Das' legacy to the world.

'The Vimla Devi Trust is a vehicle for Ayodhya's royal family to earn a name for themselves. They care little for Ayodhy'a own *pratibha* (talent),' says Sri Krishna Madhukar. 'Come with me, I can introduce you to the boy who actually wrote the poems that Yatindra published as his own in the collection, "Yada Kada,"' says a young professional. Since plagiarism is an old, and not unknown aspect of the literary world, I decline the invitation. However, I search for any goodwill that the present king and prince may have earned in Ayodhya-Faizabad, and end up not finding any. It is perhaps for this very reason that this royal family has not been able to play any role in working towards a solution to the mandir-masjid problem, despite the Raja's attempted entry into electoral politics.

'When Vinay Katiyar was put up as a candidate from these parts, the BJP had actually approached the Raja to be a candidate. But he said he is not interested in entering politics. Then what happened with Mayawati? It was a big miscalculation,' says Sri Krishna Madhukar. 'His stellar contribution to any cause can only be considered signing away the lands he owned to the VHP for the Karyashala (workshop where the stones for the Rama temple have been carved). Even though Paramhansji had control over the land, it was his, and he signed it away without consideration to the VHP.' A kothi to Mayawati and a karyashala to the VHP. At least the royal family of Ayodhya still has abundant resources to give away in this fashion across different political seasons.

Splendid isolation may be the path this royal clan has chosen for itself. But in the context of democratic, millennial India, it strikes a jarring note.

—◦◦◦—

6

Phalahari Baba
Reformed Roughneck

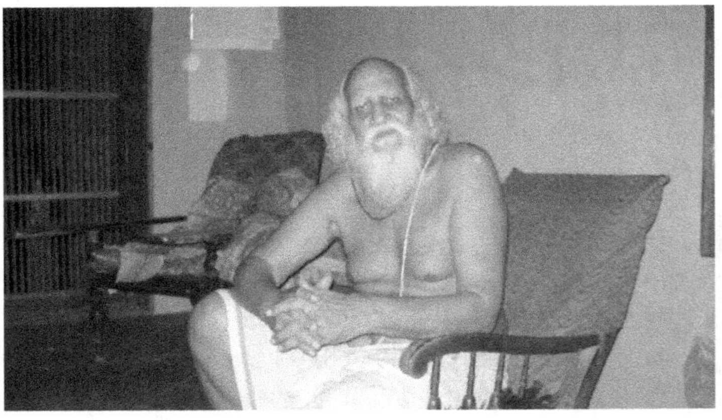

Ansuvan jal seench seench, prem bel boyee.

(I planted the vine of love, and watered it with my tears.)

—Meerabai

Heading an institution in the heart of Ayodhya is a sadhu who is known for his moderate and well-considered views. Remarkably free of all the obvious symbols of religious power in these parts, such as gunners in attendance with rifles, or men with elaborate *tilaks* on their foreheads screening visitors, Sri Kaushal Kishore – or Phalahari Baba draws respect across a wide social and political spectrum, an obvious indication of his integrity and acceptability as a spiritual person. In an Ayodhya where the biggest names among sants, mahants and sadhus are accustomed to making derisory references to each other, this overall acceptability is no mean achievement. It is even more remarkable considering that Kaushal Kishore may have completely missed becoming a sadhu, when he was better known as the terror of Balrampur.

'I was born in Balrampur,' says Phalahari Baba. 'My father, Keshav Ram Shukla, was a freedom fighter who followed Bhagat Singh and Chandrashekhar Azad's approach rather than the Gandhian one. He was jailed by the British, and after Independence, when he was released, he became a part of the Revolutionary Socialist Party, working for the poor and the landless. He strove to get the workers of the Beck Sutherland sugar mills unionized, and secure a bonus for them. When zamindari was abolished, he campaigned shoulder to shoulder with small farmers to get them their redistributed lands.'

His father's efforts on behalf of the poor were enough to disturb powerful vested interests, who had Keshav Ram Shukla murdered when his son was still a young student. 'The tragedy of my father's death disturbed my education. Since his death had been a political murder, the desire for revenge grew in me, against those I perceived to be behind his death. Unable to immediately deal with these people, I became a local rowdy instead, whom others came to for protection,' recalls Phalahariji.

'Kaushal Bhaiya', as he was then called, commanded enough clout in Balrampur to head a sizeable gang of youths. 'We were a bunch of rough and tough youngsters. But, inexplicably, a man named Pandit Badri Prasad used to have *kirtans* and *satsangs* in his house, and some of my rowdy friends used to attend these sessions.

They liked going, and spoke with great fondness of the man who sang hymns to God with such feeling that everyone was moved. This irritated me. I attended a few of Pandit Badri Prasad's "kirtans" without being particularly affected by them. I began to speak of him as a *nachaniya* (dancer), a theatrical man who was leading my friends astray. Pandit Badri Prasad, I later learnt, had come to hear of my criticism.'

Kaushal Bhaiya's protection tactics were needed around this time, when one of his friend's sister was teased by some boys at the girl's college she attended. 'Call Kaushal Bhaiya!' was the universal cry, and sure enough, he swung into action. 'I had the youth who had teased the girl beaten and paraded in a rickshaw around town, with the girl's feet planted on his chest,' he says. This was an event that the eve-teaser and his family would of course, not forget in a hurry. Seething under the humiliation meted out to him, the youth crept away after the public rickshaw ride.

A few weeks later, the film *Har Har Mahadeo* was running at a local cinema. 'My friends wanted to see the film, and such was the fear I inspired among the locals that the manager let in fifteen of them into the balcony of the theatre without their paying for the tickets! I myself, however, did not go for the film,' says Phalahari Baba. This single abstention was to lead him to the turning point of his life.

'All my friends were at the cinema. As I walked alone on the street, I was suddenly faced with the gang of the boy I had humiliated for the eve-teasing incident. They were after my blood. I ran from these men, crossing streets and neighbourhoods, walls and gutters, running for my life,' he says. It was then that he remembered the home of Pandit Badri Prasad, which had its own temple, with a door that was never locked. He ran into the temple to find the Pandit in a state of silent ecstasy before his God, tears running down his cheeks even as his eyes were closed in contemplation.

'I was afraid that the gang would enter the house in search of me, and to save myself, I had to lock the door. I tried to do this as softly as possible, but Panditji heard the sound. He opened his eyes, and turned to look at me. He could see me panting and dishevelled. He asked for no explanation, and I offered none. Then he held out a hand to me. It had a *tulsi mala*. He offered these prayer beads to me and said, "Say Sita Rama, and remember the nachaniya who leads young men astray."'

That was the moment when Kaushal Bhaiya transformed into a spiritual seeker, one who would not be satisfied with half-measures or mere ritual worship. Kaushal Kishore accepted the tulsi mala and took the first step towards becoming Phalahari Baba.

Pandit Badri Prasad passed away just a few months after this experience. After his mentor's death, Kaushal Kishore came to Ayodhya where he was given the Sitaram mantra by Pujya Sri Siya Raghunath Sharan of the Hanumat Sadan temple. He stayed at the Sadan for a few days, then returned to Balrampur, a 'tired, exhausted soul'. He began abstaining from all his prior activities, concentrating on *jap* alone, focussed chanting and meditation on Sitaram.

'I was a rogue turning to spirituality. I threw myself into it with the same passion which I had earlier shown towards my activities as Kaushal Bhaiya. I developed a desire to see God. At the same time, I felt I was not qualified for domesticity – for all the strength and resilience that a man needs to complete his duties towards family. As my practice developed, I began getting spiritual experiences,' he says.

However, this evolution from Kaushal Bhaiya to Phalahari Baba was not completed without its share of pain. 'I stayed with my mother and paternal grandparents. One night I overheard a conversation between my grandfather and grandmother. He was expressing his anguish to her. He was saying, "I had one son and he was killed. As if that loss was not sufficient, now my grandson has become a *bairagi* (renunciate) who sits all day with his tulsi-mala. I thought I would have someone feed me and look after me in my old age. Instead, I will have to support this grandson indefinitely."'

Phalahari Baba was devastated by this conversation. 'What will become of me? And what of my inability to ever be of use to anyone?' He asked this of the God whose name he chanted night and day. Even before he had received an answer, he decided that that day onwards he would not eat anything but fruits and berries, food that he could himself pick off the trees. 'I first began living on *amla* from a tree in our compound. Then, in the summer months, it was *bel* (wood apple) that I ate. This diet is what brought me the title of "Phalahari" or one who lives on fruits. Of course, over the years, it began to include all the elements permissible for those who are ritually fasting, such as rotis from the flour of *singadha* (water chestnut) and vegetables. It's no big deal today for me to be a Phalahari – I am amply nourished. But in the beginning, I was truly and exclusively living on fruits alone.'

Such austerities, and the sheer torment that had led to his asking God what would become of him, were bound to elicit an answer in some form. Kaushal Kishore, now Phalahari Baba, received his reply in a dream wherein his God reassured him, 'You are on the right path. Have faith and patience.' He attributes it to divine Grace that from around that time, elders and scholars began visiting him.

'Through some mysterious way, I seemed to have the right word and phrase for whoever came to visit me. They went away marvelling at my every word, and I would wonder, what is so great about what I have said? Anyway, I began to acquire a reputation among very educated and powerful people, while I still lived with my mother and grandparents. No one knew the pain and anguish that had led to my spiritual awakening and its aftermath. For some time, life continued on that scale. Some land was available to us for farming and food supplies. We lived a lower middle-class life.'

When Phalahari Baba left Balrampur to come and take up permanent residence in Ayodhya, he found that his instincts, the values his family had bequeathed, made him distance himself from wrongdoings. 'My father had gone on a year-long fast with Mukti Nath Upadhyay in Benares Central Jail,' he recalls. 'Mahatma Gandhi and Nehruji were concerned about his condition. At the time they had requested Sampoornanand to have daily status messages about his health to be posted in the popular newspaper *Aaj*.'

In contrast to such sacrifices for principles, Phalahari Baba found in Ayodhya, a sadhu community whose sole aims seemed to be 'to live in comfort, to collect wealth, to make a name'. His approach began to make waves soon after his arrival. 'My guru, the mahant of Hanumat Sadan, put up a proposal to appoint me as the successor of the mahant of Rajagopal Mandir, before a sabha of elder mahants. They approved of it, but when I was informed, I told them that my guru's judgement is not at fault, but I am not interested in being the mahant of a temple. Let a gurubhai of mine be appointed to the post, and I will serve him in any capacity I am asked to serve. This became a big topic of discussion in Ayodhya for some weeks. Then the topic turned to – who will be the mahant if Phalahari has refused? My guru asked me to choose a successor for the Rajagopal Mandir from among my gurubhais, and I did. I was willing to do all the work, be a servant, not a mahant. It was my attempt at starting a new work culture in Ayodhya, to remove the sense of inferiority that persisted among sadhus. It is this feeling of inadequacy that results in people setting up more and more temples, appointing themselves mahants.'

In some more years, the question of the Rajagopal Mandir came up again. By now, Mahant Gyandas, the powerful head of the Hanuman Garhi temple, had his eyes on the seat, and was keen on having his own man in place. Trustees of the Rajagopal Mandir, such as Shri Narayan Das Khatri and 'Qiladhish', the mahant of Lakshman Qila, were opposed to Gyandas' claim. Phalahari Baba was appealed to by many sadhus who asked him to occupy the Rajagopal Mandir position, as someone who could stand up to Mahant Gyandas.

Phalahari Baba took over as head of the Rajagopal Mandir and Sanskrit Mahavidyalaya on 1 July 1985. There was so much tension about this particular appointment within the sadhu community that the then SSP, Karamveer Singh, presently DGP Uttar Pradesh, had the area of the temple cordoned off. Ordinary citizens came out in support of Phalahari Baba. He has headed the institution ever since, a sprawling campus opposite the lane leading to the Chhoti Devkali temple in Ayodhya. Young boys in dhotis and the tilaks of novitiates can be seen in the ample courtyard of this place, playing cricket in the winter afternoon, or heard in the evening, singing prayers or shlokas. A sweeping circular staircase leads up to the first floor where Phalahari Babai meets visitors. He welcomes the opportunity for both spiritual and secular discourse. While I sit and speak to him about his life and times, he delivers a brilliant description of the present balance of power in South-East Asia and the self-serving interests of US foreign policy as an aside to another visitor.

This is one sadhu who remained outside the movement for a Rama temple, even while he stayed within Ayodhya's establishment the entire time the mandir agitation was raging across the town and country. He says wryly of how this happened, '*Mahamaari ke samay mein bhi kuchh log bach jate hain* (even in the time of an epidemic, some people are saved).' He was nowhere near the crowds in 1990 and 1992, or seen anywhere in the build-up to the demolition at the meetings held regularly by the VHP in Ayodhya. 'When the VHP began with a *kalash yatra* for Hindu Jagran (Hindu awakening), I too spoke at a few of their meetings as a sadhu. Initially, it was being touted as a non-political movement. But soon, it became clear that it was the grand web of a conspiracy to capture power (*raajtantra ke shadyantra ka mahajaal*) and I was repelled, and refused to have anything more to do with them,' he says. This refusal of Phalahari Baba is part of his critical approach to the whole structure of religious authority and power in Ayodhya.

'The main business of Ayodhya is religion and spirituality,' he says. 'Unfortunately, it is a culture that creates hypocrites, emphasizing form over substance. Look at the Sanskrit education being pursued here. The rural boys who study in Ayodhya would be better off being honest farmers in their villages. Teachers here are lazy, students cheat and collect certificates, everything is done mechanically, with no real interest or love for the language. Even the dozens of *pravachans* (discourses) being given here daily by sadhus and sants of all kinds are mere verbal sophistry. What do you really have to say? Is it coming from the heart? What is the use of quoting from the Gita, Puranas and Upanishads when all have gone through hundreds of editions? It is better to say something original, than to try and hide behind such scholarship.' Regretting this atmosphere of lip service and worldliness in a place supposedly meant to be a destination of faith and spirituality, Phalahari Baba asks a pointed and poignant question: 'If I make this very temple and institution grand and shining, how would I have contributed to Ayodhya?'

Like hundreds of other temples and trusts, the Rajagopal Mandir is also facing a slew of cases relating to the ownership of land and assets. 'I consider the long legal struggle on behalf of the temple to be the darkest chapter of my life!' says Phalahari Baba.

Following the demolition of the Babri Masjid on 6 December 1992, Phalahari Baba had taken the then prime minister, P.V. Narasimha Rao, roundly to task at a meeting in Delhi at which Nirmala Deshpande, Mahant Gyandas, Shitla Singh had all been present. 'I held him fully responsible for what had occurred, and did not hesitate to say to him, "All these incidents have happened with your knowledge", in front of everybody,' he recalls. The PM heard him out in stoic silence. Later, he asked his home minister to consult Phalahari Babai on what should be done in Ayodhya in the aftermath.

I do have a question, though, that remains unanswered and I present it to Phalahari Baba. What happened to Rama Lalla when the Babri Masjid came tumbling down on top of the statues that Abhiram Das and his associates had surreptitiously installed there in the intervening night of 22-23 December 1949? Many theories abound in Ayodhya about this. 'Mahant Laldas, who had been the pujari of the Rama Janmabhoomi for many years before he was removed and replaced, had alleged that looting kar-sevaks had carried away the idols of Rama Lalla, Lakshman and Sita at the time of the demolition,' says K.P. Singh, senior independent journalist who has spent years with *Jan Morcha*. 'It is highly possible that this was so, since complete anarchy reigned at the spot for over forty-eight hours. Para-military forces had to conduct a pre-dawn operation to flush out the hundreds of kar-sevaks who continued to remain at the site of the demolition. In fact, it was these determined and well-trained hordes who levelled the ground and removed the traces of the mosque, following its fall.'

If kar-sevaks had indeed carried away the idols of Rama and Sita and Lakshman from the site, then where did the present idols come from, and who placed them there? In my conversation with Phalahari Baba, it emerges that one possibility is that that they could have been placed there by an administration anxious to prevent further bloodshed and rioting. Since president's rule had been imposed immediately after the demolition, such a step becomes the brainchild of the Congress government at the centre. Was the Congress behind both the original planting of the idols in 1949 and their replacement following the demolition in 1992? In any case, locals who had been worshipping the 1949 idols and who later saw the post-1992 Rama Lalla noticed a visible difference in them.

'The Congress is less likely to have planted fresh idols in the interest of maintaining the peace,' says K.P. Singh. 'More likely it was the VHP camp itself, which hurriedly found replacements. You see, the absence of idols on the spot meant a weakening of their claim over the land. They could not have left a blank spot. Moreover, even if the idols had not been looted, they could have just got buried under the masjid debris. When the archaeological excavation began, some bodies had also been found buried under the fallen structure. If actual people could be trapped like that, of course Rama Lalla's idol could have been similarly buried.'

When you consider the descriptions of the orchestrated chaos of 1992, the words of Phalahari Baba acquire added meaning. 'The country became independent,' he says. 'But what is Independence? This is something we have not understood even today. We have failed to communicate this to our people. *Arajak chetana Bharat mein vidyaman hai* (an anarchic consciousness prevails in India). It is true that just and right thinking people have increased in numbers, but still, everybody sees justice only through the prism of self-interest.'

The sadhu who has walked the difficult path of seeking self and God, speaks with the candour of the brave and the wise.

7

Mithilesh Pande
Homemaker at the Helm

Nagar palika parishad Ayodhya aap se appeal karta hai ki:
Nal ki tontiyon ko khula na chhoden
Koodha karkat ek jagah hi ekatrit rakhen
Nagar aapka hai, ise saaf suthra rakhen.

(The Municipal Council of Ayodhya urges you to turn off taps, and collect garbage in one place. It's your town, keep it clean.)

—The Municipal Council, an Ayodhya advertisement in the
June 2007 issue of *Bharatiya Leher*

Wander the streets of Ayodhya and you cannot go a couple of hundred feet without encountering a foundation stone or embedded marble or granite board in a building or street corner that announces – 'This ____ was inaugurated by Respected Mithilesh Pande, the Chairman of the Ayodhya Nagarpalika Parishad on ____.' These boards, some with gleaming golden letters that wink in the sunlight, prepare you for an encounter with the lady elected to the Chairmanship of the Ayodhya Municipal Council, long before you actually see her.

Meeting Mithilesh Pande requires having to negotiate the hours that she may be in the kitchen cooking, or taking an afternoon siesta, or otherwise not available to visitors. The first time I manage to talk to her, accompanied by a fellow Congress party member, she is candid about the difficulties of administering a town like Ayodhya. 'There are four important melas in a calendar year, but no budgetary provision for these. We have to manage with available funds. The worst part is the dearth of sanitary workers. The town is growing in all directions. There are far more streets now than there were even ten years back. New colonies are coming up, with many more residents in each. But our staff strength remains the same, we cannot recruit afresh. Keeping the town clean is our biggest headache.'

She is a tall, fair, well-built woman whom any family would like to have as a *bahu*. As it is, she is the wife of Shailendra Mani Pande, a political stalwart of Ayodhya whose career graph has traversed the Janata Dal, the Samajwadi Janata Party, the Samajwadi Party and finally the Congress, of which both he and his wife are now members. Mithilesh considers her husband her political mentor or guru. Both are in Ayodhya from birth. While he plunged into politics after completing his MA and LL.B, winning his first election to the Municipal Council as an Independent in 1988 from the Swargdwar ward where they live, she fought her first election on a Samajwadi Party ticket against the BJP's Chandrakanti Mishra in 1995, losing to the latter by a few hundred votes.

Mithilesh Pande's election to the chairman's post was preceded by two terms, Chandrakanti Mishra's in 1995, and Mahendra Singh's victory as a Congress representative in 2000, both of which got mired in allegations of unofficial 'commission' payments and corruption. It was a time during which citizens were not able to notice any visible change in conditions or amenities. During these years, Shailendra Mani's popularity increased, and people perceived him as a firebrand, a leader with the potential to bring real change in the town.

Shailendra Mani was all set to contest and win the elections in 2006, when the seat was announced as one reserved for women. This is when the couple moved to the Congress. On 3 October 2006, they joined the Congress, and on 4 October they filed Mithilesh's nomination for the election. In November 2006 she won this election handsomely and took charge of the Municipal Council, with a band of trusted councillors as her cabinet.

'My *janmabhoomi* and *karmabhoomi* (birthplace and place where one makes a contribution with one's work) are both Ayodhya,' she says. 'Ayodhya is a religious town, different from other places. Because this is both my *sasural* and *maika* people here are fond of me, and regard me as *Ayodhya ki beti*. They therefore deal with me with affection, not with the impatience and scepticism with which they may view other officers. Officials come and go, they get transferred, promoted. But my relationship with the people is different. They know I will continue to stay among them.'

Within her home, Mithilesh has to perform the balancing act

that professional women from the city handle routinely – that of keeping family and elders happy, while staying busy and professional. 'There are definite difficulties when you're a woman,' she admits. 'If you are in politics, your visitors or aggrieved citizens do not take into account your time or space. (I am quiet about the many occasions when I've tried to meet her and have failed.) They wish to see you anyway, and family routines cannot accommodate such demands. The elderly do not like to eat the food cooked by servants. Children need attention. One has to try hard to maintain a fine balance.'

In a region as deeply feudal as Uttar Pradesh, notwithstanding its dalit woman CM, women who enter public life face all kinds of hostility from society. Having a protector, a burly political one in the form of a committed husband, is a definite asset. Shailendra Mani enters halfway through my second meeting with Mithilesh, and his presence seems to give her confidence, grant her reserve. She shifts topics, from domestic concerns to business.

'The whole experience of being elected to something like the Municipal Chair is like this,' she says. 'The first year just passes by in your getting used to the office, its functioning, the people. Then you begin to address the major problems. Before you know it, half your term is done. When I took over, our biggest problem was the huge backlog of dues in the salaries of sanitary workers. We owed them nine months of salary, and other staff up to thirteen months. How can people be motivated to work in such circumstances? When the Municipal Council of Ayodhya was separated from Faizabad, our sanitary workers were 110 in number. There has been no recruitment of sweepers in the last fifteen years. The current number of sweepers is around seventy-five, out of which everyday around fifteen or twenty are absent. Do you think this is enough to keep Ayodhya clean? We have given out seven wards on contract for private agencies to do the necessary cleaning, and this is still not enough.'

The refuse in Ayodhya is dominated by food and its by-products because of the large numbers of daily bhandaras or community eating. This is evident to anyone who walks around and spots *pattal* and *dona* (leaf plates and bowls) heaps along street corners. These in turn are rummaged by monkeys, and provide some much-needed nourishment to the hundreds of hungry bulls, calves and cows that roam the streets.

When I point this out to Mithilesh, she says, 'Temples and matts litter streets all around the clock, but our municipal sweepers have set times for their duties. How are we to keep pace? For instance, our sweepers normally clean a road and leave by twelve noon. But this would be just around the time that some mandir would offer *bhog* (the offering of food to be blessed by the deity in a temple and later distributed as prasad) and then have a bhandara! Immediately after the bhandara, the plates are thrown on the road, after which the monkeys and other animals have a whole day to spread them all around town before they can be collected and cleaned up again the next morning. It's a vicious cycle, and we don't know how to break it. Appealing to the matt or mandir does not work; we have tried it umpteen times. Sadhus will do everything their way, and no one can get them to change!' Mithilesh speaks with calm, but one can understand her anguish.

This is the most obvious example of the householder versus sadhu contradiction that plagues Ayodhya. For a town like this to keep clean, either antiquated municipal facilities have to invest heavily in getting modernized, or tradition-bound religious institutions have to develop a civic sense more in tune with the twenty-first century. When neither happens, the consistent ugliness of open and dispersed garbage in this temple town is likely to persist.

We return to the topic of the melas, the defining point in Ayodhya's calendar, that she had mentioned to me in our first meeting. 'Our budgets have been slashed from Rs 4.29 crores to Rs 2.22 crores. This cut has drastically affected performance. You see, the mela pilgrims stay at mandirs and matts, where there should have access to private toilets. Instead, they stay there, but are forced to defecate by open roads, or in nearby fields. It is a really sad situation. And we face a tough time during the mela when there is an influx of thousands, even a couple of lakhs of pilgrims, and insufficient numbers of public or private toilets.'

But hasn't sanitation been taken up as a priority by the administration at any time, I ask, shocked that a town with so many annual visitors could be this apathetic. 'It was taken up at least once, when Mr Lu was DM,' says Shailendra Mani, referring to Mr Venkateswarlu, an IAS officer hailing from Andhra Pradesh, who, for some reason, is only always referred to as 'Lu Saab' by people in Faizabad and Ayodhya. While I did not have the fortune to be in Faizabad during his tenure, I have once heard him speak on the occasion of Kabir Jayanti at the Kabir Matt in Ayodhya. That speech, delivered in a heavily accented but perfectly correct Hindi, came with a no-nonsense injunction to the audience to solve problems like ignorance and over-population. In fact, I had been struck by the officer's sincerity and his courage at taking up the whole issue of procreation in Uttar Pradesh, where the average family even in 2011 has three children, and four or five are quite common. He was definitely a memorable personality.

'So how did he take up the issue of sanitation?' I ask Shailendra

Mani. 'Well, he had asked for toilets to be constructed by all the matts and mandirs playing host to mela visitors. In fact, he had four sittings with sants and mahants to take up the matter on a war footing. But this was not done, and then he was also moved elsewhere.' As his voice trails off, the picture of indifference and neglect by successive governments becomes apparent.

This town, always in the national headlines for some mandir-related issue, is much worse off than other, smaller municipalities elsewhere in the country. 'In fact, running the municipality can only be effective if other departments and agencies also support us,' says Mithilesh Pande. Her partyman, Balkrishna Goswami, deputy chairman of the Zilla Congress Committee, who arrived somewhere during the course of our conversation, nods emphatically in agreement. 'See, look at how our facilities work,' he says to me. 'The electricity is cut off at 6 a.m. Over winter, it is still dark at this time. The water supply stops if motors cannot run. In the evenings too, the supply of electricity is erratic. What can people do in the dark? Every home cannot have inverters.' Mithilesh interrupts, 'In the municipality, though, we use generators to pump water.'

'What are the arrangements for the winter cold?' I ask. Our conversation is taking place on the coldest day of the season, with day-time temperatures hovering between five and seven degrees! Every person I encountered on the deserted roads of Ayodhya-Faizabad had a miserable expression, skin reddened and face screwed up against the icy wind. 'We have bonfires at twenty-five places in the town,' Mithilesh Pande tells me. 'We would have been able to arrange for bonfires in at least twenty-one more places, if we did not have to take up the responsibility of arranging for bonfires at all the checkposts for the security personnel for

Rama Janmabhoomi.' 'You mean, the police and central forces have separate bonfires from the people?' I ask. 'Of course,' says Mithilesh Pande with a mildly amused look at my naivete. 'We pay for their bonfires too, though these expenses should rightfully be paid for by the SSP.'

There is a short spell of silence. We have arrived at the point which is at the heart of the arrangements for this embattled temple town – the issue of permanent security. After all, a huge number of security personnel have camped in the town since 1989.

All at once, the interviewees start speaking in unison, and I struggle to unravel the threads and put them in place. 'Crores are spent on security,' says Balkrishna Goswami. 'And yet, the burden of payment falls on the municipality. If even the security guards' bonfires have to be lit by the town's funds, what is the point?'

'See, we have a sewer cleaning machine – an imported one that cost many lakhs, that was meant to be used to clear night soil in different parts of the town. This is to be used by residents. They are charged a fee of seventeen hundred rupees per truck load of waste cleared. There is a waiting list for this machine, so great is the demand. But the police force around Rama Janmabhoomi? They ask for it whenever they want,' says Shailendra Mani Pande.

'To date, there are dues of two-and-a-half lakh rupees for this machine from the police personnel,' adds Mithilesh. 'You can imagine how long they have been using it without paying.'

'Life is nothing less than hell for the people who live in the Yellow Zone, stretching from Tedhi Bazaar to Brahm Kund, Kaushalya Ghat and all the areas around the barricade,' says Balkrishna Goswami. 'They have to constantly have armed security forces breathing down their necks, and there are so many restrictions on their movement. God forbid if an aged or a pregnant woman finds herself there needing medical attention in the middle of the night! She will not even find a rickshaw-man there at that hour, it becomes so deserted.' He pauses, then says, 'And yet, the sadhus come for their extortion day and night.' 'You mean the moneylending sadhus of Hanuman Garhi?' I ask, and he nods. '*Sadhuon ko mala pe nahin, bandookon par bharosa hai* (sadhus have more faith in guns than they do in their prayer beads),' he says.

So has the agitation for the Rama Mandir really left a crippled Ayodhya, I ask. 'Of course,' says Mithilesh, looking at her companions for assent. '*Vihip Rama ki vyapari hai, Rama ki pujari nahin* (the VHP trades in the name of Rama, they do not worship him),' says Balkrishna. 'If they want to build one grand temple for Rama, can they tell us why they have been directly or indirectly responsible for destroying no less than thirty-five traditional temples on the acquired land?' asks Shailendra Mani Pande. 'Really? Thirty-five temples?' I ask, and they begin listing some of them. 'Sakshi Gopal Mandir, Sumitra Bhavan, Rama Khajana Mandir, Kohabar Bhavan, Anand Bhavan, Chauguruji Mandir – each one of these was a small bit of Ayodhya's history, each was associated with an aspect of Sri Ram's life,' says Balkrishna.

That means that the levelling of the land and the artefacts collected from it were as likely to have come from these tiny mandirs as from the supposed temple destroyed by Mir Baqi prior to 1528. I am suddenly faced with another facet – the deceit of those who have appointed themselves as the guardians of the Hindu faith. Why is it that despite being a practising Hindu, I have never felt attracted to the call of the VHP or its slogans? And I know dozens of others like me, so as not to feel like some freak of nature.

Feeling oppressed by what I have learnt during our meeting, I ask Mithilesh Pande if her time at the helm has resulted in any concrete gains for the people. Of course, the stones and inscriptions all over town praising her are very impressive, but since she is functioning under so many limitations, has she been able to do any good at all?

Her detractors incidentally had arrived at their own reason for these stones. They alleged that these plaques were the handiwork of her husband, who had to shell out a mere thousand rupees to have some marble tablet installed. Officially, these were to be place-holders and funds would get sanctioned for a building or a playground at the site. These funds would then be available for diverting elsewhere. 'Mithileshji may be an innocent in political terms but her husband has used these five years like a true politician,' some have murmured to me. Sharad Sharma's barbs about the scam of more than a crore of rupees that the *Hindustan* has been writing about in relation to the Ayodhya municipality is also on my mind. When I question her, I do so, hoping she will reel off an impressive list of achievements.

'We have laid a good network of roads, consistently cleaned sewers and garbage points, we have added dumpers and mini-loaders to our fleet,' she says. 'Also, the problem of drinking water supply has been addressed for all the seasons, particularly the parched summer months, by digging tubewells, reboring community handpumps, and laying pipelines. People have begun to notice our work because it makes a real difference to their lives.'

While Mithilesh Pande has not yet managed to press local Congress MP Nirmal Khatri to take more interest in budgetary allocations for Ayodhya, she has been trying to secure Sonia Gandhi's attention. With the typical optimism of a politician, she says, '*Hamein samay kam pad gaya. Agar mauka mila, aur janata chahegi, to aur kaam karenge* (I ran out of time. If I get another opportunity and people want me around, I will do more work).'

A few months away from the end of her term,* it is difficult to say if this mother of two teenagers will indeed get another shot at being at the helm of India's most controversial temple town. But walk around Ayodhya, and all the stone tablets will tell you that she has tried enshrining her name for posterity.

---

*This interview was conducted in late January 2011. Mithilesh Pande will remain the chairman till the local body elections are conducted in UP perhaps in December 2011, or in early 2012.

8

Baba Jairamdas
Ramlila's Rakshak

Hamun sakal balakan meela, karaun sadaa Raghunayak leela.

(I will get together with all the children and forever perform the
'lila' of Sri Rama.)

—Hanuman's dialogue in the *Hanumat Natika*
by Goswami Tulsidas

Past the landmark of Mani Ram Das ki Chhavani in Ayodhya
lies the neighbourhood of Vasudev Ghat. Down one of the
lanes in Vasudev Ghat is the Patthar Mandir, Ayodhya's largest
and most respected training centre for Ramlila, the folk theatre

performance of Sri Rama's life. Ramlila enjoys a special status just before Dussehra, when it is performed in Varanasi and Delhi, and hundreds of small towns all across North India. In Ayodhya, a daily performance sponsored by the Department of Culture of the Uttar Pradesh government is running in its seventh year, giving the opportunity to Ramlila troupes from Mathura and Brindavan, Madhya Pradesh, Bihar, Rajasthan, and even Orissa and Karnataka to present their art before an avid daily audience of at least three hundred people.

Enter the courtyard of the Patthar Mandir and you find dhoti-clad boys with long tilaks on their foreheads exercising, washing clothes, sitting or talking. These are the actors of the Ramlila, under the care and guardianship of the *vyas* (director and main narrator) of the Awadh Adarsh Ramlila Mandal, Baba Jairamdas, who is also the mahant of the Patthar Mandir.

Baba Jairamdas is always a pleasure to meet because he offers the affection and warm curiosity of someone used to dealing with people, and getting the best out of them. He always sprinkles his remarks liberally with a '*behna*' or a 'beti', and while such consistent humility can be considered a kind of form for a sadhu, it does not fail to touch those he meets. In his appearance, he bears an uncanny resemblance to the present head of the Rama Janmabhoomi Nyas, Mahant Nritya Gopal Das, a formidably powerful sadhu and mahant of the Mani Ram Das ki Chhavani. Together, the two can easily make for a 'separated at birth' captioned photo. But while Nritya Gopal Das has beetling brows and a forbidding expression, Baba Jairamdas has a wide smile. Where the former is surrounded by gunners, assistants and queues of visitors eager for a darshan, the latter is at ease sans gunners or visitors, meeting the tradespeople bringing provisions to the temple, or dealing with the boys training under him. The two sadhus are not related, and are very different from one another, whatever be the superficial resemblances they share.

Baba Jairamdas has lived in Ayodhya all his life. It is this town – its sadhu community, and traditions of worship – that has shaped his entire being.

Baba Jairamdas' father, Ram Sharan Pande, was a poor Brahmin who lived with his wife and three sons in the Sri Haridwari bazaar area around Hanuman Garhi. Ram Sharan and Devaki Devi's eldest son was born on 2 November 1940, and named Jagdish Prasad Pande. Subsequently, two more boys were born, and the last one was found to be deaf and mute. The family eked out a living by the father's twin occupations of making tulsi-malas for sale to sants, mahants, and pilgrims, and carrying notes as invitations to bhandaras. On this income, he was able to enroll his sons at a primary school at Tulsi Chaura. When Jagdish Prasad was a mere ten-year-old student of class five, his father passed away. As if this tragedy was not devastating enough for the family, a month later Jagdish Prasad's mother died too.

In 1950, three orphans, the eldest – Jagdish – only ten years old, his brother – Ram Narayan – aged seven, and the last – Ram Kumar, whom people called *gunga* (mute) – aged five, were left at the mercy of the temple town of Ayodhya. 'In the evenings *khichdi* was distributed at Hanuman Garhi or Mani Ram Das Chhavani. I used to go and pick up my share, which I then divided with my brothers,' recalls Baba Jairamdas. 'At other times, our neighbours offered us what food they could.' Unbelievable as it may seem in today's harsh circumstances, the three orphans actually managed to live like this for some time.

Then, on Independence Day 1950, Jagdish Prasad had gone to

the Patthar Mandir near Shravan Kunj in Vasudev Ghat, where the famous Ramlila of Baba Prem Das was being staged. There, along with a group of star-struck boys, he watched keenly while the regular Ramlila artistes were applying their make-up. Nearing the time of the performance, Baba Prem Das' disciple Radhe Das began shooing away the boys, clearing space around the actors. All the boys ran away, but Jagdish Prasad stayed back. Seeing the lone boy, and cursing his stubbornness, Radhe Das lifted the boy's hand up and violently flung it down, and also gave him a tight slap for emphasis.

At this, Jagdish Prasad began to cry and reproached Radhe Das loudly for hitting him. Baba Prem Das, who was sitting nearby, heard the altercation, and called the boy to his side. 'Why are you hitting such a small child?' he scolded Radhe Das. 'What is your name, *beta*? Where do you live?' he asked the boy. What he heard about the boy's stark circumstances shocked him.

'Will you stay here and learn to act in the Lila?' he asked Jagdish Prasad. 'If you agree, you will get food and clothes, and five rupees every month.'

'I have two younger brothers,' said Jagdish Prasad, hope dawning on his tear-stained face, along with a determination to get the best deal for his brothers. After all, they were dependent on his ten-year-old self.

'Okay, if you agree and learn the Lila, we shall send five rupees every month for both your brothers too,' said Baba Prem Das.

The boy felt as if a great weight had been lifted off his shoulders. 'Yes, I will join you. Just let me tell them and come,' he said, collecting himself to run home as fast as he could. There, he told a kind neighbour, Ram Lal Halwai, a sweet shop owner, of the offer he had received, and the man and his family agreed to have his younger brothers in their charge while he joined the Lila.

Ever since, Baba Jairamdas has lived in the Patthar Mandir, daily preparing to perform an art that is, in reality, only another form of devotion to Sri Rama. 'When I joined the Ramlila at Patthar Mandir, the vyas was Mahant Ramdev Dasji Maharaj, and the tabla and mridang for the performances were played by the legendary Pagal Dasji Maharaj,' he recalls. 'We had very good actors for the lead roles. I learnt to play the harmonium and sing portions of the *Ramcharitmanas* from Ram Dev himself, and it was he who named me Jairamdas.'

When Baba Prem Das passed away, the baton of carrying forward the Awadh Adarsh Ramlila Mandal was picked up by Ramdev Das. For a time, the mahant of the temple was Ram Tirath Das, but after he passed away six years later, Ramdev Das took over. So it was, in 1984, thirty-four years after he had come there as a small orphan, Baba Jairamdas took charge of both the temple and the Awadh Adarsh Ramlila Mandal and continues to lead these today. He has, however, in the tradition of the Patthar Mandir and other such institutions in Ayodhya, already appointed his successors – Sri Ram Lalan Das as vyas, Shashi Kant Das and Baba Manish Das. Ever since Baba Jairamdas led the Mandal, the Awadh Adarsh Ramlila has been performed in many different states like Assam, West Bengal, Jharkhand and Chhattisgarh, Rajasthan and Madhya Pradesh, besides being honoured by the UP Sangeet Natak Akademi and the Adivasi Lok Kala Parishad of Madhya Pradesh.

'The Patthar Mandir was set up in 1880 by a *shishya* of Gurudev Baba Raghav Das,' says Baba Jairamdas. 'We are followers of Swami Ramanandacharya. The foremost feature of our Ramlila is that it is based on the works of Goswami Tulsidas, mainly the *Ramcharitmanas*, and then other works like the *Ramachandrika* and *Hanumat Natika*. The Ramlila is Tulsidasji's great gift to humanity.

It began in Varanasi, at Assi Ghat and Tulsi Ghat, and is still celebrated today with a grand Rajyabhishek Lila performed at Tulsidas ji's *samadhi* spot every year. Awadh Ramlila is special because we stay most faithful to the texts. *Hamare liye Ramlila ek aradhana, ek samarpan hai* (for us, Ramlila is a form of worship, a surrender). After all, this is Ram's birthplace, and we are performing for him.'

In his childhood, Baba Jairamdas remembers Ayodhya as a very small place, dominated by Muslim graveyards. 'Vikramaditya's Ayodhya had been destroyed,' he says. 'Mughal invaders only wished to flatten temples and loot what they could. Like the Suraj Mandir in Kashmir was destroyed by Mohammed Ghori, Sri Ramjanmabhoomi was attacked by Babar. If it had not been for Darshan Singh, or Dadua Maharaj, who acquired land all over and had temples built, modern Ayodhya could not have been a town with over fifteen thousand temples. Ayodhya has been rebuilt from the ashes.'

Clearly recalling the euphoria of both 1947 and 1949, Baba Jairamdas says, 'When I was seven, the country became independent. Then, in 1949, the idol of Rama Lalla was installed. There was such a great outpouring of faith! Pilgrims were arriving here from Ujjain, Haridwar, Nasik. For some time, it felt as if Ayodhya was a magnet for the devout. Then, from 1949, it became the subject of dispute,' he says, his expression conveying acute regret.

'What is present-day Ayodhya like?' I ask him. 'Does it bear any resemblance to the town you remember?'

'Saints are still living here, bathing in the Sarayu, doing daily puja and kirtan, leading a quiet life,' he says. *'Rama nam ki kheti hai behna, rama nam se sab kuch chalta hai* (it is the harvest of Ram's name, sister. Everything is made possible by Ram's name).' When I press him for an explanation of how this occurs, he reveals a poignant truth. 'Where else could sadhus stay? Who will give us employment? What else do we have except the name of Sri Rama?'

Something stirs inside me. My rational self says, 'What a classic argument of the unemployable! So religion is only a means to fill one's stomach by peddling illusions.' But at a deeper level, something inside me is rejoicing. 'Truly, anything and everything is possible, if you stay true to Rama!' Baba Jairamdas' candour and commitment has pushed me to examine my own level of faith.

In today's circumstances, Baba Jairamdas feels acutely about how Ayodhya has suffered indignity and carries a tarnished reputation. '*Ayodhya ke saath anyay hua hai* (injustice has been done towards Ayodhya).' In what way, I ask. Who has been most unfair towards Ayodhya?

'Mulayam Singh Yadav,' is the unequivocal answer. 'His declarations in 1990, when he said, "*Parinda ek par nahin marega* (not a bird will be allowed to flap its wings)," about the arrangements here, were very hurtful to people's sentiments at the time. There were four or five incidents of police firing, putting Ayodhya's residents and the citizens' lives at risk. Those who died in the stampede after the firing were loaded on to trucks, carted away and disposed of in the river.' I did not question these statements, although this is the exact area where differences arise between people's accounts of 1990 and 1992. Their statistics are in exact proportion to their perspective on the temple. Those for a Rama Mandir speak of horrific atrocities, and those for a balanced and secular approach downplay the casualties.

'No one else, not Narasimha Rao, not Rajiv Gandhi or Kalyan Singh, no one has tortured Ayodhya like Mulayam has,' continues Baba Jairamdas with uncharacteristic bitterness.

'So was he there at the spot on 6 December 1992?' I ask him. 'Yes, I was at a temple called the Rama Kacheri Mandir, watching the crowds of kar-sevaks arrive from all directions,' he says. 'Truly, behna, I felt the *devas* had descended from heaven to perform a divine task. I saw a *jattha* (large group of people) arrive from Jharkhand, with bows and arrows. Another followed from Maharashtra, with naked swords. They were raising slogans making their intent clear – 'Kar-seva *rokoge, to maar seva dikhayenge!* (If you stop us from performing kar-seva, we shall show you violent *maar-seva*, brutality.)' It was a charged atmosphere. I feel it is nothing short of a miracle that events unfolded the way they did. Or who could have brought down a structure made of bricks and mortar and stone and tested over centuries?'

This protector of the Ramlila tradition may be ascribing a divine meaning to events described elsewhere as frightening, murderous of the Constitution, and India's darkest hour. But if so, his words only mirror the truth of these lines of Goswami Tulsidas, *'Jaaki rahi bhavana jaisi, prabhu moorat dekhi tinh taisi* (it is our own individual feelings that define our perception of God).'

In a land as driven by faith as ours, we have not been able to develop a system of justice and common good that can unite differing perceptions.

9

Mahant Satyendra Das
Manning the Epicentre

Sarvesham anukool ved niyamo dharmah – jo sabhi ke anukool ho, ved sahmat ho, aise karma hi dharma kehlayenge.

(Those acts that guarantee the well-being of all, and are in accordance with the Vedas, only such acts can be considered 'dharma'.)

—Mahant Satyendra Das quoting from the scriptures

'Rama Lalla', the infant form of Lord Rama, has been at the centre of controversy ever since the VHP chose to link Ayodhya with 'Hindu identity'. In fact, this relatively obscure deity was thrust into prominence through the courts around the beginning of the present-day Rama Janmabhoomi movement in 1989, thanks to a case filed on his behalf by Deoki Nandan Agarwal, a senior advocate who retired as a judge of the Allahabad High Court. From that time, the label 'Rama Lalla' began being used to describe the infant god whose birthplace was the disputed site in Ayodhya. Since March 1992, this deity has been worshipped and served by Mahant Satyendra Das, the priest appointed by the government to officiate at Rama Janmabhoomi.

When all hell broke loose around him on 6 December 1992, it was Satyendra Das who was responsible for the safety of the idols under the central dome of the mosque. He has since continued working in the position, acutely aware that the crown of Mahant-hood comes with thorns.

For a person regarded as one of the most learned men of religion in Ayodhya, Mahant Satyendra Das had a remarkably late start in the world of letters and scriptures. He was born in Basti, now Sant Kabir Nagar, in a village at the meeting point of the Sarayu and Kuano rivers, on 12 November 1938. As a child, he felt deeply attracted to the character and story of Hanuman. 'I went to Ayodhya as a child and loved the place. I used to want to return there as often as possible, to have darshan of Hanumanji,' he says.

The simple rural boy was nearly twenty when he met Abhiram Das on 2 February 1958. Abhiram Das, the sadhu from Bihar who was the leader of the team that placed idols in the Babri Masjid on the intervening night of 22-23 December 1949, asked the young Satyendra a simple question: 'Do you want to study?' When the boy replied in the affirmative, he took him under his wing, and thus began his education.

'I had to begin studying from the primary level, so my age was misrepresented; it was suggested that I was younger than I actually was. I studied for some time and got a fifth class passing certificate, then I entered the Hanumat Sanskrit Mahavidyalaya to study for the *madhyama* or secondary level,' recalls Mahant Satyendra Das. His late start notwithstanding, he showed an aptitude for classical studies, and graduated as a Sanskrit Shastri and Acharya from the Dakshinamoorti Sanskrit Mahavidyalaya at Varanasi with a special qualification in *vyakaran* (grammar). In 1976, he began teaching at the Tridandi Dev Sanskrit Mahavidyalaya at Koshlesh Sadan, Ayodhya, continuing to study alongside by appearing for his Vedanta examination and earning his Master of Arts from Awadh University in 1979-80.

A mild-mannered, non-controversial, scholarly sadhu, Satyendra Das was appointed the mahant of the Rama Janmabhoomi on 1 March 1992. 'The court-appointed receiver, J.P. Singh, had died on 20 February 1992. After that, the district administration was in charge of the temple at Rama Janmabhoomi. I was appointed by Umesh Tiwari, the then ADM, and took charge on 1 March,' he says. The process of appointment for this post says a lot about the calibre and qualifications of Ayodhya's sadhus. The administration was hard pressed to find a sadhu who had never had an FIR registered against him, was not involved in any case, and had no obvious political party affiliation. Many names were suggested, which included Baba Dharamdas, Satyendra Das' *gurubhai* (fellow disciple of Abhiram Das), Govardhan Pujari, Bajrang Das and Janardan Das, but they fell short of one or more of these conditions. In Ayodhya, where every small temple or matt was mired in legal claims and counterclaims, it was difficult to find a suitable personality, free of such cases. 'My qualifications and general personality did help the administration arrive at a decision,' admits Satyendra Das, when I question him about how he came to be their choice.

The bright and outspoken Mahant Laldas had earlier occupied this post. He is best seen in the Anand Patwardhan documentary, *Raam ke Naam*, and is subsequently quoted in *Creating a Nationality: The Rama Janmabhumi Movement and Fear of the Self* by Ashis Nandy and others (Oxford India, 2005). His very ability to call a spade a spade went against Laldas. Bitterly opposed to the politics of the VHP in Ayodhya, he was removed by the administration when they came under pressure, ostensibly because of there being several cases against him, and on account of his having quarrelled with the then City Magistrate. Satyendra Das succeeded this colourful personality in a very quiet way, with a total of three appointed assistants, chief of whom was Ram Narayan Das.

Before this appointment, Satyendra Das had lived through the trauma of the police firing in 1990 along with other Ayodhya citizens. 'We were told to sit down by the police,' he recalls. 'In fact, we had all sat down peacefully, and chanted, "Sitaram, Sitaram." The police fired on such a crowd. Innocent people died on that day. I knew of at least three from Ayodhya, Ramesh Pandey, Rajendra Dharkar and one Gupta. I believe the final figure of people who had died was thirty-two,' he says. While different sides were giving different figures at that time, the unanimous view was that the incident was extremely traumatic. It was unthinkable that people engaging in satsang could fall to police bullets, even if some of the members of the crowd were slogan shouting, headband sporting kar-sevaks out to flout every constitutional authority.

When the masjid was stormed into and demolished by thousands of kar-sevaks, Satyendra Das was performing his duties as priest. He was present at the very spot. 'I was in the temple. At 11 a.m., I was told by the leaders of kar-sevaks, "Give us a coconut and some cloth, and we will do a puja." Meanwhile, regular announcements were being made, ordering kar-sevaks not to crowd and rush towards the chabutara just outside the structure where people traditionally place their offerings. They were being urged to bring sand and water from the Sarayu instead to perform a symbolic puja for the temple, and hand this over to us. From the stage that had been erected there by the VHP, it was announced, "With the water and sand that you have brought, the chabutara will be washed and the puja will be performed." At this announcement, some young boys started shouting and rushed towards the structure. This form of distant worship when they had been made to believe that they would actually begin the process of making the Rama temple with their bare hands was too much for them to accept. They picked up the materials that had been kept nearby for the construction of the Seshavtar Mandir – bricks, iron rods, wooden planks. They began attacking the structure with whatever they could find.'

Recalling the sequence that led up to the fateful day, Mahant Satyendra Das says, 'The VHP did not have any intention of building the temple. On 4 December, a judgement was expected in the Ayodhya title suit regarding whether a symbolic puja could be conducted on the disputed 2.77 acres of land just adjacent to the mosque. The court did not pass a judgement on that day, and instead, scheduled the next hearing for 11 December, meaning that the parties concerned were to wait for the decision. Instead, the VHP preempted any order by announcing a kar-seva on the sixth, a mere two days after the last hearing. The spot at which shilanyas had been permitted earlier, was chosen as the site for a symbolic construction with people bringing water and sand.'

Enraged at being deprived of the opportunity to contribute in any real or meaningful sense, crowds of kar-sevaks began shouting violent slogans and rushing towards the mosque. 'The top brass of the VHP could not control the crowds,' says Satyendra Das. 'They just had to flee in fear. After that, no announcements worked. Events took their own turn. The domes began to fall and people from Ayodhya began to carry away mud, bricks, even pieces of the metal barricading, to their homes.'

What about the idols, I wonder. Did the dome fall on them? There have been suggestions by some that the idols were buried under the debris, and later substituted by the VHP, because the VHP's claim would not exist without there being idols on the spot. This is a charge that had been voiced by Laldas before he was murdered. Were the idols lost and the throne, ornaments, etc., of the deity looted by kar-sevak mobs? Mahant Satyendra Das is angry at the mere suggestion.

'How could I have allowed such a thing to happen?' he asks in anguish. 'Before the first dome came down, seeing the ugly turn of events, I had the idols removed to a place of safety with my attendant pujaris.' He does not specify where. 'In fact, they were reinstated there the very next morning, and have been in place since. I could not offer bhog for prasad on the sixth, and this caused me so much grief that I spent the next twelve years living on phalahar alone,' he says.

The question of what had become of the idols on the day of the demolition is not a trifling one, however. It was raised on the floor of the Lok Sabha and Home Minister S.B. Chavan had to clarify that there had been an investigation into the matter and the idols, their ornaments and throne had all been found to be the same as before the demolition. 'Anyone who suggests that this Rama Lalla is different from the one who was in the temple earlier is doing me a grave injustice,' says a visibly upset Satyendra Das, for whom the issue is indeed loaded with significance. After all, it was his guru, Abhiram Das, who placed the original idols in the mosque.

The events of 6 December 1992 have impacted Satyendra Das' life in very direct and difficult ways. They have forever changed the shape of things, so that the daily routine of worship and service – the very basis for his existence – has become dry and barren official duties. 'It used to be a different world before 1992,' he says. 'There were so many little shops for pilgrims. *Chehel pehel rehti thi* (it used to be very lively). *Rama Lalla purna roop se surakshit the, puja vidhi vidhan se hoti thi* (Rama Lalla was completely secure, pujas used to be conducted in the prescribed manner). Now, Rama Lalla is affected by the sun, wind and rain. The curtains around him flap in the strong breeze, the rain falls on the tent and wets it. It is terrible. When Sri Rama has said, "*Main bhakt adheena* (I am under the protection of my devotees)," it makes it more important for a true devotee to guard his or her *aaradhya* (adored one, deity) more securely than his own life.'

In fact, the conditions Mahant Satyendra Das describes cause several devotees to weep openly at the spot. 'It is a very difficult situation for a devotee to accept,' continues the mahant. 'I cannot have an *akhand deep* (eternal lamp) burning all round the clock; no one stays long enough. Only curtains hang between Rama Lalla and the elements. The *maryada* (etiquette) of a temple cannot be observed, such as putting the deity to sleep, or waking him up with special puja.'

Instead, Rama Lalla has to be attended to according to a roster that covers four assistant pujaris and four workers. 'We are all assigned our separate duties. I go as required. On a typical day, I reach there at 10 a.m., offer bhog at 11.30 a.m. Other pujaris do their roster to cover the duration for which the place stays open for darshan. We are really troubled by the monkeys. They are a real nuisance. The food items for bhog have often been snatched or have fallen down on the ground in the time it takes to cover the distance from Manas Bhavan to the Janmabhoomi (a few hundred yards). Everyday, the bhog has to be carried under elaborate protection. People hold lathis to scare away the monkeys, and in spite of this, two of my pujaris have had serious monkey bites,' says Mahant Satyendra Das.

So fed up did the mahant become with the constant threat posed by the monkeys that he has learnt a special recipe for monkey bites, one that Ram Vilas Das of Vasisht Bhavan had been taught by his guru. 'I make it myself regularly for people bitten by monkeys,' he says.

Underlining his dissatisfaction with the bleak conditions around Rama Lalla, the mahant says, '*Rama Lalla ki dayaniya dasha dekh kar lagta hai ki un logon ne Raja Rama ko bhikhari bana diya* (the pitiable conditions in which Rama Lalla is placed makes one think that those people turned King Rama into a beggar).' He is referring to the people behind the havoc of 6 December 1992. It is because of them that today most of us struggle to redefine our duties and responsibilities as citizens of a free, fair, and secular India.

Hari Dayal Mishra, who has a ready wit (*see* Chapter 2), has classified the three disciples of Abhiram Das who are prominent in Ayodhya in the following way: Satyendra Das is the *vidwan* (scholar), Dharamdas is the *pehelwan* (wrestler) and Ram Vilas

Vedanti, VHP ideologue and former BJP member of Parliament, is inspired by a *shaitan* or the devil.

Mahant Satyendra Das' reiteration that the VHP did not intend to build a temple for Rama, highlights that the conflict may have been a grand political game. 'History may have taken a different turn if the Congress had continued in power in UP,' he says. 'They are veterans and know how to manage difficult situations, such as the placing of the idols or the shilanyas. They offer a middle ground, a solution that is acceptable to all. Bullets in Ayodhya, the masjid falling, everything happened after the Congress lost power in UP.' Since the Congress was last in power in Uttar Pradesh in the first week of December 1989, and doesn't look like it will come into office any time soon, this seems like a forlorn assessment. Besides, others have hinted at the culpability of players like former Prime Minister P.V. Narasimha Rao and former Home Minister Buta Singh in matters relating to Ayodhya. The managerial skills of the Congress have repeatedly been tested and they have often failed in the process of safeguarding our nationhood.

However, Mahant Satyendra Das' sentiments can be appreciated and identified with. Yearning for a state such as that described in the Uttarkand of Tulsidas' *Ramcharitmanas*, wherein '*sab nar karain paraspar preeti*' (all people live in harmony, with affection for each other), he says that future policies have to be decided carefully. They need to benefit all. '*Sarvajanhitaya karma hi dharm hai*.'

Tending to a deity that is as much a symbol of India's inability to manage her contradictions as it is of the faith and devotion of many, Mahant Satyendra Das hopes and prays for a better world.

⟨⟨⟨⟩⟩⟩

10

Rani Awasthi

Auntie of the Differently Abled

Utho, jaago aur tab tak rukon nahin jab tak manzil prapt na ho jaaye.

(Arise, awake, and stop not till the goal is reached.)

—Swami Vivekananda

For a lone woman, being able to carve a niche for oneself in a patriarchal world is often an act of absolute heroism. Surviving the stares and taunts of a male-dominated society and continuing on one's chosen path with undiminished confidence makes this even more remarkable. Rani Awasthi's achievements in Ayodhya reflect one such saga.

Rani was born on 11 October 1955 in Allahabad. Her father was the manager of a printing press, while her mother was staunchly religious and a traditionalist who believed in doing all the housework. Rani was the third daughter, with two younger brothers. Her elder sister was studious. The father doted on Rani, calling her 'Dulari' or 'Dulariya' or 'Mem' because she was very fair. She thus knew she could rely on her father's protection. Rani got away with all the mischief for which her sister might have been scolded or punished. A direct consequence of this was that she developed a close relationship with her younger brothers, who motivated her to do something daring!

Because she was beautiful, Rani's family received a proposal for her, when she was very young, from a very rich family. There were no dowry demands made, the groom's family had a thriving business dealing in foreign liquor. Rani's parents married her off at nineteen to one of the sons of this well-known family. 'At that age, marriage for me meant travelling in a car, wearing jewellery. I wasn't thinking of the complications or the responsibilities,' she recalls. 'I was sure that I wanted to continue studying and did so, even though my in-laws disapproved. My husband's elder brother's wife had had to give up her academic career a few years earlier. Since I was the younger bahu, kitchen duties began to get thrust on me, so I had little time to study. It was hoped that I'd be forced to discontinue, but I was determined.'

Rani could have even borne her personal struggle with equanimity if it wasn't for the oppressive atmosphere at home relating to the division of the large family-held property among the brothers. At that time, her husband was the one who was spending the maximum amount of time at the family's shops and office. The arguments and discussions around the division of property were upsetting, but what caused Rani the most distress was the acute attack of food poisoning suffered by her husband. Unable to shake off the feeling that his own family could be responsible for his illness, she experienced what she calls *moh-bhang* (the breakdown of attachment) with her in-laws. 'The money, the house, everything began to depress me, and I wanted to leave. I came to Ayodhya in 1980-81 for a darshan like any ordinary pilgrim,' she says.

She loved the place the instant she set foot in it. For a reason she could not then fathom, she wanted to live there. It was during this trip that she met someone who would become a long-term associate – Kripa Shankar Tiwari, and through him, Rang Narayan Tiwari, who was running a school in Faizabad, the Meghdoot Shiksha Niketan at Reidganj. 'Come and live in Ayodhya, and run my school,' Rang Narayan Tiwari invited her, and this was enough to convince Rani that she would do just that.

Rani left the oppressive home of her rich in-laws and began living in Ayodhya. She ran the Meghdoot Shiksha Niketan for four years. Then her neighbours in Ayodhya began telling her, 'You live in Ayodhya, but go and work and teach in Faizabad! Surely you can do something for us. This town needs you.' Their words had a salutary effect.

On 25 April 1984, Rani founded an institution that had two separate initiatives under it – the Prominent Public School was started as a good mainstream school for children seeking a better education in Ayodhya. 'A revenue-earning school that would help pay teachers for the specially-abled children,' is how Rani puts it. Alongside this, the Mand Buddhi Mook Badhir Vidyalaya was started to educate hearing and speech-impaired and mentally-challenged children and help them overcome their handicaps. Both wings of Rani's institution have continued to be in operation since that day, and her school for special children has enabled hundreds of them to find their place in society.

Establishing a vital institution did not mean that Rani was able to shake off the family troubles that had motivated her arrival in Ayodhya in the first place. Pressure from her in-laws to return to the home in Allahabad was increasing around this time, so she convinced her husband to come and stay with her too. Here, he set up a small business of his own, the Rani Medical Stores at Maatgaind Chauraha. When, following her husband's arrival in Ayodhya, family pressure continued to mount on the couple to return to Allahabad, Rani and her husband decided to stay on in Ayodhya even if it meant maintaining a low profile during the property division. The family business was declining. Land and shops kept getting sold. Rani and her husband had to fight for their rights even as they tried to keep a distance from the bitterness and politics around the division of property.

Rani's husband fell ill in 1996. Even though he had several relatives in the medical profession, the couple chose to have him treated at the SGPGI hospital in Lucknow, the government hospital offering the best treatment. Years of bitterness had taken their toll on family relationships, and her husband's family learnt of his illness much later from his sister. On 27 February 1997, he died after a year of treatment. 'That was an intensely difficult period for me,' says Rani. 'Even now, I find it difficult to visit a sick friend in that particular hospital, where we spent months. The memories are still so painful. Looking after my husband, keeping the establishment in Ayodhya going – life was a tough struggle. I remember, my younger son was in the seventh or eighth class at the time. Once, he had gone to fetch something and got stuck in the hospital lift at 2 a.m. I was so frantic at that moment. I never want to relive such times.'

With four children of different ages to think of, Rani could not let the devastation caused by her husband's death overwhelm her. 'I didn't want the children to see me cry, and cry in turn. Instead, work seemed the best therapy. I threw myself even more into my profession.' Kripa Shankar Tiwari provided much-needed support to her during this period, and helped run the school and institution, of which he is the manager.

Today, years later, Rani is entirely in command. She deals with several rural, semi-literate people daily – the parents of children born with speech or hearing or learning difficulties. I watch her make a speech at a function of her school at the Tulsi Smarak Bhavan in Ayodhya, wherein she emphasizes that these children are special, not lifelong burdens. I can see how her task of making people more sensitive and aware in a society riddled with superstition, where a lame man is still called 'langda', is a tall one indeed. At the function, Rani's students perform little group dances to simple Radha-Krishna songs, the kind that are often heard playing at tea shops and bus stands, which can only be called 'pop folk'. Their costumes and make-up, and the parents clapping in the audience serve to keep the children excited and happy. One thing that is striking is the large police presence at the school function. Rani Awasthi often invites the local police bigwigs to her school programmes, which is as much a reflection of her need to be secure and protected in the feudal and occasionally dangerous world she inhabits, as it is of the fact that her younger brother, the one with whom she plotted some mischief in her childhood, now works in the CBI.

About her work, Rani says, 'I love children – enjoy being with these specially abled ones. We have teachers who develop a lifelong bond with them because of the nature of their work. People whom I have taught come back to see me with their own families and children. It is such a wonderful feeling! These children are selfless, and often very intuitive. They can smell dishonesty, and if they ever suspect they are being fooled or cheated, they become very angry and agitated. A large part of our work is dealing with these stress factors for them, in the environment in which they live. Many of these children are hypersensitive, particularly around adolescence, and turn suicidal. We have to be very alert. Mentally-challenged children are innocent, an incarnation of God.'

Rani's own children today have grown up and have gradually begun to leave the nest. In Ayodhya, this is inevitable, she knows. 'The young cannot have their ambitions satisfied. There are no prospects for business or employment. For a religious or a retired person, or a writer,' she pauses, smiling at me, 'this place is great! But not for young people who want to get out and do something with their lives.' On the other hand, Rani's long years in Ayodhya have only strengthened her own resolve to be here always. 'Hearing Sitaram all the time produces its own inner satisfaction,' she says. 'The chant gets into you, becomes a part of your being.'

Rani stays along the banks of the Sarayu at Gola Ghat, opposite another sadhu featured in this book in Chapter 12, the Dhrupad singing Gauri Shankar Das, and from her home, she can still see the crowds of pilgrims arriving for Ayodhya's *parikrama* and melas. So how did the events of 1990 and 1992 affect her life in the town?

Rani speaks from the heart. 'My father used to speak of the Rama temple movement of the 1990s being like the freedom movement,' she says. 'In those days, my house used to be open to kar-sevaks, just like thousands of homes in Ayodhya. I loved it! A seventeen-year-old boy from Gorakhpur had come here, who lost two brothers in the firing in 1990. "So what if two are gone? Two of us are still alive. We will build the temple!" he told me. I was humbled by his spirit of sacrifice. In 1992 also, nearly five hundred people must have been coming and going through my home. People were lying and sitting everywhere. They had the right.'

Rani was an eyewitness to the events on 6 December at the disputed site. 'I was there, and heard the speeches. There was firing. I participated in towing away rubble from the spot. Everyone was trying to take home a brick, some mud from the spot, even my son was doing so. In fact, I truly believed that the structure falling down would signal the start of something good. I believed the temple would put Ayodhya on the world map for international tourists, and on the fast track for development.'

Subsequent incidents have saddened Rani, who now asks, 'The VHP should maintain and care for all the temples lying in a state of decay in Ayodhya. Why single out only the Janmabhoomi? This whole town belongs to Rama.' Speaking purely from the point of view of an ordinary devotee and temple-goer who is attached to Rama and Hanuman, Rani remembers Ayodhya before the masjid came down. 'When we first came here, a single Home Guard watched over the Rama Janmabhoomi. We were free to go up to the idols and do our puja any way we wished. They could have had a new Janmabhoomi temple without disturbing the old one! This present situation is really sad and intolerable.'

When I look around her drawing room, I see pictures of her

with several personalities, and Baba Ramdev holds a prominent place. Is she an admirer and supporter? 'Yes, but I did not like the fact that he entered politics directly. He should be more of an inspiration, a teaching force for the people. Corruption flows from the top, downwards. If Ramdev, or any other political party can bring about an "inner revolution" amongst the upper classes, ensure that people start operating from their conscience, then we will have a modern-day Gandhi!' she says.

Being a prominent citizen of Ayodhya engaged in community service has not kept Rani Awasthi totally safe and immune to the idle talk and gossip about women that is so much a part of this society. She acknowledges that such sniping and backbiting exists. 'Discrimination against women is indeed felt at every step. The first way in which people seek to belittle you is by casting aspersions on your character. I have not been an exception in this regard, have faced it all. But one must learn to get away from such things, rise above such distractions.'

For the fair and smiling auntie of Gola Ghat, the needs of her specially abled charges come before other existential worries.

11

Baba Dharamdas
Beguiling Muscle

(Hanuman joined his friends. He could uproot large trees in sheer playfulness, or break up veritable mountains.)

—*Hanuman Sathika* by Goswami Tulsidas

The mahant of Hanuman Garhi, often referred to in these pages, Mahant Gyandas, has been an expert wrestler. This is entirely in keeping with the tradition of the famous akharas of Hanuman Garhi, where young men who had chosen sadhuhood as a way of life have been trained in wrestling and exercise. In the past, this was not only to improve their physical prowess but also underlined their constant readiness to battle for their faith. While the akharas still exist, what is more fascinating is the lore that has sprung around them – stories of sadhus who were unstoppable wrestlers – the WWF champions of their time.

Baba Dharamdas is one such living legend.

Born in 1945, in Dumari village of Bihar's Buxar district into a Bhumihar family, Baba Dharmadas is tall and well-built, which accounts for the immediate awe one feel in his presence. His white hair and beard notwithstanding, he shows no sign of enfeeblement. He is also bashful about his wrestling tales, retreating into a gruff acknowledgement of sundry details, while others outline the heroic narrative.

Baba Dharamdas came to Ayodhya as a teenager. What brought you here, I ask. Was it curiosity? 'Not curiosity,' he replies. '*Prarabdha* (destiny). In the past, every village had sadhu role models, men who had left their homes to pursue a different life. In our childhood, we could see such people around us. Becoming a sadhu is a soul journey. Many factors play a part – *purva janma sanskar, jahan anna daana paani likha hai, bhagwan ke bhajan, bhagwan ke naam se lagav, bairagya* (past life karma, where one is destined to receive food and water, the attachment one begins to feel for God's name, the final sense of detachment from other ties). I came alone to Ayodhya, not on some family outing, but for myself.'

It was here that he met Abhiramdas, on the banks of the Sarayu. The senior sadhu from Bihar was returning after a bath. The two got talking and Abhiramdas offered to take on the teenager as a disciple, to which he agreed. Thus began a life in Ayodhya, one where the boy 'used to feel the presence of God everywhere.'

Abhiramdas is in fact the key figure of the gang that placed the idols of infant Rama, Lakshman, Bharat and Shatrughna in the Babri Masjid on the intervening night of 22-23 December 1949. When I meet Baba Dharamdas in the small room he occupies next to the Hanuman Garhi temple, I am standing in the same space occupied by Dharamdas' guru. The area is dominated by a portrait of Abhiramdas painted by an unknown artist. Dharamdas, on his part, insists on having his picture taken holding a black and white photograph of himself as a young sadhu with his guru Abhiramdas.

As to the relationship shared by the two, Dharamdas' good friend and fellow Bihari, Hari Dayal Mishra (*see* Chapter 2) describes an occasion when Baba Dharamdas was inspired to give a discourse (*pravachan*) on some aspect of devotion to Rama. While he sat on stage and held forth, his guru arrived and was enraged to see his disciple having assumed such a lofty position. He stormed towards the stage and cuffed Dharamdas, sending the latter flying into the bewildered audience. Later, he thundered at his penitent disciple, 'There's no need for you to be messing around with the Ramayana and Bhagwat. You stick to wrestling and protecting the Lord from attack. For all the learning and Sanskrit, we have Satyendra, don't we (*see* Chapter 9)?' Dharamdas himself puts it another way. 'I wanted to be a learned sadhu too, but Guruji assigned to me the duty of wrestling, so this is the path I followed.'

Baba Dharamdas represents an important link to the mandir-masjid controversy in many ways. First, he provides me with a clue as to why Rajiv Gandhi, grandson of Jawaharlal Nehru, and leader of India's supposedly most secular party, the Congress, should have taken the inexplicable step of having the locks of the disputed site opened in 1986. This in turn provided a boost to pro-mandir groups, and granted momentum to the movement for a Rama temple in Ayodhya. Whatever Rajiv Gandhi's other political compulsions may have been, one thing that emerges from knowing Baba Dharamdas more closely is that the late prime minister had great admiration for wrestler sadhus at one point in time.

As the story gets told, I learn that one of Baba Dharamdas' disciples, a young wrestler, had become very close to Rajiv Gandhi. Once, Baba Dharamdas had occasion to accompany him when he was going to the prime minister's residence in Delhi. As the two orange-robed figures were walking towards the PM's house, the armed security guards who were familiar with only one of them, challenged the other sadhu, Baba Dharamdas. Baba Dharamdas ignored their calls and continued walking. When the guards rushed towards him to stop him physically, he threw them both to the ground in seconds with a few deft movements. '*Unko patak diya*' is the succinct description. This incident is reported to have brought much amusement to Rajiv Gandhi, who is supposed to have then asked his security guards, 'Why shouldn't my security be assigned to these powerful sadhus, instead of to you?'

When I ask Baba Dharamdas to corroborate this incident, he mutters, 'All exaggeration,' and looks down, pretending to read from a small holy book. 'But did you really get challenged by the guards? Did this happen?' I persist. He nods in assent. 'They called me, I didn't listen, that's all. Then they tried to catch me,' he stops, not wanting to say more. But when asked about Rajiv Gandhi's fascination for the wrestling sadhus from Hanuman

Garhi, he is more open. 'Yes, he was a wonderful man, a really good human being. He genuinely liked and respected us,' he says.

The other association that Baba Dharamdas has with the mandir-masjid controversy is that he grabbed land at the disputed site over which he then had control by continuous occupation. It was this land, earlier part of the Nirmohi Akhara's holdings, that he gave to the VHP in 1984, out of a belief that his guru would have wished him to contribute towards a temple for Rama at the place of his birth. Ask Baba Dharamdas about the separate Nirmohi Akhara claim on Rama Janmabhoomi, and he says, 'It is all *char-sau-bisi* (referring to Sec. 420 of the I.P.C. – cheating).' Ask Tarunjeet Varma, whose family has long represented the Nirmohi Akhara, about Baba Dharamdas, and he turns pale and says, 'Oh he is a very bad and dangerous man! He burnt or threw in a well many precious documents relating to the disputed land, destroying some proof forever, besides snatching the land in the first place.'

Baba Dharamdas, who won second position in the Twenty-fourth International Wrestling Meet when it was held in Shimla, has wrestled for Hanuman Garhi in several places in Jammu and Kashmir, like the Rani Mandir at Jammu, besides matches at Muthi and Akhnoor. His guru, Abhiramdas, breathed his last on 3 December 1981 at Varanasi, after naming Dharamdas his successor and keeper of all his landed property. Sometime before or after this date, it is not exactly clear, Baba Dharamdas and a few others forcibly occupied portions of the land around the Babri Masjid which was then under the control of the Nirmohi Akhara. They also looted some household goods and other articles of daily use from the site.

A case of looting and encroachment was registered against Baba Dharamdas and others, and he spent two months in jail before being granted bail. In 1984, he gave the portion of the land that he had forcibly occupied to the VHP. 'I gave the land on the condition that the temple would be built with my help,' he says. 'A lot of people told me that they (the VHP) are shopkeepers, not true Rambhakts, but I gave them the land anyway, as my *gilehri prayas* for Rama.' Baba Dharamdas, of course, wishes to compare himself to the squirrel or gilehri in the story of Rama who fetches pebbles and sand in her mouth to build the bridge to Lanka.

Avoiding further questions on his involvement with the land around the disputed site, Baba Dharamdas says, 'If I say anything about the matter now, it may be used in favour of the other side (the Muslims). That is why I will keep quiet.' However, he is clear about a few things. 'Hanumanji will take care of everything for me. The judgement has come in our favour. I expect even the Supreme Court to decide by Chait-Baisakh (April-May). All will belong to Rama Lalla at the end and all will be clear for a temple to be built,' he says. When I ask him if the leadership for a Rama temple will ever be the same after the death of Paramhans Ramachandra Das, he bristles and says, 'Paramhans became the face of the temple movement only because of the VHP and the media. The real hero of the Rama temple was and is Abhiramdas.'

On the fate of the idols his Guru had placed in December 1949 under the dome of the masjid, I share with Baba Dharamdas the anguish his gurubhai, Mahant Satyendra Das felt when it was suggested that he had failed to protect the idols of Rama Lalla and his brothers. Baba looks up, 'Satyendra protected the idols? Why would he do that? It wasn't his job.'

'He told me he took Rama Lalla away to a safe place before the domes fell down, and did phalahar for twelve years because bhog could not be offered on that day,' I tell Baba Dharamdas.

A snort is heard in reply. Baba Dharamdas says, 'I carried away the idols in a *gamchha* (cloth worn on the upper body) and kept them in a trunk for some hours when things started getting ugly. Satyendra did not have to trouble himself. Such situations are not for the likes of him. It was my duty to protect the idols and I did it. As for the phalahar, why did he do it for twelve years? The domes fell only late in the afternoon. Bhagwan had already had his bhog many hours prior. And late that night, even before the morning of 7 December, the idols had been placed back in their spot.'

It looks like I have stumbled upon a rivalry of gurubhais. Taking Dharamdas' emphatic words as a cue to veer away from the subject of the temple, I instead talk to him about another episode that has come to my knowledge. Apparently, when Baba Dharamdas was once on a long sojourn in Delhi, a wrestling challenger appeared who had defeated every wrestler sadhu in Hanuman Garhi. 'There isn't a man who can defeat me here!' he boasted. Elderly sadhu Hari Shankar Das, whose protégés were the defeated wrestlers, was most perturbed. 'Go to Delhi, tell Dharamdas that I have been taken ill, and ask him to come immediately,' he instructed some disciples. This was accordingly done, and Dharamdas arrived in Ayodhya. 'Give him badam and milk, a good oil massage, and ask him to come ready for a fight tomorrow,' said Hari Shankar Das. When Dharamdas, expecting to see a sick Hari Shankar Das, learnt of the reason for the summons, he was prepared to fight immediately! However, he was persuaded to wait for the morrow, and the fight duly took place between the challenger and Dharamdas, resulting in a thumping victory for the latter. As he was being garlanded and carried around as the saviour of the prestige (*pratishtha*) of Hanuman Garhi, Dharamdas felt a surge of power and pride.

'Who is there who can defeat me now, within Hanuman Garhi?' he asked Hari Shankar Das a few days later. 'I can defeat anybody for miles around.'

'Even me? Can you defeat me?' asked Hari Shankar Das. 'Yes,' said Dharamdas.

The elderly wrestler then took on his young protégé and in the first few seconds of the match, cracked his left wrist so hard that Dharamdas to date has a knobbly protuberance at the point his wrist did not join properly. As for Hari Shankar Das, he was not more lucky – Dharamdas felled him with a twist that resulted in a knee fracture for the elderly sadhu. The match was therefore a draw.

'Who was the challenger you defeated?' I ask Dharamdas.

'Surender Singh, from the military,' he says gruffly, taking refuge once more in his little holy book.

The benefit of being the victor who had saved the reputation of Hanuman Garhi was a lifelong supply of additional rations for Dharamdas – from mustard oil to dry fruits. Still entitled to such wrestler's wealth, he has never used it exclusively for himself. In fact, every year, he observes a day at Hanuman Garhi when the additional rations he is entitled to are distributed among his akhara mates. Today's wrestlers still have reason to feel a close bond with this sixty-six-year-old sadhu.

When I ask Baba Dharamdas to describe the difference between the Ayodhya of his youth and the present day, he gives me a reply that is typical of his peculiar mix of philosophical concepts couched in everyday words. 'Ayodhya is no different, really,' he says at first. Then, seeing my scepticism, he tries to explain, 'How does her mother's home (*maika*) appear to a girl? It seems different when she is an unfettered child, different when she is leaving home, then when she comes back as a married woman, and when she is older. Places remain the same, it is our feelings that change. Ayodhya is still good for me.'

When I look around, I notice, Baba Dharamdas' room is not bigger or better appointed than that of any of the other sadhus I have visited. By now I have become used to the cramped lodgings, the jumble of a few belongings that mark the existence of these holy men.

On the occasions when I have visited him, Baba Dharamdas is always caught up in some little worldly crisis. Sometimes, signing a cheque is a big production when it comes back to him with a small mistake in dates or spellings, after the original filling out had taken a long enough time! Sometimes, he worries over the brass knob of his official cane being cleaned, the ceremonial staff that he has inherited from Abhiramdas, so his assistants discuss the matter endlessly ('Should it be washed with Nirma or tamarind?'). On one occasion, a PVC bathroom door is carried in by masons in the middle of our conversation, momentarily acting like a big brown screen between us. Baba explains that he is getting an accommodation built and refurbished right there, next to Hanuman Garhi, and the door is for one of those bathrooms. Endless little distractions, arrivals and departures, always mark time with Baba Dharamdas.

I don't mind at all. I like evidence that shows us that sadhus are human, not seeking to be some 'godmen' to be worshipped. For me, one of the bonuses of visiting Baba Dharamdas is a meeting with his little disciple, Neel Mani Das . Neel Mani represents the sharp, jaunty, urchin panda-pujari-sadhu trainees who roam in big numbers all around Ayodhya.

Baba Dharamdas is a man of contradictions. He is a lovable

giant of a sadhu, but he is also deeply connected with the conspiracy that has thrown our nation into a state of turmoil ever since Hindu idols were planted in a mosque in December 1949. How does one evaluate an individual like him? As a human being who occasionally errs? Or as a Bhumihar bully who represents the worst of caste and communalism? I think long and hard about how Baba Dharamdas' life as an ordinary mortal has posed a challenge to independent India and her constitutional values.

Has Baba Dharamdas failed India? Or has India failed to stand up to this wrestler devotee of Hanuman?

12

Gauri Shankar Das
Kanak Behari's Minstrel

Kesav! Kaaran kaun gosain?
Jehi apraadh asaadh jaani mohi tajeu agyaki naiee.

(O Keshav! What is the reason? Keeping which sin of mine in mind are you casting me aside like an absolute stranger?)

—*Vinay Patrika* by Goswami Tulsidas

The Kanak Behari temple in Ayodhya is one of the best places to pass an evening in happy contentment. Before or after one has had a darshan of the white marble deities of Rama, Sita and Lakshman, it is good to sit on the shallow steps around the black and white checkered inner courtyard and watch other pilgrims come and go. Or look up at the evening sky and watch the stars emerge while the breeze from the Sarayu blows pleasantly.

In one corner of the courtyard, just outside the sanctum of the temple, a singer usually sits with a harmonium, accompanied by a tabla or *dholak* player, singing bhajans.

Gauri Shankar Das has been one such singer for twenty-five years. He is today Ayodhya's only true-blue classical Dhrupad artiste.

Born in the Tulsi Bari area of Ayodhya on Shivaratri in 1939, Gauri Shankar Das is a sadhu who lives in the typical single-room dwelling of the ascetic. However, what makes his place somewhat forbidding is its proximity to the Sarayu river, a few hundred yards from the water line. On the occasions I have visited him, always in winter, the strong and chilly winds blowing in from over the water make it difficult to open the door or window a mere crack. Only in the afternoons does Gauri Shankar open his house to receive students. Otherwise, he has to stay entombed in his small room at Sadguru Sadan at Gola Ghat, waiting for the season to change. Moreover, since he doesn't have a private vehicle, and lives in this comparatively distant neighbourhood, he is cut off from the more oft-visited areas. To top it all, he was the most fragile looking of all the sadhus I met, which made me worry about his health and well-being.

'My father was a sadhu too,' recollects Gauri Shankar Das. 'He was a pujari at the Jaunpuria Mandir, a poor Brahmin who lived on the offerings of people who visited the temple or called him to conduct pujas. Food, and donations of cloth, grain and other provisions, this is what used to help our family get along. Such charity and generosity was possible in the Ayodhya of that time. It was an Ayodhya full of mahatmas – the Badi Chhavani, Mani Ram Chhavani, Tapasviji ki Chhavani – all had sadhus living in them who were truly spiritual. At the time, the Sarayu flowed very close to the town, was never very far from us. There were only pontoon bridges on the river, not big bridges like there are now.'

In the Ramanandi tradition, most of the sadhus have Vaishnav names, most often derivatives of 'Rama' like Ram Sharan, Ram Kripal, etc. How Gauri Shankar got his name is an interesting story. 'My mother said I was born at 4 a.m. on Shivaratri. Our home was in Gudiyana, where my paternal grandmother lived. She was told by my uncle, "A son has been born," but she misheard it as a daughter and exclaimed, "Gauri has arrived!" Later, on learning that the child was a boy, the name was changed to Gauri Shankar. Thus I have an unusual name for Ayodhya.'

Recalling that his childhood was spent during the years when Rajendra Prasad and Jawaharlal Nehru led our country, Gauri Shankar Das says, 'I got admitted to school. The teachers were lazy, but I learnt from other students, who demanded sweets in exchange for such lessons! My father consequently took me to a guru who taught me by bribing me with *channa-gur* (roasted black gram and jaggery) and sweets. This was my first guru, a disciple of Shri 108 Sri Janaki Rasik Sharan of Mani Parbat. He taught me the alphabet and words, as well as the musical *sa-re-ga-ma*. From the beginning, I found it easier to learn the music, than the letters!'

Gauri Shankar Das' erratic efforts at studying attracted the notice of a school inspector who arrived to test the students one day.

When he was caught for lagging behind in his lessons, his school teacher took the inspector to meet his guruji. This gentleman said nothing, just asked his student to bring the harmonium. Once the school principal and the inspector heard the boy play, they struck his name off from regular school and declared that he should be devoted to music full time.

'I began doing duty at Kanak Bhavan from the age of ten or twelve,' says Gauri Shankar Das. I sang bhajans both in the morning and evening for eighteen rupees a month. I used to learn the *taal* from Bhagwan Das, the guru of Pagal Das. Another teacher, Ram Kishor, was a big critic, listening to me sing, then pointing out where I was going wrong. However, after a while, he too expressed an interest in teaching me, and I learnt from him as well.'

Gauri Shankarji's initiation into sadhuhood was another matter. 'I took *diksha* (initiation into a spiritual or artistic practice) at the age of eighteen or twenty from Sri Ram Kamta Sharanji from Jhansi. He used to come to Ayodhya around Rama Navami and special occasions.' While a musician by choice, Gauri Shankarji also trained physically – like all sadhus in Ayodhya. Gauri Shankar Das used to exercise at the Hanuman Garhi Akhara. 'At Kanak Bhavan, I used to have listeners who came specially to hear me sing bhajans both in the morning and evening,' he says. 'I was there regularly till 1975, then gave in my resignation. I hadn't received my salary, but that was not the only reason I left. I had also begun to differ with the management on matters of spirituality.'

Gradually, Gauri Shankar Das' ties with the world began to fade. His mother passed away in 1960, his guruji in 1965. 'After I left Kanak Bhavan, I felt free, especially with respect to music. I sang at many temples, and also travelled. I reached Sadguru Sadan at Gola Ghat in 1994.'

Our conversation takes place in front of one of Gauri Shankar Das' students. Shalini Shukla listens attentively as her guruji explains a *pad* (short devotional poem) from Tulsidas' *Vinay Patrika* to her, and sings the opening lines. 'I have completed my BA, and am now learning music from Guruji,' she says. 'It is truly what brings me the greatest happiness today. I love coming here. He sometimes scolds us, but is really very kind. We are fortunate indeed to have a good guru like him.'

In fact, unlike the music schools that can be seen in many neighbourhoods in cities and also in smaller towns, Gauri Shankar Das does not charge any fee. 'I teach students not for cash, but for whatever they feel like offering, be it fruits or provisions,' he says. 'What is regrettable is that today I find it hard to get students who are serious, who are willing to put in the kind of rigorous practice that is needed to make them really fine musicians. I sing in the *dhrupad ang* and this is not a light and easy style of singing. It demands a serious level of commitment that is tough to find today.'

With Gauri Shankar Das, all my conversations are centred around music and its scope in Ayodhya then and now. This gentle soul is really not interested in discussing anything else, and I don't push him for his views on the demolition, or Mulayam and the events of 1990. In any case, now, having asked dozens of people about the same events, it is obvious that there is a lot more to Ayodhya than just the scars left by the collective madness of the past.

• • •

One of our conversations is in the courtyard of the Hanumat Vishwakala Sangeetashram in the Pramod Van area, dominated by a single *amla* tree in the centre. The thatch-roofed cottage of its founder, Pagal Das, faces the portals of the institution. Our host at the Hanumat Sangeetashram is Vijay Ram Das, who earned the title 'Taalmani' as a percussionist, and arrived from Bihar in July 1987 to become Pagal Das' disciple. He regales us with stories of his guru, one of Ayodhya's legends, and the only one in recent times to have put Ayodhya in the reckoning on the national music scene.

Dr Ramshankar Das, or 'Pagal' Das, a title that well described his devotion to music that transcended ordinary boundaries, was born in Deoria on 15 August 1920, and ran away at the age of fourteen to arrive in Ayodhya. He received his initial diksha from Mahant Ramkishun Das, known as Bengali Baba. He then began staying in Hanuman Garhi under the guardianship of Baba Sukhram Das, and left a year later to tour Bihar with various drama companies. He returned to Ayodhya to continue growing as a percussionist under various gurus, notably Swami Bhagwandas, Baba Thakur Das and Sri Rammohini Sharan, which amounted to about twenty years of training in the mridang. From Pandit Sant Sharan 'Mast' he learnt to accompany classical singers on the tabla for ten years. His own growth as a percussionist was so remarkable that he drew great praise from Ustad Allauddin Khan, who hailed him as 'Manas Putra' (an honorific praising his sensibility) and the second Kodau Singh, after a legendary percussionist from whom flows the 'Awadhi Gharana' style of playing. In fact, Pagal Das is credited with the revival of the *pakhawaj* and mridang in classical music – two instruments that were on the decline before his arrival.

'On 10 October 1972, when Swami Bhagwandas was laying the foundation of this ashram, the mridang was being played,' Vijay Ram Das tells us. 'Guruji's mastery of this instrument was so complete that he inspired Acharya Brihaspat to coin the slogan, "Jai Mridang!" Let me tell you the story behind the slogan. In 1960, at a music festival in Gwalior, Guruji had begged for time to play the mridang. "Who wants to hear such an instrument?" the organizers asked him. Guruji said nothing, and a short distance away from the performance venue where Bismillah Khan, Ustad Allah Rakha and another equally renowned flautist were giving a recital, he began playing. A huge and appreciative crowd gathered. People began to leave the main concert to come and hear him play. That is when this slogan came into being. On another occasion, a festival organizer said to him, "People go for tea when the mridang is played." Guruji was unfazed. He placed a wad of notes on the table and said to the man, "Okay, here's ten thousand rupees. Now announce that I'm going to play the mridang and let's see who leaves!"'

We all pause to consider the supreme self-confidence of a maestro who was able to challenge the apathy of the establishment towards his beloved instrument. 'There is so little appreciation and interest in true music in Ayodhya,' says Gauri Shankar Dasji. 'One of the reasons is also the lack of artistes who can stand up to event organizers and government functionaries.'

'Yes,' agrees Vijay Ram Das. 'As it is, a system of "commission" operates in All India Radio for us to get programmes. Then, there is no provision for even transport for an artiste like Gauri Shankar Das from his home to the radio station – a distance of a good ten or eleven kilometres! As for the programmes of the Vimla Devi Foundation, you know the story (*see* Chapter 5 on the Raja of Ayodhya). Musicians in Ayodhya are a threatened species.'

'*Kalakaaron ka koi sangathan nahin hai* (there is no united organization to represent artistes),' says Gauri Shankar Das. 'One has to be vigilant on so many counts. The situation here is such that you may even have been dead for three years or more, but someone in the Post Office will be drawing your pension and taking the money from your deposits. Worse, you may find after moving to a different neighbourhood, that you have been pronounced as dead!'

'Guruji himself had begun to feel towards the end of his days that perhaps his *zid* (strong insistence) to live in Ayodhya had been a wrong choice. Perhaps he should have taken the chances repeatedly offered him over the years,' says Vijay Ram Das.

One such offer was made by the late Prithviraj Kapoor to Pagal Das. He had a private museum in which he had collected many instruments. He showed this to the pakhawaj player, and asked him to come and stay in Mumbai. 'You have all the instruments, except their *baap*,' said Pagal Das, referring to the mridang and pakhawaj. Prithviraj promised to repair the omission immediately. Pagal Das turned down the offer to live in Mumbai because his heart belonged to Ayodhya.

'Much is made of the Ganga-Jamuni tehzeeb or *sanskriti* of this region,' says Vijay Ram Das, referring to the commingling of different faiths that has been such a part of the history of Awadh. 'Music is the link for the Ganga-Jamuni sanskriti. It binds performers and audiences of all faiths. But it cannot survive without government patronage and help.'

In another incident that illustrates Pagal Das' ability to cock a snook at authority, Vijay Ram Das describes the inauguration of the Cultural Centre in Ayodhya during President's Rule, when Motilal Vora was the governor. The performing artiste on that occasion was none other than Pagal Das. After the programme, a beaming Vora gushed and asked Pagal Das to visit him when he came to Lucknow. '*Bhagwan na kare ki mujhe bhi aapke durbar mein pratyashi ban kar aana pade* (God forbid that I should also have to come to your durbar as a supplicant),' was the reply. Vora then sent his emissary, Indu Rani to Ayodhya, and she came to visit Pagal Das and asked, 'What do you want done here?' 'Whatever you do, let it be for keeps,' he replied. He wasn't interested in half-hearted or temporary measures.

The winter evening has advanced, as I take leave of Vijay Ram Das and prepare to accompany Gauri Shankar Das back to his freezing room at Gola Ghat. I can't help being overwhelmed by a feeling of sadness and regret – regret that so much of what is worth preserving in our midst has to fight for a toehold in the overwhelming callousness, greed and self-aggrandizement around us.

I am on the verge of sinking into real depression when something inside me says, 'Jai Mridang!' and I remember that ten to twelve good students are trained annually from Pagal Das' institution in Ayodhya. Smiling in the winter gloom, I give thanks for the mad genius of Ayodhya who had the foresight to build a Sangeetashram.

13

Nritya Gopal Das

Formidable Foe

Lakhi subesh jag banchak jeu, besh pratap pujiahin teu.
Ughare ant na hoi nibahu, kaalnemi jimi raavan rahu.

(Even devious men in saintly clothing can draw respect from the
world for a while, but eventually their true nature is unmasked,
as in the case of Kaalnemi, Raavan and Rahu.)

—*Ramcharitmanas* by Goswami Tulsidas

Chhavani or cantonment is a term used commonly in North Indian towns to describe those areas where the erstwhile British army used to have their settlements for troops, transport and ammunition. In Ayodhya, it is used to describe buildings and temples set up specifically as sadhu settlements, meant to provide them with shelter and food so that they continue to safeguard the Hindu faith. There are several such chhavanis in the town, but the two biggest are the Mani Ram Das ki Chhavani at Vasudev Ghat and the Raghunath Das ki Chhavani near the Ravidas Mandir. Some locals hold that both Mani Ram Das and Raghunath Das were sepoys in the British army, and these chhavanis were built post 1857, when they embraced sadhuhood. But the Ayodhya Shodh Sansthan publication, *Sakshi*, only emphasizes the sadhu lineage of these two places, revealing that Mani Ram Das had his chhavani built after spending twelve years in Chitrakoot and having Hanuman appear before him. This sadhu from the Kurmi community set up an institution for the worship of Sri Rama and Hanuman, for service to sadhus, pilgrim guests and cows.

Mani Ram Das ki Chhavani is inappropriately called 'chhoti chhavani' in Ayodhya. It is, in fact, a sprawling complex of buildings and compounds that include the Rama Janaki, Sri Hanuman, Sri Rangnath and Char Dham temples besides the imposing edifice of Maharshi Valmiki Ramayana Bhavan. The Bhavan's marble walls are covered with the text of the Valmiki Ramayana, and it houses a library of texts related to Sri Rama in many languages, including some rare palm leaf manuscripts. Over three hundred sadhus find shelter and food in the chhavani, and students learn Sanskrit and are instructed in the Srimad Bhagavat, the stories of the avatars of Vishnu. Daily satsangs and kirtans and bhandaras are some of the other notable features of this complex.

Mahant Nritya Gopal Das is the sixth Peethadheeswar (ceremonial and administrative head) of the Mani Ram Das ki Chhavani, which some would say is the richest institution in Ayodhya in terms of offerings and donations received. Hanuman Garhi is the nearest rival in this regard. All other temples and matts in Ayodhya come far behind. He is also the present head of the Rama Janmabhoomi Nyas, a position whose former occupant was the mercurial Paramhans Ramachandra Das, once the face of the movement for a Rama temple in Ayodhya.

All these designations reflect immense power and clout in the real world, or rather, they represent such clout if the holder wields it in a certain way. Paramhans Ramachandra Das was regarded as a *phakkad* sadhu, a man who was truly free of worldly attachments, who could receive ten thousand rupees in cash from a devotee only to have another come and beg it off him the next minute, or spend the entire ten thousand immediately on *channa* for the monkeys he loved to feed. No one has yet accused Mahant Nritya Gopal Das of such phakkad-ness.

Instead, he is spoken of with exaggerated respect by men like Sharad Sharma, the head of the media cell of the VHP, who will phrase a sentence thus: '*Maharajji ke sannidhya mein*', meaning 'in the grace and presence of Maharajji'. Or he is mentioned with exaggerated dread, as displayed by an advocate in the Faizabad courts periphery, who said to me, 'Nritya Gopal Das is the biggest example of the *bhoo-mafia* (land grabbing mafia). In fact, it was not a lie some years back to say that if you had a house or plot that he liked, you had only two options: either give the land or house to him, or die. There was no third option.' To substantiate his claim the advocate told me of his own acquaintance, a retired government servant who had had a house in the Pramod Van area of Ayodhya.

When Nritya Gopal Das saw and liked the house, he sent emissaries several times to make offers for the property. But the retired man stayed obstinate, refusing to part with his retirement home. He was fatally knifed in the street by unknown men, and his grieving family had to subsequently make arrangements to move away from Ayodhya to a neighbouring state.

The Bindu Sarovar attached to the Mani Ram Das ki Chhavani has a huge Hanuman statue installed in its temple. Triveni Das was once mahant of this temple, who fell foul of Nritya Gopal Das on some internal matter. One dark morning at the pre-dawn hour of 4 a.m., when he had gone for a bath in the Sarayu, he was run over and killed by a truck. Such hit-and-run incidents only serve to add to the 'defy-only-at-your-own-peril' aura that surrounds the Peethadheeswar of the Mani Ram Chhavani.

However, what is remembered as the worst instance of Mahant Nritya Gopal Das' land-grabbing tactics is the takeover of the Marwadi Dharamshala in Ayodhya in 1986-87 by his men. This dharamshala was home to around fifty to sixty rural students from nearby villages. At 11 a.m. one day when they were at college, the takeover of the dharamshala happened with guns and rifles. The students' belongings and papers were collected at one spot and set on fire. These poor rural youths lost valuable degrees and mark sheets, along with more ordinary belongings. Fifty-two students made a representation to the then DM, Ram Sharan Srivastava, who had an FIR filed against Nritya Gopal Das and others for cognizable offences under Sections 347, 348 and 436 of the I.P.C (wrongful confinement for extortion, or for restoration of property, arson to destroy home).

To understand the reputation that precedes Nritya Gopal Das, one needs to digress for a moment, delve into the recent history of

Ayodhya's holy men and come to grips with the notoriety they enjoy. To be fair, Nritya Gopal Das is not the only sadhu to have such a dreaded reputation. In fact, this is something that has become an established part of Ayodhya lore – that regular incidents of shootings, killings, kidnappings are to be associated with the inmates of various matts and mandirs. Amarnath Verma, a journalist with *Jan Morcha*, who was associated with the Communists from 1985 to 1993, says, '*Baba samaj nihayat kaamchor, aur h****khor samaj hai. Us mein milenge ardha vikshipt, ghor palayanvaadi, niraasha se bhare hue, aur kuchh chor lutere.* (The community of *babas* is lazy and parasitic. In this community, you will find half-crazed escapists and pessimists, as well as some thieves and thugs.)'

If the movement for a Rama temple achieved anything, it was awarding a sense of great importance and significance to the sadhus, sants and mahants of Ayodhya. Men who may have remained unknown and obscure all their lives suddenly became figures on national TV, with their utterances being given great importance by the media. The petty property disputes and fights for the control of temples – which had long been a fact of life among Ayodhya's sadhus – acquired prominence, even as the whole Ayodhya issue began to revolve around a property dispute. As the sadhus grew in stature, they began to seek security for themselves from the government. Having a retinue of private and government 'gunners' became a status symbol for Ayodhya's holy men.

'In fact, these sadhus don't need gunners to protect them from ordinary people; they need them to protect themselves from each other,' says Verma. 'These temples and matts have secret chambers and doors. Anything can, and does happen inside them.'

A Congress worker I meet in Faizabad tells me of an alleged incident in the kitchen of Mani Ram Das ki Chhavani. Two sadhus had an argument while cooking, and one picked up the huge ladle with which he was stirring a giant pot and smashed the other's skull with it. His victim fell down dead, following which the corpse was hidden in a pile of hay in the *goshala* (cow shelter) and later taken under cover of dark to be cast away in the river Sarayu. '*Arre, in logon ke saath yeh sab aam baatein hain* (such things are commonplace within the sadhu community),' says the man identifying himself only as Babloo.

The criminalization of Ayodhya's mandirs and matts has been reported regularly in the press. When dreaded gangster, Kamdev Singh of Begusarai in Bihar, who was responsible for murdering many grassroot Communists in the region, was killed in a police encounter in 1983, his gang dispersed and many found shelter as sadhus in Ayodhya. Chief amongst these men was Ram Kripal Das, an expert bomb-maker, who came to run a successful criminal business of extortions, murder and land grabbing in Ayodhya, notching up two dozen cases of murder and loot before being killed in November 1996.

The Week is one publication that has tracked the surge of crime in Ayodhya's sadhu community through several stories. Kanhaiya Bhelari wrote a cover story on 23 November 1997 in which the Bihar-Ayodhya nexus of crime was detailed with some shocking facts. He stated: 'Some sadhus even have paramours. A visit to one cost Ram Sharan Das of Hanuman Garhi his life. Wanted in a dozen criminal cases, he was on his way to the Faizabad district hospital to see his ailing paramour when he suddenly found the police on his tail. He whipped out his revolver and shot at them, but they shot him instead.

Two years later, in 1993, Ram Prakash Das of Hanuman Garhi was chased by the police and shot in an encounter at Barahata

Majha area of Ayodhya. According to the police records, Ram Prakash, 19, belonged to Bihar and was fleeing after spraying bullets on Ladoo Das of the matt. When he opened fire on the police, they retaliated.

There have been several clashes inside Hanuman Garhi. In 1976, the Gadhi Nasheen,* Dinabandhu Das survived an attempt on his life, when another mahant, Ram Kripal Das, opened fire at him when he was seated on the Gadhi. The next year two groups of Nagas clashed inside the matt using spears, country pistols and bombs. The same year a Naga, Bajrangdas, was killed. More killings followed: Dinabandhu Das in 1987, Harbhajan Das in 1990 and Ramagya Das in 1995.'

Ajay Uprety's report in *The Week*, dated 11 July 1999 continues with a list of names of both victims and perpetrators in Ayodhya's institutions: 'In September 1991, the 70-year-old mahant of Janki Ghat, Barasthan, was strangled in his bedroom. Three sadhus, Janmejai Sharan, Balgovind Das and Kamlesh Das, were accused of killing him to usurp the temple property worth Rs 15 crore. Janmejai became the mahant while the case is pending.'

There have been several killings for control of the Hanuman Ghari temple complex, where six-hundred sadhus live. It started in 1984, when Mahant Harbhajan Das was shot dead by his own men. In 1992, Deen Bandhu Das, the head of the temple complex was killed; three years later it was the turn of the mahant of Hanuman Ghari, Baba Ram Agya Das. Das was at loggerheads with his guru, Baba Triyugi Das, over a piece of temple land.

In a fight for the mahant's seat at Lakshman Quila temple last year, country bombs were lobbed into the room of Mahant Maithali

---

*The Persian name of the head of the Hanuman Garhi temple.

Sharanacharya. The appointment of Sharanacharya was challenged by Sanjay Jha alias Maithali Raman Sharan, a former mahant's driver who had the support of Rama Janmabhoomi Nyas chief Ramchandra Paramhans and BJP state vice-president Vinay Katiyar. Raman Sharan usurped the mahant's seat, and the sadhus supporting Sharanacharya launched an agitation in protest.

Finally, the district administration intervened and handed over the temple keys to the agitating sadhus in March this year. Sometimes the local people also have to pay with their lives for the greed of the sants. Thus in November 1998, disciples of Mohan Das alias Mauni Baba opened fire on the residents of Guptar Ghat, killing four persons. The Baba and his disciples had allegedly planned to grab the land adjacent to their Guptar Ghat ashram.

Baba Gyan Das, mahant of Sagaria Patti, admitted that many criminals had made matts their hideouts. He blamed the Vishwa Hindu Parishad (VHP) for the criminalization of Ayodhya. 'The VHP wants to control all the temples and it has turned many mahants into killers,' he said.

In the same article, Guru Ram Kripal Das, mahant of Bhakt Mal Bhavan, narrates the harassment he was undergoing in 1998. He had then blamed Mahant Nritya Gopal Das, deputy chief of the Rama Janmabhoomi Nyas as the prime mover behind these threats and harassment, because he said that Nritya Gopal Das was in pursuit of the Bhakt Mal Bhavan property.

Finally, after all the references to the infiltration of Ayodhya's matts by criminals from Bihar and eastern UP, we come back to the personality presently at the acme of power and mahant-hood in Ayodhya. A man who is not from Bihar, but from another holy town in UP, Mathura, who has studied not at some rural roughneck college, but at Varanasi, the seat of classical learning. Mahant

Nritya Gopal Das has not escaped unscathed from his widely-hinted trysts with violence. He survived an attempt on his life in late May 2001 when country-made bombs were flung at him and his disciples at a time when they were going to have a holy dip in the Sarayu at 5 a.m. The Mahant sustained pellet injuries on the chest and lower body. Initially, Mahant Nritya Gopal Das blamed the ISI for this attack, though later, it was discovered that the crime had been triggered off by a property dispute – the desire to control the Rama Vallabh temple. Nritya Gopal Das had had the Mahant Devram Das Vedanti removed, and the disgruntled former priest sought revenge.

In fact, if there is a single redeeming feature about Mahant Nritya Gopal Das' tenure it is the international 'Sitaram' bank headquartered at the Valmiki Bhavan. At this bank, devotees collect notebooks which they then fill by writing 'Sitaram' in red ink in any one of more than a dozen Indian languages and a few international ones. The filled notebooks are returned to the bank, which has, reportedly, several billion (*kai arab*) of such copies in its vaults. There is an incentive attached. A person writing 1.25 lakh 'Sitarams' gets membership at the bank, and as the number grows, there are rewards of bronze, silver and gold being offered. For fifty lakh names, there's a silver medal; a crore inscriptions fetch a gold medal. Through this ingenious and much sought-after scheme, Nritya Gopal Das can be said to have etched 'Sitaram' in the common man's mind. Whether his actions have strengthened faith in 'Sitaram' in their hearts is another matter.

On the occasions when I have been ushered in to the presence of Mahant Nritya Gopal Das, referred to as 'Maharajji' by his assistants and visitors, it is nearly always to bring some local issue to his attention. I have tried to get him to take an interest in the 'mini-monkey sanctuaries' project for Faizabad-Ayodhya,* and represented to him the concerns of farmers on the Sarayu riverbank whose land was being considered for takeover by a posh residential colony. He comes across as remarkably shrewd, but not forthcoming with any assurances of help. My hopes that the religious establishment will understand the concerns of the ordinary citizen of Ayodhya, and be moved to lend their voice for addressing these, have always been dashed at his court.

I am ushered to his audience room for visitors once more as I seek his blessings for a chapter on him in this book. It is a cold winter afternoon and his forbidding countenance – he has a rugged, swarthy face with beetling brows – is rendered less threatening by a white woollen band he wears across his ears and tied under his chin in a grandmotherly manner. As always, there are at least six or eight people in the narrow room on the first floor of the Chhavani temple.

After paying the usual respects, I tell him about the book, that it features twenty-five personalities from Ayodhya and of course, there has to be a chapter on him too. Nritya Gopal Das is very fond of the Urdu expression of encouragement and appreciation 'Wah!' He will interject his sentences with the word several times in any conversation. He begins with 'wah' and I am emboldened to talk a little more about the book. 'I feel only through the varied stories of actual people will readers get a good sense of Ayodhya's recent history,' I say.

---

*The author had submitted a proposal to municipal, state and central authorities for the creation of monkey enclosures as recreational spaces at several places in Faizabad-Ayodhya in order to address the man-animal conflict there. She also organized a public campaign to press for such sanctuaries. Nritya Gopal Das' support was sought for this scheme.

He looks at me keenly from under his brows. 'Who are these twenty-four other people you are featuring?' he asks.

I begin listing names while he listens. He says 'wah' only to some, stays silent for others. It is clear whom he approves of, and whom he considers a regrettable choice. After going through my list, my voice tapers away. There is silence.

Then, speaking softly but with unmistakable intent, Mahant Nritya Gopal Das tells me, 'Do not feature me in your book. This is my request.' When he delivers the statement sitting in his *durbar* like a king, it is not a request, but a command. I try to change his mind, stressing that the book will be incomplete without him. He cuts me short with a wave of his hand.

'It is my belief that a sadhu's worth cannot be measured in his lifetime. It can only be evaluated after his death,' he says. 'What is the point of writing about us when we are alive? Whether in *vyavaharik* terms (the business of daily living) or in terms of *paramarth* (the ultimate truth) we have not reached anywhere.'

I am silenced. I cannot argue with him, though I want to say that it is not my place to evaluate his worth as a sadhu. All I can do is provide readers with an introduction to his personality, like I have done with the other subjects. The people in the room are keenly listening to every word we speak. In front of them I cannot be seen to be questioning the mahant's views or authority. It is my cue to pay my respects and leave. As I rise, Maharajji softens his refusal by offering me prasad.

A week later, I am sitting in the winter sunshine with Vineet Maurya (*see* Chapter 1) recounting my ejection from Nritya Gopal Das' durbar. 'I don't mind his refusal to being featured,' I say. 'After all, there are authorized biographies and unauthorized biographies. So this can be an unauthorized portrait. What really hurt was the way he told me, "Give channa to the monkeys" when I mentioned the monkey project. Does he really think I built the whole monkey sanctuary scheme without ever having fed them? Should I produce Nuchu and her friends for proof?' I ask, referring to the troupe of monkeys that has been consistently visiting my home for the last two-and-a-half years.

'Oh don't worry about such comments from him,' says Vineet. 'After all, who is he to award certificates of devotion to monkeys? You know, there is a big difference in the way Paramhans Ramachandra Das fed monkeys, and how Nritya Gopal Das feeds them.'

I look at my friend questioningly. 'Paramhans bought fruit and vegetables from passing vendors, sometimes whole cartloads, to feed the monkeys. Both monkeys and humans were happy. Nritya Gopal Das does no such thing. So many sackloads of grain and pulses are received everyday at the chhavani to feed the sadhus. After sifting and sorting, the bad grain is thrown to the monkeys. His strategy is to draw the maximum amount of mileage and earn *punya* (good karma) without losing any real money.' We both laugh, and I am not so noble that I can draw no comfort from this observation of the mahant's meanness after my recent encounter.

Still later, I reflect once more on the murky world of the sadhus of Ayodhya, and how events in Ayodhya have repeatedly thrown the nation into a state of turmoil. Some troubling questions emerge.

While a man like Nritya Gopal Das is entitled to his religious authority and the stature he commands because of it, can such authority be superior to the laws of this land? Can sadhus, who are renunciates, ever truly reflect the interests of the vast majority of people who are enmeshed in the daily issues of survival for themselves and their families (the *grihastha* versus *virakt* debate of Ayodhya)? And would we, as a country, have landed in such a mess over the Ayodhya issue, if a large majority of our citizens had not been mistakenly seeking certificates in faith and patriotism from ill-qualified parties?

Perhaps the only hope for our democracy is this – that each individual comes to rely on his conscience.

PART III

PEOPLE LIKE US

The cost of vegetables and the lack of facilities, the future of our children and the thoughts of our forefathers – people in Ayodhya are subject to many of the same dilemmas that face us elsewhere. What does it mean to hold a job, raise children, make ends meet, in short, survive in a deeply religious and tradition-bound town? Meet the men and women who daily face these and similar challenges.

14

Padmavati
Bahujan Beti

(Mayawati makes the government, and Mulayam fills water at the well. Our *didi* is large-hearted, people are cheering for her!)

—Popular lines sung by rural children following
BSP's victory over SP in 2007

It is an evening in early October. In their recently constructed house near Ayodhya railway station, Padmavati and her husband, Sri Krishna Murari are both resting when I arrive to meet her.

The phase of panchayat elections in which she has been a candidate has concluded just the previous day. The largest democratic exercise in the world, the Uttar Pradesh panchayat elections, covers seventy-one districts and fifty-two thousand constituencies. In the 2010 elections, thousands of seats were reserved for women candidates, and their posters have been dotting the countryside for weeks before this meeting. Driving through any village meant seeing posters and hoardings showing a woman with her head demurely covered, with her hands folded in a namaste, asking people to vote for her. But for each Savitri Devi, or Basanti Devi, or Urmila Singh, there are always smaller images, the faces of their husbands peeking out at you from the bottom right corner of the poster or hoarding.

In Uttar Pradesh, you often find examples of the old cliché, though somewhat modified. Here, behind every successful woman, there is a man, and probably one who actually calls the shots.

At Padmavati's home, I find both husband and wife heavy-eyed and fatigued, her voice showing the strain of long weeks of campaigning. But they are welcoming nevertheless, eager to share whatever it is I am seeking from them. I settle down in the midst of sounds of easy domesticity – children's voices, tea being made, instructions given. Padmavati sits comfortably opposite me, right in front of a large picture of Kanshi Ram, who has been a guide and mentor figure for her family.

'Both of us are from Basti district,' she says of herself and her husband. Basti is 43 km from Ayodhya, en route to Gorakhpur. 'That is where I was born on 1 July 1968. We are from the *chamar* community (whose most famous representative is present-day UP Chief Minister Mayawati) and my father was a postmaster. The thing is, even though I had three elder sisters, we grew up in a liberal atmosphere. At home, we were not treated any less than sons, and were encouraged to study. I studied up to the first year MA level in Sanskrit, but I had got married slightly earlier, when I was an undergraduate.'

Indira Gandhi visited the district when Padmavati was a young girl, and gave a speech on the occasion of Ravidas Jayanti. Seeing a woman leader for the first time was a great inspiration for Padmavati. She wanted to be up on that stage, giving a speech herself. But while her father was most encouraging and understanding of such ambitions, she found that in a deeply feudal society, women were her first and worst enemies. 'So you think you will be a *neta*?' some taunted. Others spoke about her among themselves, alternately sniggering or making horrified comments like, 'She thinks nothing of eating before the men have eaten – I have seen her eat in front of ten men without any sense of shame!'

Undeterred by such pettiness, Padmavati got her first opportunity to learn of political manoeuvrings with the emergence of Kanshi Ram. In the decades that he asked for 'one vote and one note', and mobilized large numbers of dalit government servants under the umbrella of BAMCEF (The All India Backward and Minority Communities' Employees Federation), he also often came by Basti. He was in direct contact with Padmavati's family. 'In those days, meetings used to be held in people's homes. I must have been only fifteen years old, when I had the pleasure of cooking for Kanshi Ramji. He liked it so much that on every subsequent visit he would specifically ask for me to make something for him!' Padmavati says with obvious pleasure at being thus sought out by the iconic figure.

This was also the period when a pony-tailed Mayawati addressed meetings with her mentor. Padmavati remembers going and receiving her at the station for a meeting in Basti. More thrilling were her own forays – she went up to Delhi with other political workers for rallies and meetings. Travelling independently, without family protection, was completely unheard of at that time. But Padmavati defied convention.

By 1995, she had gained enough political stature to contest the Zilla Panchayat elections on a BSP ticket. Although she lost to a Congress candidate who was a sitting Zilla Parishad member, the narrow margin of her loss, only 135 votes, meant that she began to be taken seriously as an election candidate.

Padmavati recalls Ayodhya at that time. 'After the events of 1992, we just knew Ayodhya as a centre of controversy,' she says. 'From a small village in Basti, we depended on the accounts of people who had gone to the town. Those who had returned from parikrama were not too encouraging in their reports. Although we lived less than fifty kilometres away, we were reluctant to even visit this place,' she says.

Little did Padmavati know that her husband's posting as a Lekhpal (official in the Land Records office) for the UP government would bring the entire family to Ayodhya in 2003 for permanent residence. When they came, they brought along their children – the eldest daughter, Satya Jyoti; the son, Shilp Sen Gautam; and two younger daughters, Swapna Jyoti and Sunaina Jyoti, who were three- and two-year-old toddlers respectively.

While their involvement with the BSP had allowed the family to pursue upwardly mobile ideas and dreams in Basti, Padmavati and Krishna Murari found that Ayodhya took them back by nearly two decades. 'If you remove the big temples from Ayodhya, which people come to visit from all over the country, and if you stand at any street corner, you will discover that Ayodhya is no better than any village,' says Padmavati. 'Ayodhya is a very backward place, in terms of thinking, education and facilities'

From the beginning, Padmavati shielded her children from the regressive influences they would invariably find around them in Ayodhya. 'Stay well away from the disputes of this place!' she and her husband told the children. 'Don't allow all this to affect your academic life.' It is definitely because Padmavati and her husband reinforced the liberal traditions set by Padmavati's postmaster-father that the children have grown up relatively unaffected. The two youngest daughters, bright, inquisitive and pert in their replies, play chess at the national level, and have participated in tournaments in far-flung venues.

'My wife is completely behind both of them being able to get this far in chess,' says Krishna Murari. 'It is her patience, her being able to motivate them, and accompany them to tournaments that has propelled our daughters this far. I haven't gone for a single event!' However the children benefit from their father's talent and interest in art. On my first visit to the family in 2008, I noticed an entire wall painted as a mural by Krishna Murari, a very arresting sight in little Ayodhya. And I knew I was in the presence of an artist.

But all this talent and desire to better their circumstances has not spared Padmavati's family from the casteism that is rampant. 'Even wearing good clothes is seen as an offence,' says Padmavati. 'I just have to wear a beautiful saree for one of my neighbours to remark, "Look at these chamars, strutting in their fine clothes!" They don't spare the children also. "How can such low-caste children play in the nationals?" they ask each other. It is another matter that they have not tried to do any such thing either for themselves, or for their children.'

'You see, religion is the main means of livelihood in Ayodhya,' says Krishna Murari, finally breaking a brief spell of silence. 'Because they need religion to earn their daily bread, these people also reinforce all the backward beliefs and practices associated with religion. If their religion teaches them contentment as a philosophical concept, they interpret it to mean that one must not aspire for any improvement! If you look around, you will find that all the decent-looking houses, all of them, belong to newcomers or people who have arrived here from elsewhere. The original inhabitants of Ayodhya live in ruined houses without proper toilets, and still aspire for nothing more than they have.'

'If you ask me, religion is the very reason Ayodhya stays undeveloped,' says Padmavati emphatically. '*Mattadhishon ne kabhi paise ko shiksha ke liye istemal nahin kiya* (the heads of religious matts have never used their money to educate). You find babas and sadhus with fat bank balances. But buildings lie in ruins, most property is caught in some dispute, and belongs to some temple. It cannot be developed by anyone else, and the temples won't do a thing either. Objects just lie in a state of decay. Most importantly, the merchant class, those with the means to do something, want to avoid any dispute with religious authorities. So they also stay put, and things stay exactly as they are.'

So is it the overall prevalence of religion, not the mandir-masjid dispute, that is responsible for the lack of development for the locals? 'Not exactly,' says Padmavati. 'The hold of religious authority makes people have backward ideas. But the actual blocks to progress have been the demolition and the aftermath. For people here, the continuation of the Hindu-Muslim debate and dispute means their livelihoods get affected. *"Agar ghar mein khana hoga, tab hi to na hum mandir banayenge* (if we have food to eat at home, only then can we build a temple, right?).” Now people feel it very strongly, that is why they reject all the champions of the temple that once walked so tall amongst them. How can they encourage such people now, after they have been so badly hit? When their stomachs are half-full and their children lack basic amenities, they cannot sustain the dream of a temple with any conviction.’

Even the 30 September 2010 Lucknow High Court judgement in the title suit of the Rama Janmabhoomi is seen by the people today only through the lens of how it will affect their livelihood, if one goes by Padmavati’s version. ‘The most devoted people from both communities just want some judgement. Let there be a verdict, whatever it is, and let us get on with our lives, is the sentiment today. After all, can Ayodhya escape the increasingly business-like approach of today’s world? In the old days, we used to have people coming from our village to do what was known as *kalpavas* in Ayodhya. It meant bathing daily in the Sarayu, visiting all the temples, staying for an extended period, listening to discourses, doing bhajan-kirtan. Today we don’t see anybody having the time or resources for this. Even the puja or katha that is being done for the household is executed in such a hurry. “*Panditji, jaldi kariye*! (Hurry up, Panditji!)” is what people are urging, more often than not.’

The woman who has held the post of Zilla Sangathan Mantri of Basti for the BSP chose Vikramjyot for her panchayat candidature, chiefly for its proximity to Ayodhya and the fact that it was a scheduled caste reserved seat. ‘There were eleven men standing against the lone woman candidate, Padmavati,’ says Krishna Murari, with obvious pride. ‘Yagnesh Pandey, who had won the post in 2000, placed his tractor driver, Akhilesh as a candidate, because it had become a reserved seat. The posters all carried the Brahmin's photo, although it was the dalit boy who was standing. But we are giving them a tough fight.'

Checking in with Padmavati on the phone in early November 2010, I learn that she lost the election and the Brahmin's driver won amidst speculation of manipulation, and lakhs of rupees being spent on a steady supply of liquor and treats for the voters. I share a few minutes of enquiry about the election and counting process with her, then call off, with a pang of regret that she could not make a breakthrough in the male- and caste-dominated bastions of rural Uttar Pradesh. But Padmavati herself does not sound unduly upset.

This doughty Bahujan beti proves that defeat is defined by the death of hope or possibility. Padmavati believes she is a winner.

15

Raghuvar Sharan
Romance as Worship

Ek tadap ka naam jo satya aur shanti chahti hai, par uske swaroop ko nahin janti, uske marg ka bhi theek thaak pata nahin. Idhar udhar daudti hai, hazaar anubhav ki chaukhat par sir patakti hai, aur kabhi apni kenchil mein past padi rehti hai.

(Call it an anguish that yearns for peace and truth, but does not know how to get there. Runs here and there, bangs its head against the threshold of a thousand experiences, and sometimes lies inside its own dead (snake)skin, completely exhausted.)

—Raghuvar, describing himself in the context of Ayodhya

The Rasik Nivas temple in Ayodhya – that has been home to Raghuvar Sharan since his birth – has an interesting history. It was built as an edifice expressing love for Rama between 1770 and 1785. An atmosphere of great gaiety marked the entire process of construction, with the people who were offering kar-seva to build the temple wearing *ghungroos* on their feet, and singing as they carried bricks from the nearby kilns to the temple site.

This expression of love for their beloved Rama marks the Rasik Sampradaya. Its founder, Rasik Ali (the Hindi 'ali' meaning friend), is considered the fourth but most direct Acharya or teacher of the tradition, the earlier three being Rama, Sita and Hanuman. Rasik Ali's followers take the appendage 'sharan' (taking shelter in) after their names, signifying a complete surrender, as displayed by a beloved towards her lover, towards God. In fact, in this manner, the tradition shares elements with the way in which Krishna is worshipped in Mathura-Brindavan. Raghuvar admits that the Rasik Dhara contains '*Rama ki upaasana mein Krishna ki upaasana ki chhaya* (the reflection of Krishna worship in the worship of Rama).' But he adds that his father and other elders of the tradition would have frowned on such an admission. The Rasik Sampradaya adherents among Ramanandi Vaishnavites plainly consider their surrender to be of a deeper nature and distinct from the Krishna-and-gopis adoration of Brindavan.

Since the other sadhus of the Vaishnav tradition in Ayodhya have 'Das' (servant) after their names, it signifies the unique approach they have towards their deity. For the Rasik Sampradaya, the most important festival to be celebrated in relation to Rama is the 'Rama vivaah' (Rama's wedding), observed every year on the Agahan Shukla Panchami day, which comes somewhere around December or January.

The Rasik Nivas temple was built by Gopal Narayan Singh on five *bighas* (a measure of land varying from a third of an acre to an acre) of land. This had been gifted to Rasik Ali by a nawab whom he had cured of an illness by blessing him. The different relationships between these three characters, and the circumstances of the temple coming into existence are typical of the episodes with which Ayodhya's history is replete.

Rasik Ali's biography is most interesting. According to Raghuvar, Rasik Ali stayed in a small cottage at Sita Kund, where he met and spoke to few people. When he did interact with anyone, it was to grant blessings. There he met a boy, to whom he said, 'Go! You will be king!' The astonished boy, depressed and hungry, protested, 'What? How? Even if I do become king as you say, what do I do now? I am hungry.' The saint, showing his ready compassion, served the boy a meal of *sattu* (a multi-grain powder offered in the form of a paste). The youth returned to Tikari in Bihar, neighbouring Gaya, where the queen and her nephew had had an argument which had so incensed her that she told her minister, 'Go and get any boy from the banks of the Ganga and make him king!'

The boy, whom the minister found, was Gopal Narayan Singh, who had been blessed by Rasik Ali. On being crowned the king of Gaya, he returned to Rasik Ali and begged to be allowed to stay with him. 'No, your duty is to now go serve your people,' the saint told him.

Meanwhile the saint continued to bless many others, one of whom was an ailing nawab whom he met at Janaki Ghat. When this man was cured of his illness, he recalled the saint's blessings and gifted him the land on which Gopal Narayan Singh had a temple built for the saint.

Today, this patch of earth is inhabited by Raghuvar.

Raghuvar was born on 4 June 1968 and raised in the temple that stands here. His father, who had come to Ayodhya around 1930 to study Sanskrit, had stayed on and eventually been anointed as the mahant of Rasik Nivas. 'When I was a child, there was enough wilderness around the house and temple for us to be able to see deer and jackals, porcupines, mongoose, and of course, monkeys. They were in our midst as we played. It was a very happy world. Even as I engaged in usual boyish pursuits, I was aware of God as the unseen presence. I felt the spiritual current flowing through the people who came to the temple.'

Raghuvar's father's priestly duties included daily pujas and more elaborate festive rituals. But it was his father's constant connection to the God he worshipped that left the deepest impression. From him he imbibed the sense of *'hardam bhagvat smaran karna, manasik jap karna* (the need to engross the body and mind in the contemplation of God)' and in the peculiar bliss this produced.

To begin with, Raghuvar was not an overtly religious child who participated in rites. Instead he grew up believing *'bhagwan ek chaitanya satta hai, nitya nirantar ka saathi* (God is a conscious power over us all, with us in every sleeping, waking, eating, smiling moment).' In a hazy, unformed way Raghuvar also felt responsible towards his father and the temple, as if he should eventually do something of his own for the place of worship.

But such thoughts and joyous memories were to be seriously tested by the onslaught of reality. When Raghuvar was in class five, his father suffered a paralytic stroke, throwing the family into disarray. His elder brother, used to being the pampered child of gentle parents, had a breakdown – the beginning of many years of instability. He did not take up the responsibility of the temple from his father.

Raghuvar sensed the strain. All these years, he had grown up as most lads in Ayodhya did, with yoga and wrestling lessons at the akhara, and swimming jaunts in the Sarayu. He had wanted to grow up and become a sub-inspector in police uniform. 'I thought the IAS was beyond me, and the post of a policeman seemed the best compromise under the circumstances. I even wrote the exam,' he says.

These khaki dreams were shattered due to his father's ill-health, and Raghuvar went on to pursue his MA in ancient history from Saket Degree College. It was during this period that he developed an attachment for academic life, discovering the pleasure to be had in learning for learning's sake.

Raghuvar's father had passed away when Raghuvar was studying for his Bachelor's. Since then, he had taken up some of the temple duties with his mother. In his postgraduate years, he became a creative writer, penning essays and poetry, and reading newspapers with great care and attention. He was attracted to the moderate and slightly highbrow journalism of the *Navbharat Times*.

Raghuvar met his wife, Renu when they were studying in Saket. After he completed his postgraduation degree, the couple got married in 1995, by which time Raghuvar had become a journalist. He spent years with the mainstream *Dainik Jagran* in Faizabad, before moving to its rival *Amar Ujala* in late 2010. Today, he also lectures at his alma mater, Saket.

However, these mature vocational choices came after his days as a student leader of the ABVP or Akhil Bharatiya Vidyarthi Parishad. 'In 1990, I was most irritated and upset by Mulayam's utterances, like nearly everybody in Ayodhya,' he says. 'I had decided to offer kar-seva. On 30 October and 2 November, both the days, Mulayam's police had turned Ayodhya into a garrison. I was surprised by the masses of kar-sevaks arriving into the town inspite of the barricades at all the entry points. People in Ayodhya were inspired by these numbers and came out in support of them.'

While nearly everyone has mentioned the firing at Lal Kothi area on 30 October, what Raghuvar remembers is that the police were misguiding people on that day and giving them wrong directions so that kar-sevaks would not be able to reach the disputed structure at all. Despite that, some determined kar-sevaks reached the structure and hoisted a flag there. Raghuvar's recollection is that two or three people died on that day, not more. This is the wild difference in figures that we keep encountering from one account to another.

'On 2 November, the VHP had decided to surround the disputed structure and do kirtan around it. On this day, even more kar-sevaks had assembled. Their mood was euphoric, eager. "We have defeated the might of Mulayam," they were thinking. No one imagined there would be bullets again,' says Raghuvar. 'When there was firing again, people were caught unawares. What upset me most was that while the VHP had decided to surround the disputed structure and do kirtan around it, they did not reveal their true plans either to the public or the administration. The police chased the kar-sevaks a great distance from the masjid and thrashed them. Meanwhile, there was a complete absence of responsibility on the part of the VHP. No one was there to call back the kar-sevaks who were getting fired upon.'

Shocked by these events of 1990, Raghuvar went through a great deal of disillusionment with the leadership and policies of the Rama Janmabhoomi movement over the next couple of years, a process that reached its culmination on 6 December 1992, when the Babri Masjid was brought down. 'I was frightened by the militant nature of the crowds,' he recalls, with the pictures still vivid in his memory. 'I had never seen anything like this, and I devoutly hope I never have to see it again – so many naked weapons – swords, *trishuls*, spears, and slogan-shouting crowds! Their slogans were violent to the point of being hurtful just to listen to. I did not see Rama bhakti or respect for any of Ayodhya's traditions in any of their faces,' he says.

There was a sharp contrast between the way Raghuvar had been brought up in the Rasik Dhara tradition of Ayodhya, rubbing shoulders with sadhus and pilgrims without any feelings of animosity for his Muslim neighbours, and the raw, anti-Muslim sentiment exhibited on the streets. All this was too much for him. Worst of all, these violent crowds were completely unsupervised and unchecked. The leadership that should have been guiding or inspiring them was totally absent on the streets. 'If any revered Ayodhya personality had also come in their path on that day, they would not have survived those crowds,' says Raghuvar.

At the disputed site, things were not better; in fact they turned much worse. Here, the VHP leadership was present. A stage had been set up for leaders to address the crowds and instruct them. 'But as the pressure of the masses built up, it was very obvious that these people had neither foreseen the onslaught of the crowds, nor could they do anything to contain them. Even those leaders who had earlier been making very polite and civil announcements like "get down, stand back, let us begin to offer our kar-seva" began saying, "*ek dhakka aur do*, push, push". Complete anarchy reigned. I don't care for any of these leaders, but on that day I feared for the lives of even the likes of Ashok Singhal. As the angry swarms of people seethed around the VHP leaders, the latter had to retreat. Staying there meant getting hurt, badly.'

As a journalist, Raghuvar has documented the seamier aspects of Ayodhya, including the criminalization of its matts and mandirs. Yet, as an individual who has spent nearly every waking moment in this town, he cannot help but retain a romantic and wistful view of the place. Aside from the violent events of 1992, I ask him what he regrets about the Ayodhya of today. 'What I regret the most is the shrinking space for true spiritual search,' he replies. 'I don't know whether this is due to Ayodhya's own peculiar history or just the pace of change everywhere else.'

Does he mean that it is not just the politicization of religion that has led to the depletion of spiritual spaces, but also globalization and the whole change in our approach to life? 'Perhaps,' says Raghuvar, in part-agreement. 'It is true that getting more bridges and buildings built, making things bigger and shinier is not the solution for Ayodhya. After all, the big matt heads are anyway engaged in a fight for economic supremacy, competing with each other for the acquisition and development of bigger property. No, what hurts is the loss of the Ayodhya that used to be considered a *siddhon ka sarai* (a haven for realized souls),' he says.

The gentler, quieter pace of life of the childhood that Raghuvar has described to me so graphically in many earlier conversations begins to dance before my eyes as he speaks – the temple frequented by lovers of God, his father in silent contemplation of Rama, the small animals, many friends, and the sweet proximity to the Sarayu. It is difficult not to be moved by his nostalgia for a kinder world. 'What I am trying to say is that there was space for those who felt disturbed or dissatisfied by society and its mad rush in Ayodhya in the past. Rebels and misfits, spiritual seekers, all could find quiet here for a meaningful inner dialogue. Sadhus could really find solitude, a retreat from worldliness that would give them greater depth and understanding. *Ab toh atma-samvaad bhi us tarah ka sambhav nahin dikhta* (now even that kind of dialogue with oneself seems an impossibility in Ayodhya).'

We pause. I can relate to his observations because I have similarly noticed a business-like attitude in the pilgrims that visit the town. This has disturbed me and has made me contrast Ayodhya with profoundly spiritual places like Thiruvannamalai or Varanasi. There is a lack in Ayodhya and both Raghuvar and I are acutely aware of it at that moment. It is as if even the business of seeking God or spirituality is ruled by a brisk, business-like tempo. The complete abandon or absence of attachment to many worldly duties and concepts that are visible in some other towns is not characteristic of Ayodhya.

So what hope do you hold out for the future, I ask Raghuvar. Is it possible to put the whole dispute and its aftermath behind us? He replies, '*Ab prakriti jo kare so kare. Koi vyakti iske bare mein kuchh sarthak prayas karta nahin dikh raha* (now time will do what it does. I don't see any individual making any meaningful impact on the resolution that follows).'

Many in Ayodhya have placed their trust in the healing quality of time, rather than on individual or collective efforts. It is as though, after over six decades of independence, we are left with little to believe in.

16

Hashim Ansari
'Chacha' to All

Hukumat talwar ki mazboot nahin hoti, mohabbat ki hoti hai.

(The rule of the sword can never be as solid or stable as that of love.)

—Hashim Ansari, speaking on why, eventually,
all will be well in Ayodhya

The twin towns of Faizabad and Ayodhya are home to two elderly Muslims, both of whom have made a living by running a cycle repair shop. One of them, Mohammed Sharif of Khidki Alibag in Faizabad, is a man who tends to the destitute at the District Hospital, and provides a decent burial or cremation to unclaimed bodies. His deeply humanitarian efforts have given hundreds of dying people comfort in their last moments, as he feeds them and cares for them when their families have abandoned them. As for providing the last rites for unclaimed bodies, Sharif was moved to do this after his own young son was murdered in Sultanpur, around sixty kilometres away, and Sharif received only the boy's watch and belt from the police. 'No corpse should be allowed to rot in a hospital, or be eaten by dogs,' he decided. He has worked tirelessly to restore human dignity, each day of the month, for the last fifteen years or more.

The other elderly Muslim, Hashim Ansari, also does not fail to elicit affection and recognition every time his name is mentioned. Ansari has also had a long stint as a cycle repair shop owner. Now, of course, his name is known across the country as the man who has fought a sixty-year long legal battle in the title suit of the Babri Masjid-Rama Janmabhoomi dispute. The 30 September 2010 judgement of the Lucknow bench of the Allahabad High Court in response to this suit had caused life in Ayodhya to come to a near standstill. In the days and weeks following the verdict, there were different statements by the players involved. While some like the Sunni Central Wakf Board spoke of going to a higher court, others like the Rama Janmabhoomi Nyas held celebratory meetings at Karsevakpuram. Alongside this, another effort was seen in Ayodhya – a dialogue between Hashim Ansari and Mahant Gyandas, the head of the Hanuman Garhi temple, and members of both Hindu and Muslim communities, to seek an out of court solution.

This initiative is greeted with scepticism and scorn by some, respect and regard by others. However, whether or not it yields any long-term results, Hashim Ansari, who was in 2010 the longest serving litigant in the Ayodhya title suit, made waves for some weeks with his meetings with Mahant Gyandas.

Hashim Ansari is plaintiff No. 7 in the case filed by the Sunni Central Wakf Board in 1961 in the Ayodhya title suit. There are a total of eleven plaintiffs in that suit. Ansari was reportedly roped in to become a plaintiff because he was a young man with a lot of time on his hands. He was perceived as honest, because he did not hanker after big money or a high public profile. Instead, he needed only kind words, a small treat in the form of samosas and tea or similar offerings, to keep going faithfully to the courts for every hearing.

Even as he began talks with Mahant Gyandas, the local media began to speculate that Hashim would choose to keep out of the legal battle now, and concentrate on out of court efforts instead. But when the Sunni Central Wakf Board filed their appeal in the Supreme Court in November 2010, sure enough there was a power of attorney from Hashim signalling his continued involvement in the case. He thus remains an important symbolic presence for his community in the title suit.

When I arrive at his home to talk to him, Ansari is eating his lunch and peers out of a window, a tell-tale grain of rice sticking to one side of his mouth. I apologize for barging in, but he is unfazed and tells me he will join me in a few minutes. In the months following the judgement, and through the last two decades, he has been accustomed to dealing with media persons from around the country. I wait for him in a tent erected for security personnel across the road from his house, and the policemen there very courteously clear space on a bench in the warm sunlight for me. They get a plastic chair ready for Hashim. This is a routine they are also familiar with. They may be PAC men, but they are not above social niceties, especially for this man, whom every passer-by on the street stops to greet with a, '*Namaste, Chacha*! How goes it? *Sab theek hai?*'

It is Hashim Ansari's peace dialogue that has earned him all this goodwill. Ansari admits, 'It feels good to be in touch with people who appreciate our efforts at starting a dialogue. 'Ninety per cent of those who come forward to speak to me or meet me are Hindus. They come from all over the country, even abroad. I have not appealed to the Supreme Court, but I will continue my out of court efforts. After all, I am not a *mohtaj* (refugee) of the courts for this.'

Hashim Ansari was born in Ayodhya 'around 1918', and his father was a tailor with a shop in Sringar Haat. Taking over this traditional occupation, he ran his father's shop till the Emergency struck, when it closed down. After that, he was a part of his brother's cycle repair shop, the same shop that brought him close to the Naali Wale Baba (*see* Chapter 4 on Ram Sharan Das).

'It was my mother who pulled me away from my brother's business,' he reveals. 'Why did she do that? Were you and he having some personal problems?' I ask him. 'No,' he says. 'She was disappointed with my growing social and political involvement. "*Tum to raajneeti mein aane lage ho, jail jane lage ho* (you have started entering politics, going to jail),' she told me. But I was not chasing any political goal. Rather, I was inspired by good leaders, *imaandaar* men, irrespective of which party they belonged to. Even my involvement with the case was never out of a desire to be in the news. I was one of the smaller parties, but Faizabad's big lawyers made my case into a big one.'

I ask him about the long legal battle for Babri Masjid-Rama Janmabhoomi that has preoccupied the nation since 1984. What does Hashim feel about it all? 'There were four cases that have been lumped together for the court to decide on the title suit. The first was filed by Gopal Singh Visharad, a lawyer from Gwalior, the second was filed by Paramhans Ramachandra Das, the third was the Nirmohi Akhara case and the fourth was filed by the Sunni Central Wakf Board. The last of the lot entered the fray after the idols had been placed, because the masjid was Wakf property.

'You have to understand that this is a dispute that has been created not out of hard facts, but out of a whole lot of imagination. The very first case should have been dismissed. But look at the limitations of the administration, they allowed the second case to be filed too, and when the idols had been placed in the masjid, Nehru called the state administration after four days. The chief minister here told him that removing the idols would disturb the peace, and there was a danger of things getting out of hand. That was when the seeds were planted for this dispute to be used for political purposes. The second case was withdrawn by Paramhans in 1990, because he was fed up by then of attending court. The third case was a property dispute that had begun in 1870 or 1880, it was that old. What was the need for it to be taken further? Several tracts of the disputed land had become so tough to identify because Dharamdas, the chela of Abhiramdas, the man who placed the idols in the masjid, had forcibly taken over the land and burnt all the papers. Then he gave the land he had occupied to the Rama

Janmabhoomi Nyas. All through this long history there were so many decisions that the courts and administration could have taken, but they did not. *Congress ki laparwahi se firka parast partiyan mazboot hui hain* (it is because of the negligence of the Congress that communal parties have been strengthened).'

Hashim does not mention the most political case of them all – the fifth case filed in 1989 by Deoki Nandan Agarwal on behalf of 'Rama Lalla' – the installed deity of the Rama Janmabhoomi, who is supposedly a 'minor' in legal terms and could not file a case on his own. This is the case that has resulted in 'Rama Lalla' being given independent status in the 30 September 2010 judgement.

'On the surface, this matter appears to be a religious one, but look deeper and it translates into politics alone,' says Hashim Ansari. '*Yeh mulk is maamle mein kab tak jalta rahega?* (How long will the country keep burning in this particular matter?)'

But hasn't his religion turned Hashim Ansari into an important litigant for members of the minority community? 'Yes, my religion does make me an important litigant in the title suit, and the Sunni committee backed me, and yet Hindus respect me. Why?' he asks me, and goes on to provide an answer. 'They respect me because they know that I have suffered expenses, but neither did I allow my case to become political, nor did I use it to collect money.'

'Paramhans and I were childhood friends,' he continues, referring to his legendary bonding with Paramhans Ramachandra Das. 'We stayed friends till the end. His nephews and chelas still give me a lot of respect.' Ayodhya lore has accounts of how the two used to share transport to go to the court where they were engaged in fighting each other.

Hashim Ansari compares this with the petty politics he sees around him. 'Look at the communal parties; can they even deliver what they promised? They set up Karsevakpuram* with great fanfare in Ayodhya at the height of their movement. Karsevakpuram was nothing but a haven for the black money of the *seths* from other states. Initially they served long-grained rice and good quality daal. Slowly, even this is closing down. Today the people of Ayodhya don't support them.'

Hashim Ansari has stayed an ordinary man despite being at the centre of the legal tangle that expressed Ayodhya's most visible dispute. His family has got by, still living in a small house, with his sons taking up everyday vocations. One of his sons is a driver of the tempo taxis plying between Faizabad and Ayodhya. Yet, Hashim Ansari holds forth like a man with a great deal to say. Listening to him, one cannot help noticing the difference between his account and the routine ranting of us educated, middle-class citizens against the system. Often, such comments are made in the comfort of our homes, among like-minded friends, entailing no risk. But Hashim Ansari, being a man of humble means, has had to deal with officials of all sorts from the lower courts to the Lucknow bench, and has had several years to grapple with the ground-level realities of the judicial system.

Hashim Ansari continues speaking, 'For the record, we have four *melas* here every year. But the provisions made for them are so very negligible. The need for facilities is much greater than the

---

*Karsevakpuram is a large and sprawling campus on the outskirts of Ayodhya, which was used for the assembly of VHP cadres and kar-sevaks who had arrived from different parts of the country. It was here that many strategies of the movement for the Rama temple were planned and it was given its local edge. Reportedly, it was set up on land owned formerly by the Ayodhya royal family (*See* Chapter 5). Today it is a semi-deserted place that is merely the local headquarters of the VHP.

actual supply. I went to Mecca last year. I saw the arrangements the government there makes for water, sanitation, accommodation. We were able to have good food, stayed in a good hotel, had good transport and medical help, despite not being the richest pilgrims. Compared to that, what does the government here do for the melas? If anyone were to have a major problem during the melas here, God help them!'

If his criticism of the system reflects his personal experience, his next comments reveal a deep political wisdom too. A moment after extolling the conditions for pilgrims in Saudi Arabia, Hashim Ansari's expression sobers. He brings up another fundamental difference. 'For all the facilities they possess in those parts of the world, there is also an important difference. Here, I can speak out against the prime minister, if I want to. There, the people have to toe the American line for all matters.'

I decide to change subjects. Since he has seen nearly a century in this temple town, I ask him about Ayodhya then and now. 'The town has not really changed for me,' he says. 'All my friends and well-wishers still exist. No development has taken place, however.' He pauses, pondering over the town's history.

'Earlier, Faizabad and Ayodhya had a common municipal council. Some people here wanted a separate municipality, and I saw their point of view. I too pushed for it. It happened like this – when the Emergency happened, and I was imprisoned, along with several important leaders. I got close to them. I spoke to these leaders about Ayodhya's need for a separate municipality. However, I now consider it a mistake.'

But didn't the bifurcation mean better, more streamlined municipalities for both places? 'No, not really,' says Hashim Ansari. 'Senior functionaries were sent from Faizabad to Ayodhya in the beginning – teams of responsible people. Later new people emerged and they lacked accountability. This is because, where earlier, people fought municipal elections to earn a good name, now they fought elections to earn money. The money that got sanctioned from Delhi or Lucknow would get distributed amongst the leaders from Faizabad, and commission cuts would keep happening. By the time it would reach us, it would be whittled away to a fraction of what it was.'

Since Faizabad is the district headquarters and administrative hub, allocation of funds for Ayodhya via Faizabad has created a network of corporators-intermidiaries-contractors that creates the same obstacles to development as seen in many other small towns across the country. Besides, the scale of funding sanctioned by the government is also different for a municipal corporation, as against for a mere municipality, and these differences have been defined in the Uttar Pradesh Municipalities Act, 1916 as well as the UP Municipal Corporation Adhiniyam, 1959.

'What does being a legislator mean in today's India? Shouldn't these elected representatives have some sympathy for the people they represent? You have so many fancy titles, so many Chairmen these days – one for lighting, one for water – and no action anywhere. What I find most difficult to digest is, *hamare neta sach bolne se kyon darte hain? Jo mandir ke naam par rajneeti karte hain, woh vikas ke naam par chunav kyon nahin ladte* (why are our leaders afraid of speaking the truth? Those who play politics in the name of the temple or mosque, why don't they fight elections in the name of development?)'

How does he see events panning out for Ayodhya in the days to come, I ask him. 'My peace efforts with Gyandas have been opposed by political elements in both communities, Muslim and

Hindu. The work we started, if it could have gone a bit further, we could have communicated to the highest authorities that the twenty-five lakhs spent daily on the fourteen companies of PAC (Provincial Armed Constabulary), seven companies of CRP (Central Reserve Police), the special contingent of women police and the two police dogs could be spent on the development of this town instead. Now I think time will provide the best solution in the form of younger, more creative leaders. *Aaj ka mulk naujawanon ki taraf dekh raha hai. Yeh faisla tab hoga jab naujawan desh mein raaj karenge* (today the country is looking towards its youth. This matter will be solved when young people are leaders of this country).'

By now, Gaurav Tiwari 'Beeru' has turned up and is listening to our last few minutes of conversation. Several people on the road, having greeted 'Chacha', have been listening appreciatively as well. The ninety-two-year-old litigant of Ayodhya looks at me. Pointing towards Beeru, he says, 'Look at this young man. Comes to see me with a mouth stuffed with tobacco, but didn't think of getting me a cigarette too!' Abashed at being thus reminded, Beeru hurries away to procure the much-needed smoke, while I take leave of this remarkable old man.

The harshest words one can hear about Hashim Ansari in Ayodhya are that he is a bit player or pawn of more powerful interests in the Muslim community, and his efforts to broker peace in the Ayodhya imbroglio through talks with Mahant Gyandas are inconsequential. Such cynical evaluations, which Ansari continually refers to, since they appear to have got under his skin, remain the only criticism of 'Chacha' across many conversations with people across the social hierarchy. On the other hand, an equal amount of people regard him as a hero and a good-hearted man who is very approachable. His daily struggles for survival ensure that a vast majority of Ayodhya's impoverished population identifies with him. A tea stall owner at the Tedhi Bazaar *chauraha*, not far from Hashim Ansari's home, raised his palms and gazed skywards when I asked him about the old man. 'What can one say? Chacha is a *farishta* (angel),' he said. While this is typical of the hyperbole that prevails in this Awadh region of Uttar Pradesh, it would hardly be offered if it was untrue. Whether he is on the winning or losing side in the Ayodhya title suit, Hashim Ansari will never lack for people to buy him tea or a samosa in Ayodhya.

17

Sharad Sharma
Hindutva's Hope

Koti koti Hindu jan ka, hum jwaar uthakar manenge.
Saugandh Rama ki khate hain, hum mandir bhavya banayenge.

(We shall not rest till we have created a human tide of crores and crores of Hindus.
We take a vow before Rama, that we shall build a magnificent temple.)

—From the VHP document,
Sri Rama Janmabhoomi: Ayodhya ko Samjhen

Sharad Sharma was born on Independence Day, 1973, which makes him one of the youngest subjects of this book. However, his youth has not prevented him from being closely entwined with the recent history of his birth place, Ayodhya. As the head of the Vishwa Hindu Parishad's media cell in Ayodhya, he has been a familiar name and face for press persons arriving from all over the country for the past twelve years or more.

Speaking to Sharad Sharma at Karsevakpuram, the sprawling campus near Rama Ghat on the outskirts of Ayodhya, from where the VHP strategy for the construction of a Rama temple unfolded in a series of dramatic events, one is struck by his obvious sincerity. This man truly believes in his cause, even if it draws him little mileage in terms of local affection and support today. He also articulates the well-crafted plan that the VHP had put together to galvanize the Hindu majority into declaring themselves above the law and the Constitution of India. His is not a sophisticated, glib presentation. Rather it is the account of someone who still believes that the men whom he looked up to, the values he thought they represented, are intact and relevant today.

In 1989, the year Karsevakpuram was set up as the VHP headquarters in Ayodhya, Sharad Sharma was a sixteen-year-old who watched kar-sevaks arriving from all over the country and was impressed by their passion and zeal, just like his contemporary, Gaurav Tiwari 'Beeru'. 'We saw young people arriving in large numbers. We also saw and heard speakers and personalities like Ashok Singhal and Acharya Giriraj Kishore. I was inspired and felt I wanted to move closer to them, learn from them.'

Sharad Sharma was rapidly accepted into the Sangh fold and began to play a small but significant role. In 1990, he became the city coordinator for the Bajrang Dal. By 1998, his inclination to become a journalist asserted itself, partly because his father had been a journalist. He had also completed his education by then. He began to be given the tasks of preparing press releases and notes for the media by the VHP at Karsevakpuram. Later in 2001, he was made the media head for the whole state of Uttar Pradesh. Simultaneously, Sharma began an initiative of his own which is still in operation – the publication of the newspaper, *Ayodhya Samvaad* (Ayodhya Dialogue) which today reaches fifteen thousand subscribers.

By the time they gave the teenaged Sharad Sharma a foothold in their organization, the VHP along with the RSS, BJP, Bajrang Dal and other Sangh outfits had succeeded in laying the foundation of the movement for a Rama Mandir at the disputed site in Ayodhya. They claimed that a grand temple to mark the spot of Sri Rama's birth had existed at this spot and had been razed by invading conqueror Babar. They also described the structure of the Babri Masjid built in AD 1528 by Babar's general Mir Baqi as a dhaancha or skeletal structure that had been erected with the sole purpose of covering the remains of the ancient temple.

As a part of their strategy to evoke a strong sense of grievance among Hindus, the VHP recommended the construction of a temple for Sri Rama on the disputed site as a necessary step in the restoration of Hindu pride. They cited historical accounts, such as those in the diary of a travelling Austrian priest who had wandered across India between 1740 to 1785, and claimed that Hindus had made no less than seventy-six attempts to recapture the spot of Rama's birth through bloody battles between 1528 and 1949. In fact, they suggested that in 1934, local Hindus stormed into the structure and inflicted damage on it.

The VHP claim was bolstered in the public imagination by

several factors. The first was the presence of 'Rama Lalla' or infant Sri Rama under the central dome of the Babri Masjid since the night of 22-23 December 1949. Subsequently this was shown to be a clear act of human conspiracy and not a *prakatya* (appearance/incarnation) event as claimed by the VHP.

The placing of the idols happened when Jawaharlal Nehru was the prime minister and G.B. Pant was the chief minister of Uttar Pradesh, both Congressmen. Only K.K. Nayar, the then Collector of Faizabad was a man with links to the Jan Sangh. After the idols were placed inside the masjid, they were worshipped everyday by local and arriving pilgrims in a relatively peaceful manner till 1982-83, when the grievance-laden propaganda of the VHP began to sweep across the country. During this long spell, the idols remained inside, and a grille, with a lock on it, separated devotees from Rama Lalla. However, poojas and aartis happened daily, and food was offered to Rama Lalla and distributed as prasad. No one was really unhappy with this situation, except the strategists of the VHP, and perhaps the litigants in the title suit, fighting over the historical claim as much as they were fighting for the piece of land.

On 8 April 1984, a Sant Sabha (gathering of saints) at Vigyan Bhavan in Delhi called for the opening of the locks on the grille behind which Rama Lalla was worshipped. Using Rama Janki Raths, vehicles improvised as travelling propaganda instruments, they began to spread awareness about this demand, and drum up public support. On 1 February 1986, the Faizabad District Judge K.M. Pandey ordered that the locks be opened. At this time, Veer Bahadur Singh was the chief minister of UP and Rajiv Gandhi was the prime minister, both Congressmen.

This was a turning point in many ways. First, it meant that the Sunni Central Wakf Board which had entered the legal dispute over the site in 1961 challenged the District Judge's order. Second, it paved way for the many rallying functions of the VHP, who began to project the construction of the Rama temple at Rama Janmabhoomi as a certainty. The grandson of the architect of the modern temple at Somnath, C. B. Sompura, was appointed the architect of the proposed temple and he drew up a plan which became a model shown to large crowds at several venues.

In January 2001, when I was at the Mahakumbh Mela in Allahabad, the biggest crowds forming long, serpentine queues were assembled in front of the VHP tent to get a glimpse of the model of this temple. I did not dare to negotiate this queue even out of idle curiosity. It would have meant a day of waiting.

Following the opening of the locks, the VHP organized Shila Pujan and Shilanyas, two separate events, rather processes, which allowed them to build a huge public following for the proposed temple. Three lakh bricks, or *shilas* were worshipped in individual homes and sent to Ayodhya for the temple. But since the model of the temple proposed the use of stone – one wonders what was done with the bricks, and where they are now, these little candles of people's hope and solidarity. The first of the kar-sevas, meant to allow ordinary people to devote their labour to the creation of the temple, happened to occur during the term of a chief minister of Uttar Pradesh, christened as 'Mulla' Mulayam by his detractors, the man who won lakhs of Muslim votes for the Samajwadi Party by taking an aggressive stand against the kar-seva. Those two days in 1990 are repeatedly mentioned by the subjects of this book: 30 October 1990 and 2 November 1990, when Mulayam Singh turned Ayodhya into a fortress. The firing that ensued resulted in casualties.

With the fall of the Mulayam Singh government after he had

tendered his resignation in 1991, Kalyan Singh of the BJP became chief minister of the state. One of his first acts was to acquire forty-two acres of land around the disputed site for a Rama Katha Park, and gift this to the Rama Janmabhoomi Nyas. This was towards the southern and eastern portions of the masjid, and we have seen how this acquisition affected the lives of individuals like Vineet Maurya (*see* Chapter 1). In addition, 2.77 acres were acquired for a centre to house pilgrims. When this land was being levelled by the UP government in June 1991, the VHP document describes inscribed stones, broken statues of Shiva and Parvati, a half lotus shaped like the sun and other artefacts being found on the site. It is not clear what happened to these archaeological finds, and whether these were examined and dated by competent authorities. However, the Tulsi Smarak Bhavan in Ayodhya, where the Department of Culture aided Ayodhya Shodh Sansthan has its office, has a museum with several exhibits that have been recovered from the disputed site. Whether these were found after December 1992, or during Kalyan Singh's levelling excursions, is not clearly explained.

The firing in October and November 1990 on kar-sevaks in Ayodhya resulted in the VHP obtaining its first martyrs. The remains of two brothers from Kolkata, the Kothari brothers, were taken to different parts of the country where they were made a convenient focal point for inflammatory speeches and slogans. After being thus offered puja (in the words of the Sangh) at many places, the ashes were finally immersed in the holy waters of the Sangam at Allahabad, on 14 January 1991.

With a clever synthesis of actual Hindu religious practices and actions designed to evoke the maximum outrage, the VHP had another chance to tour the country with the *padukas* (wooden sandals) of Sri Rama. The paduka pujan (worship of the sandals) harked back to the time of Bharat, Sri Rama's brother, who had ruled Ayodhya during the time of his brother's exile with a pair of these sandals placed on the throne.

Alongside these events, to draw public support, the VHP was also engaged in a game of brinksmanship with the Narasimha Rao government. The shilanyas programme had been conducted along the periphery of the disputed site, and a Seshavatar Mandir was under construction next to this. From 9 July 1992, the VHP began a process invoking the blessings of all the gods and getting the foundation stones for the temple readied at the shilanyas spot. The prime minister appealed to the VHP to defer the process of laying a foundation for the building. They listened to his appeal, devoting themselves instead to completing the foundation and construction of the Seshavatar Mandir.

The second phase of kar-seva began with a gathering of sants in Delhi on 30 October 1992. Lakhs of pilgrims and kar-sevaks began to be mobilized to reach Ayodhya to offer kar-seva for the temple. This second wave of arrivals finally culminated in the events of 6 December 1992, with the razing of the Babri Masjid.

For young Sharad Sharma, the sequence of shila pujan, shilanyas and paduka pujan proved that now ordinary people could be a part of something much bigger, grander than just the humdrum life of a small town. Perhaps this is how megalomania begins. If Ayodhya was the focus of national attention, if events here were determining what happened elsewhere in the country, then it gave many in Ayodhya an inflated sense of their own importance.

On 6 December, far from being among the crowds cheering the falling of the domes of the Babri Masjid, Sharad Sharma was several kilometres away, at Karsevakpuram, playing host to those who had arrived from different parts of the country. 'It was our duty, being a part of the Bajrang Dal, to see that everything went well for all who came here,' he explains. 'So you wouldn't know if the demolition of the domes was a planned act, or because the VHP had lost control of the crowds who arrived?' I ask him.

'It is true that the VHP had completely lost control of the crowds who came for kar-seva on that day,' he says. 'This was something that everyone present there had admitted. People were getting angry when our volunteers were asking them to retreat. One group from Madhya Pradesh asked, "Why have you called us, if you will not let us do the kar-seva we want to do?" It was a very difficult situation.'

As for the fact that an ancient structure could be destroyed in a short span of time (when such buildings are normally strong and resistant), Sharad Sharma shrugs it off as divine intervention. 'See, for me, the blessings of Hanumanji have been visible throughout our campaign. In 1986, when the order for opening the locks was passed in the Faizabad court, a big male monkey was seen sitting on top of the court. Again, in 1990, when the kar-seva first began, a big monkey made his appearance. When Mulayam Singh had completely barricaded the site in 1990, not allowing kar-sevaks any entry, then a sadhu driving a jeep came out of nowhere and crashed through the barricades near Hanuman Garhi. This sadhu was never seen again. How do you explain this, except as a divine act? As for materials with which the kar-sevaks broke the dhaancha, they did not need external implements. It was the metal barricading itself which they broke with their bare hands and used pieces of it to break the structure.'

I do not make any response to this, though my brain is reeling with the ramifications of it all. I may be a devotee of Hanuman, but how can he literally be viewed as a monkey on a roof? Is that really doing justice to what he represents for humanity as a whole?

Since 2008, I have been trying to canvass for popular support, to the idea of setting up mini-sanctuaries for monkeys in different parts of Faizabad and Ayodhya. I began working towards a public campaign for such sanctuaries because of a desire to protect monkeys from the revulsion and hatred they inspire among the local folk, due to their snatch-and-grab antics. If monkeys misbehave, it is the natural result of their losing their habitat and living in urban areas with humans. To this day, I yearn to find another soul in Faizabad-Ayodhya who shares my passion for monkeys and other animals, a passion that translates into treating them with sensitivity and compassion. Instead, all I find are scared and suspicious people who greet monkeys, dogs, cows, calves and bulls with a loud 'haaat, shoo!' hurling a stick or a stone. If Hanumanji were indeed raining his blessings on the magistrate at Faizabad that day in 1986, why did he not similarly fill the hearts and minds of people here with some real love and respect for his simian cousins? All that Sharad Sharma's talk of divine intervention does for me is make me worry about the literal translation of many genuinely valuable beliefs and practices by unscrupulous forces.

Shifting gear, I question Sharad Sharma about the tacit support that the VHP initiatives for the temple seemed to enjoy within the Congress. He dismisses this. 'The Congress only supported the temple movement when they sensed the popular mood going against them,' he says. Then, going on the offensive, he alleges, '*Saara vatavaran banane mein mandir virodhi shaktiyon ne bhoomika nibhai. Na aakrosh utpann hota, na dhaancha dhwast hota* (those forces opposing the temple played a big role in creating the whole atmosphere. If so much anger had not developed, the structure would not have fallen).' In other words, Sharad Sharma is attributing 6 December 1992 to Mulayam Singh and the Congress, and those independent secular people who dared to speak against the idea of a temple in those days. Apparently, these people were responsible for the mass hysteria, the violent slogans and the naked weapons seen in Ayodhya on that day.

There is more. Sharma is optimistic about the further spread of a movement for the restoration of many temples in the country to bring back Hindu pride. 'After all, Hindu samaj is only asking for those sites to be returned that have been taken over by foreign invaders. If Somnath could be liberated, why can't Ayodhya? If a beautiful, world-class temple is built here, Ayodhya will definitely see development. The Centre should pass a legislation and hand over the construction of the temple to the Rama Janmabhoomi Nyas,' he says. He has finally touched the fine thread I have been searching for that is common in the hours of conversation I have had about Ayodhya with so many people – the real desire for development.

'What about the role of local people and the town's own municipality in development?' I ask him. 'Shouldn't this come before Central schemes for a grand temple?' Sharma is caustic about the Ayodhya municipality, whose chairperson is a Congresswoman (*see* Chapter 7 on Mithilesh Pande). 'The municipality of Ayodhya cannot run away from its responsibilities. There is Rs 1.5 crore scam by the Ayodhya municipality reported today in *Hindustan* (21 December 2010). Theirs is a very significant office and they are neglecting their duties. Why can't they do more for the cleanliness of this town? Why can't they stop the use of polythene bags here, along the lines of what has been done at Haridwar?' Sharma grows quite indignant.

To stem the flow, I cannot help needling him with a question – doesn't he face sarcastic people on the streets of Ayodhya ever so often who ask him, '*Kaho! Mandir kab banai?* Hey there! Tell us, when will the temple be built?' 'Yes, of course, I do,' says Sharma, finally admitting to the general sense of disillusionment with the VHP in Ayodhya that is responsible for the green moss covering the stones for the Rama temple in the VHP *karyashala* or workshop, and the deserted look of Karsevakpuram. 'But I tell them – it is your desire, your *sankalp* (vow of determination) that will build the temple.'

But are people really ready or willing for such a vow? 'Hindus lack the killer instinct,' says Sharma. '*Samaj mein akramakta aani chahiye. Isi akramakta ko hum prerna se bana rahe hain. Jwala bani rehni chahiye* (there should be an attacking edge to the general behaviour of society. We are engaged in building this killer instinct by providing inspiration. The flame should continue to burn).'

Sharma gets a little emotional when he recalls the three martyrs to the cause of the temple from Ayodhya – Vasudev Gupta, Ramesh Pande and Rajendra Dharkar – all men with families. 'Their sacrifice should not go in vain,' he says. The only reason I do not ask him then about what was being done for these men's families, particularly Rajendra Dharkar's mother in her quest for a BPL card (*see* Chapter 20 on Gaurav Tiwari 'Beeru') is because I do not know their story yet.

More recently, Sharad Sharma felt enthused by the recitation of Hanuman Chalisa eleven whole times between 17 September 2010 and 17 October 2010 at various places across the country. People prayed for a good judgement in the Ayodhya title suit. The judgement was finally delivered by the Lucknow bench of the Allahabad High Court on 30 September 2010. Following the judgement, there was even a celebratory meeting at Karsevakpuram, at which the head of the Rama Janmabhoomi Nyas, Mahant Nritya Gopal Das announced that the judgement had endorsed Rama Lalla's claim over the entire site, and the obstacles to the temple had been removed. 'We are happy with the judgement,' had been the line then. Sharad Sharma elaborates, 'When you are dividing the site – well, nobody asked for it, but when you are, then why are you dismissing the Nirmohi Akhara and Sunni Wakf Board's claims and reserving the portion under the central dome for Rama Lalla? Obviously because it is the sole rightful claim.'

Sharma is a young man with a wife and child who gets up at 5 a.m. daily, and does all his Hanuman prayers without fail. There is no reason to take a dislike to him, for there are no visible personal flaws. And yet, the journey he has revealed, the events he has participated in, have a disquieting effect. These are the events that have left Ayodhya a derelict battle zone, complete with barbed-wire fencing and a massive police presence. For days, I keep returning in my mind to the madness of the nineties and whether we are at risk of succumbing again to such emotive grandiloquence.

There are so many questions that worry me. How many more speeches will the VHP members have to make, before they find in us a 'killer instinct'? Have Hindus ever been prevented from practising their faith in the manner they wished, in homes and temples across the land, before the VHP and its cohorts engineered the collapse of the masjid? Are we finally moving towards solving those issues of justice and inclusive development that will allow people to resist the manipulation of their feelings by politicians who deliver nothing?

I am troubled by these thoughts and more for a long while. In comparison, Sharad Sharma is fortunate. Secure in the beliefs instilled in him by years of being in a cadre-based organization, he is only worried about the incompleteness of his mission. Quoting from the *Sundar Kand* of Tulsidas' *Ramcharitmanas,* he says, '*Rama kaaj keenh binu, mohe kahan vishram?* (Without having completed the work given to me by Sri Rama, how can I rest?)' And finally, he concludes, '*Ek pavitra karya hai ye. Tamam log jute hue hain. Swapna zaroor poora hoga* (this is a holy task. Many people are engaged in carrying it out. This dream will surely come true).'

18

Naga Vijay Narayan Das
'Mauni Baba'
Sadhu With A Stick

Janmabhoomi mah puri suhawan, uttar dish Sarayu ati paavan.

(My birthplace is a beautiful town, north of which flows the holy Sarayu.)

—*Ramcharitmanas* by Goswami Tulsidas

The temple of Hanuman Garhi represents the focal point of Ayodhya. It is a towering temple, built along the lines of a fort, surrounded by lanes selling puja articles and prasad laddoos, photos of gods and goddesses and CDs of the Ramayana. The deity at Hanuman Garhi, a bright orange-coloured stone representing Hanuman, is worshipped daily by thousands and draws lakhs of worshippers during the mela and parikrama seasons. Such is the hold that Hanuman Garhi has over Ayodhya that the locals know the truth of the saying, '*Ramji ki nagari aur raja Hanumanji!* (The town of Rama, where the king is Hanuman!)'

Over six hundred sadhus are attached to this particular temple, living in rooms in and around the towering structure. When I first met one of them, the fair and portly Naga Vijay Narayan Das, we were both a part of the audience at Tulsi Smarak Bhavan, a short walk from the temple, where a daily performance of the Ramlila has been staged since May 2004 under the sponsorship of the Uttar Pradesh government's Department of Culture and the Ayodhya Shodh Sansthan. Vijay Narayan Das entered midway through an evening's performance, wading through the crowds seated on the floor in front of the stage. He reached the side of the hall, where some chairs are generally grouped together, and brandished a stick to unseat a bunch of kids who were occupying them. Then he sat down and watched the show.

I used to go to the Ramlila a lot in those days to gather research material, and Vijay Narayan Das was always there, always arriving at roughly the same time, always coming round to unseat the urchins, and then watch the programme till the end with great appreciation. That is how we started saying 'namaste' to each other in 2008. I learnt his name and the fact that he was attached to the Hanuman Garhi temple. It was inevitable that we would renew our acquaintance with this book.

The social structure and hierarchy of the sadhus in Hanuman Garhi needs elaboration. For that we need a bird's-eye view first. Ayodhya is dominated by three akharas of Ramanandi Vaishav sadhus – the Digambari, Nirmohi and Nirvani. Akharas had been set up as training grounds for bands of warrior sadhus to guard *sanatan dharma* (the eternal faith, as Hinduism is sometimes called), and therefore emphasized physical training in *hatha* yoga, wrestling, and tests of endurance. They also emphasized training using weaponry like spears and trishuls, now mainly symbolic, carried by Naga sadhus, many of whom are followers of the trident-wielding Shiva.

Not every sadhu can become a Naga. For this one has to undergo an initiation and a long period of training. There are also levels of expertise or achievement that denote one's seniority in the Naga order. The most important distinction between an ordinary sadhu and a Naga is however related to the accumulation of disciples or chelas. Any ordinary person can become a sadhu in Ramanandi Vaishnavism, choosing to take up the life of an ascetic for spiritual goals. With years of *sadhana* and after some acceptance within the sadhu community, such a person can acquire other disciples. However, a Naga cannot acquire disciples. In fact, good potential candidates for Naga-hood are often picked up from the disciples of senior sadhus. The brotherhood of Nagas receives men from the larger community of sadhus, but after becoming Nagas, these men attain a different identity. They are called by different titles, according to their level or years of 'Naga'hood, and they also appear different. The ash-smeared naked sadhus with dreadlocks who carry trishuls for their ritual baths at the Mahakumbh melas are the most memorable and stereotypical examples of such Nagas.

Hanuman Garhi is a part of modern Ayodhya – temples and akharas set up on land given willingly by the nawabs who controlled it at that time. The temple was constructed in the middle of the tenth century on land donated by the Nawab of Awadh. At the time when this was being done, the three main akharas were given their respective villages – portions of Ayodhya – over which they would wield their influence. The Nirvani Akhara controls the temple of Hanuman Garhi. This important akhara is further divided into four *pattis* for the purposes of sadhu identity and administration. Thus the Ujjaini, Basanti, Haridwari and Sagariya pattis of the Nirvani Akhara administer the Hanuman Garhi temple in rotation all round the year. This means that the preparation of prasad, the bhandaras, the liaison with security agencies and most significantly, the receipt of chadhava or donations at the temple get handled by each of the four pattis in turn.

In addition to the post of a mahant from different pattis, there is also the highly ceremonial post of the *gaddinashin* (enthroned) mahant at Hanuman Garhi. The gaddinashin literally does not put his feet on the ground. He is carried in a palanquin, fanned by attendants, appears for significant and symbolic occasions, and is treated with the respect and care lavished on a king. While all the sadhus at Hanuman Garhi form a brotherhood, the charisma of individual mahants also contributes to the weight of a particular patti, and the resultant self-importance of its sadhus.

The twist in this tale is undoubtedly that of caste. While Ramanandi Vaishnavism has been accepting non-Brahmins into the fold of sadhuhood since the fourteenth century, and there are a number of sadhus from the backward castes at Hanuman Garhi, the mahant posts are reserved for Brahmins alone. So, as in the case of Baba Bhavnath Das, a prominent Hanuman Garhi sadhu from the Yadav community, you can become the head of the Samajwadi Sant Sabha, the sadhu wing of the Samajwadi Party, but you cannot dream of replacing Mahant Gyandas unless you are a Brahmin sadhu aspirant.

Mahant Gyandas of the Sagariya Patti is the head mahant of Hanuman Garhi, with other mahants under him such as Sant Ram Das of the Ujjaini Patti, Ram Charan Das of the Basanti Patti, and Murali Das of the Haridwari Patti. This powerful mahant has also been the head of the Akhil Bharatiya Akhada Parishad (ABAP), the governing body for sadhus and akharas across India, for many years. His long tenure has often been challenged during Akhada Parishad elections, and he has been engaged in a powerful tussle for continuing in his post against another claimant. Since the required number of attending sadhus have not been able to assemble for the Akhada Parishad deliberations till September 2011, it has not been able to establish clearly whether Gyandas will continue to hold authority, or have to cede to a successor who enjoys majority support. The parishad is a parent body to whom both Vaishnavite and Shaivite akharas of sadhus belong. Meanwhile, he is said to be trying to gather all Vaishnav akharas under his leadership, so that if differences over his candidature produce a clear Vaishnavite-Shaivite divide, then he can be considered the undisputed leader of all the Vaishnavite akharas, and the Shaivite sadhus can have another leader.

Vijay Narayan Das is one of the approximately three hundred sadhus of the Basanti Patti at Hanuman Garhi. He was born on 7 October 1951, at a village called Sangam Dubey at Gosainganj, around thirty kilometres from Ayodhya. He's the son of a pujari and farmer called Ram Pratap Dubey. He remembers a childhood dominated by the idea of Ayodhya being a very important place for pilgrims and worship, a very special place. 'I was one of four brothers and three sisters,' he recalls. 'I was the most interested in *puja-paath*. My mother was also a very pious lady. She used to often offer food to wandering sadhus, and this was a part of our lives while growing up. Seeing such men and the lives they led – wandering freely, without any attachments – the desire to become a sadhu was born in me.'

A visit to Vijay Narayan Das' home is an experience rife with distractions. A mouse will suddenly run out and across your feet (but this is a fact of life in Faizabad-Ayodhya!), Vijay Das himself will dash about the small room, one half of which has rudimentary kitchen utensils and another half, a bed. 'Have some water! Here, eat these laddoos! Shall I make tea?' he will ask. Then, calling to his neighbour, he will say, 'Hey what happened to that milk? Shall we make tea?' and the other is likely to peek in a few seconds later and say, 'The milk got spoilt. Only a little bit was left anyway.' 'Oh never mind,' Vijay Narayan Das will say. Rummaging through a cloth bag, he will produce some fruit. 'Have some banana?' he'll enquire. The entire process is repeated each time, whether you visit for a few minutes, or a longer spell. He does not sit still, or complete his sentences, which are stammered for the most part. He is always concerned about being as hospitable as possible, in spite of living an ascetic's life, with all his belongings bundled into a shelf in the wall. This zig-zag style of conversation reminds one of another sadhu from Basanti Patti, Baba Dharamdas (*see* Chapter 11).

As I accept a banana, I ask him how he happened to come to Ayodhya. 'When I came here in my childhood, I loved the place,' he says. 'Hanumanji helped me. He made me one of his warriors.'

'Tell me something about your training to become a Naga,' I suggest. 'See, about 672 years ago, there were terrible battles between Hindus and Muslims,' he begins. 'They were destroying our temples, making it difficult for us to pray. That is when the Naga order was established – both kinds of Nagas – Vastradhari (clothed) and Tyagi (complete renunciates). I am a Vastradhari Naga.' 'Right,' I say. So that is the difference between him and some of the more colourful, naked Naga sadhus I have seen at the Mahakumbh.

'After my initiation as a Naga sadhu, I went through all the rigours of the akhara for twelve years. There is a gradual trajectory of progress as one embraces Nagahood,' he reveals. 'You join as a Naga, then become a *hud-dangi* (hell-raiser), then an *ateet* (old, mature) and much later, if you have spiritual worth, you are made the mahant of a temple.'

It sounds like a long journey, I tell him. He nods in agreement. 'After you have completed your first twelve years of training to become a Naga, there is a grand ceremony, a wedding-like feast before the *charan padukas* (holy wooden sandals) of Sri Ramanand,' he says.

At this point, some men arrive from a new branch of a bank. They want time with Naga Vijay to convince him about some investments. He deals with them and returns. 'Everyone wants that last bit of money!' he is muttering under his breath.

I slip in another question. 'What about the moneylending sadhus at Hanuman Garhi?' He looks at me. 'What about them?' he asks. 'Do they exploit helpless people, charge exorbitant interest, land up at people's homes at night to ask them for their money?' He gives me a straight look, 'I daresay they do. But I am not one of them. Now if you take someone like him,' he says, pointing towards a boy who is trying to get a cycle to work by repairing something in its pedal and chain, 'I had given him four thousand rupees when he needed it. So he keeps in touch, helps me out, returns some of the money now and then. What's wrong with that?'

'Nothing at all,' I say, with perfect truth. I have heard horror stories about the moneylending tradition among the sadhus of Hanuman Garhi. This convention goes back centuries, to a time of barter, when wandering sadhus used to sell asafoetida (*hing*) to farmers' families in villages with the slogan, '*Hing hingadi, baisakh karaari*. Here is the hing for immediate consumption; pay us after the harvest in Baisakh.' The unsuspecting families, who bought this precious condiment, managed to pile up tons of debt which made them dread the arrival of the sadhus in later times. In the modern era, professional moneylending has been practised regularly by certain mahants who became well-known for this among Ayodhya citizens. I accept Naga Vijay Das' disclaimer, but the usurious reputations of some other sadhus are too well-established to ignore. While I struggle to put this in words, he reads my mind, and says, 'Some people become sadhus to hide their criminal antecedents. Then what will they do? If your mind is that of a criminal, you will commit crime wherever you are.'

So are there several people of this sort in Ayodhya? Is it really a place where crime has acquired the respectable garb of religion? 'No, that is a wrong perception,' he says. 'Do you feel like that? Tell your friends, "Come to Ayodhya – saints still live here." That is the truth. As for the rest, *kuchh log toh keechad uchhalte rehte hain*. Some people keep casting aspersions.'

Naga Vijay Narayan Das acquired the label of *Mauni Baba* (the silent one) when he refused to speak for approximately ten years. 'I went to Jammu and Kashmir as a tourist, then stayed on with my guru,' he says, referring to him with the traditional honorific as '108 times Sri Pandit Ram Charitra Dasji Bhagawat Bhushan from Basti.' 'I stayed at Jammu, at Kathua and Udhampur. I still have disciples in Udhampur. I broke my *maun vrat* (vow of silence) on Mauni Amavasya day in Jammu, after the Rama katha, in the presence of my guru.'

'So you had a long spell away from Ayodhya?' I ask him. 'Yes, I did. But I finally returned to stay in Ayodhya in 1995. God willed it.' I am a bit disappointed. I had hoped that he would provide me with an eyewitness account of the events of 1990-92. 'You were not here when the firing happened, or the dhaancha fell down?' I probe. He responds, 'I felt very upset and unsettled by the developments in Ayodhya when I was in Jammu, particularly when the devotees were fired at. Who wouldn't? But I was actually in Ayodhya on the day of the demolition in 1992, trying to return to Jammu. It was very, very tough to get back by train on that day. I could see people coming away from the site of the demolition, carrying mud, bricks. They were very happy. I was struggling to reach the station, and the trains were packed when I did get there. I had to stand in the train, all the way to Moradabad!'

'Do you think the falling of the structure achieved anything? What did it do for Ayodhya?' I question. He grimaces, then mutters, 'People are scared to come here. It changed things, made everything much worse.'

Like so many people I speak to in Faizabad-Ayodhya, Naga Vijay Narayan Das is involved in a property dispute. Such litigations seem to be almost a hobby in these parts, and sadhus, supposed ascetics, are not immune to the charms of court houses. In fact, if advocate Tarunjeet Verma is to be believed, they form a sizeable number of the litigants themselves. 'They come to court ready with packs of cards to pass time. They love to eat the *channa-laiya-bhujia* mix, readily available in carts near the court. People in Ayodhya, including sadhus, are born litigants!'

On one occasion as I wait outside Naga Vijay Narayan Das'

room near Hanuman Garhi, watching the antics of monkeys in the compound, Vijay Das comes hurrying home from court. 'It's my Gurubhai,' he explains, referring to a fellow sadhu. 'He had been made sole heir to my guru's property and room, but the fellow is immoral. He got married, accumulated huge riches. I am fighting to get my rights and get everything sorted out in legal terms. Mahant Gyandas helped me a lot with this dispute,' he says, acknowledging the powerful Hanuman Garhi head. 'Also, if my disciples in the army had not been there to lend me moral support . . .,' his voice trails away, he is off on a familiar dash around the room. Suddenly noticing my acute bewilderment, he adds after a moment, 'I made many disciples in the army during my time in J&K.'

A few minutes later, after bustling around his room, he finds it difficult to fold his legs and winces as he squats on the floor to get something from under the bed. 'Joint pain?' I ask in sympathy. 'Yes,' he says. 'It is easy to be a sadhu in one's youth. Much more difficult when one ages.' I nod in agreement, wondering at these lives – the severe restrictions imposed on these ascetics, coupled with crippling winters and the most primitive of facilities.

Maybe this goes against the very concept of suffering to meet a spiritual goal, but if it were up to me, I would give the sadhus of Ayodhya habitable quarters with the conveniences most of us take for granted.

Ayodhya is obviously getting to me.

19

Dr Premalata Tripathi
Domestic Divination

Jo Rama, so Rama, doosra kauno kaam nahin.

(What I do, I do for Rama. I don't have any other work.)

—Dr Premalata Tripathi,
describing her life and daily routine.

Off Parikrama Marg, between Faizabad and Ayodhya, is a white-washed house where troubled souls can be spotted seeking counsel and comfort. A small, marble floored temple to one side of the house has several deities who are worshipped daily and propitiated during special *havans* to heal afflicted horoscopes. This is the home of Dr Premalata Tripathi, an astrologer of some renown, who is consulted by people from this town and far away.

Premalata Tripathi has been an Ayodhya citizen from birth. Her father, Dr Ram Raksha Tripathi, a scholar, went by the literary name of *Nirbhik* (Fearless), and was the collaborator of the work of at least one international scholar who focussed on Ayodhya, Peter Van der Veer. He was learned in Hindi, Urdu, Sanskrit and Persian, and the author of two important books on the town – *Ayodhya ka Rakt-Ranjit Itihas* (The Blood Soaked History of Ayodhya) and *Ayodhya ka Yugantkari Itihas* (The Epoch Making History of Ayodhya). In addition, he offered a cerebral, grounded resistance to the sadhu hold over Ayodhya's intellectual and cultural life. Consequently, he brought out a paper for some years called *Grihastha* (Householder) to counter an important publication at that time which had the backing of the sadhus, *Virakt* (meaning 'renunciate' here, although its literal meaning is 'detached'). 'My father brought out this paper despite strong opposition from many sadhus, including Paramhans Ramachandra Das,' says Premalata Tripathi. 'He was a poet and a much sought-after speaker, but very humble. Scholars seeking to know more about Ayodhya came to our home from all over the world. He passed away on 12 July 1988. At the time, the VHP's influence on Ayodhya was only just being felt.'

Premalata completed an MA in Sanskrit and a Bachelor's in Education before being admitted at the Inter-College level in Gonda in 1973 and Jaunpur in 1974, where she taught till June 1978. She got married in June 1973 to an advocate, Harihar Prasad

Tiwari, and, along the way, three sons and a daughter were born to the couple. Her PhD thesis in Sanskrit was on the topic, '*Vedon mein Rama ki Prishthabhoomi* (Rama's Role in the Vedas)', which she prepared fully, but did not get typed. Another thesis for which she had completed the work was '*Sanskrit Sahitya mein Ayodhya ka Yogdan* (Ayodhya's Contribution to Sanskrit Literature).' However, in what she regards as the supremely ironic twist to her life, her academic career was derailed by her vocation as an astrologer.

'I studied a lot, know a lot about the *shastras*, people still approach me with doubts when they are studying these topics. But I ended up practising astrology all my life, a subject that I never studied formally,' she says.

Becoming an astrologer was the result of quirky circumstances beginning with her fascination with a *purohit* who was a regular advisor to her mother. 'I used to love listening to him advising my mother, using phrases like "*Sadhe saati chal rahi hai* (Saturn is going to afflict your chart for seven-and-a-half years)," or "*Adhaiyya chal rahi hai* (a planet is going to affect you for two-and-a-half years)." Because I was such a devoted listener and a very enthusiastic member of my mother's kitchen durbar, once, when I was around ten years of age, they covered one of my nails with *kajal* and asked me to predict from a question paper how an uncle of mine who had appeared for an exam had fared. I happily did so. He passed that particular exam and people praised my intuition. This set a trend. While I would never have had the guts to do such things before my father, or the intellectual people who came to meet him, it was fine in my mother's inner circle to predict "pass" or "fail" for a lot of exam candidates! By the time I was twelve or thirteen, people had got used to the veracity of my predictions.'

Strange circumstances again played a part in reinforcing

Premalata's career as an astrologer, when she inadvertently predicted the demise of a dear friend. 'We were three very close friends in college. One of my friends was from the Raja of Ayodhya's family, and the other was the daughter of a famous Bengali doctor. Just jokingly, they asked me to predict when they would get married. I told them their fortunes, quite off the cuff. I told the Bengali girl that if she still wanted to know about her marriage a year later, I would tell her, but not till then. Three days later, she had washed her long, calf-length hair, and was drying it on an open terrace. Somehow, because of her hair getting tangled up in a railing, she lost her balance and fell headlong to the ground. For some time, she was in a coma, then passed away. It was a huge shock. But people remembered my words to her and began treating me with awe. The loss of a dear friend was a big price to pay for such a reputation.'

Premalata practised her astrology from the Navi Nagar Mandir in Ayodhya from July 1980 to April 2007, sitting on a *takhat* while people came to consult her for a myriad domestic problems. Her deeply religious nature meant that she would be immersed in puja until 2 p.m.

'It is the grace of God that despite my puja and my astrology timings, my children have never been seen with leaky noses, or my house in a dirty condition,' she says, obviously feeling the need to justify her sense of responsibility as a housekeeper in Ayodhya's traditional set-up. In the last decade, she has found a devoted helper in the form of Saroj Gupta, who attends to kitchen and household duties, leaving Premalata with more time to deal with her solution-seeking clients. 'One thing I have never been seen doing in my life is idle gossip and passing time in an irresponsible manner,' she emphasizes.

Such a long stint as an astrologer in a town as religious and politically sensitive as Ayodhya must definitely have brought her significant encounters with politicians of all kinds. 'Vinay Katiyar came to ask me about his election prospects,' says Premalata, referring to the three-time MP from Faizabad from the Bharatiya Janata Party. 'Ashok Singhal had longed to perform a *shat-chandi* yagna (an elaborate ritual for Devi) for a long time. He had been travelling through South India, when he called and deputed Shri Champak Rai to find out where this yagna could be performed in Ayodhya. Champak Rai went to Paramhansji, but the yagna could not be performed there. Meanwhile, I had arranged to perform the yagna for my own satisfaction at the Shyam Sadhanalaya during the Chait Navadurga (summer Navaratri) days. When Ashok Singhal arrived at Ayodhya, he learnt about my yagna through a friend. He called me immediately and asked if he could join my *sankalp* and when I accepted, he presented himself in record time, wearing a yellow silk dhoti for the havan.'

Continuing to describe the occasion, Tripathi says, 'You see, I align myself with *bhakti* for my own pleasure, not to earn publicity or money. But Singhalji was so satisfied, he told me that he had felt as if Devi herself had appeared at the havan to partake of the prasad.'

Does she collaborate with any other Ayodhya sadhus to do any special pujas, I ask her. She gives me a look which speaks volumes. 'It is better to maintain a distance from all the babas, sadhus, temples in Ayodhya for the sake of one's own integrity,' she says. 'Look at the way people speak of Sunita Shastri and Mandakini. Such learned women, and yet always spoken of in a demeaning way in this male-dominated society.'

What she says with such bitterness is indeed true. Sunita Shastri is a learned scholar attached to the Lakshman Qila temple in Ayodhya who is nearly always referred to as the mistress of the temple's late mahant, the respected Qiladhishji, in casual conversation. Mandakini is a renowned Rama katha expert, whose discourses are much sought after in India and abroad. The disciple of Sri Ram Kinkar Upadhyaya, she is referred to in a similar snide fashion, with people recalling that she first came to Ayodhya 'wearing jeans'. This is hardly surprising, since she is perhaps the only one with an Ayodhya presence to be equally at home giving sermons in Hindi or in English. Trying to bring down such women a notch or two by making suggestive comments about them is an Ayodhya pastime.

We have worked our way around all the usual territory to finally be faced with the defining events of 1990 and 1992. Premalata Tripathi is ready to relive both years. 'An atmosphere of police terror prevailed during Mulayam's rule in 1990,' she says. 'It was so bad that we could peep out of our houses, but we could not come out. My husband used to sneak out past the security forces to feed the monkeys. The poor things were starving! He used to return bringing stories of the kar-sevak crowds and the atrocities of the police.' I say nothing, but the mention of starving monkeys is all that has moved me in this account. I remember seeing visuals of the monkeys on the deserted streets of Ayodhya in 1990 on national television, and worrying about them two thousand kilometres away.

'Jab tak mandir nahin banega, koi shanti nahin hogi (till the temple is built there can be no peace),' continues Premalata Tripathi. 'Politicians are inciting people any which way. But true peace can be realized only after the temple is constructed. The need to have a temple creates a dissatisfaction inside us which is like a

chemical reaction. Until the temple is built, this issue will produce disquiet.'

But is it necessary to have a temple alone? What about a space for public use, like a memorial, a hospital, even a library, I ask her. Won't the people of Ayodhya find that beneficial? 'Why should we waste our energies on this and that? Why not a temple?' Tripathi asks me in response, bristling slightly. 'Even future generations will have this desire for a temple. *Mandir to ban ke hi rahega* (the mandir will definitely be built),' she says.

About the day of the demolition of the masjid, Premalata has this to share. 'We had come to see the kar-seva from room numbers 54 and 56 of Manas Bhavan, right next to the Janmabhoomi. I had been praying since 3.30 a.m for the success of that day's kar-seva. I said to my husband, let's cook and eat quickly, so we can witness the events of 9.30 a.m. (the time announced earlier by the VHP for kar-seva). By 9.30 we were all holding a plate of *tehri* (a kind of vegetable pulao, popular in winter) in our hands. We saw the crowds of kar-sevaks push and break barriers near my house. We saw the structure falling down, and wondered about who was under the falling rubble. One Ramesh from Ayodhya died beneath the falling bricks and mortar. I kept wondering about the safety of the idols. The throne for Rama Lalla has been provided by my friend's family, by Pappu Bhaiya, the present Raja of Ayodhya. Has the throne been looted, what will happen, I was thinking. Around us, people were euphoric. All of a sudden, we felt as if the temple would take concrete shape soon.'

But that did not happen, I say. A flat feeling seems to have come over her. '*Kaleja nikaal ke de diya Bhajapa ko* (we took out a piece of our heart and gave it to the BJP),' she says. '*Bada dhokha kiya. Ab toh virodh karne ka man karta hai* (they betrayed us badly. Now we feel like opposing them).' Then, brightening up slightly, she voices what I am increasingly encountering across all parts of Ayodhya, 'Looks like the Congress will get us the temple.'

Do you see the temple as a necessary milestone in Ayodhya's development, I ask her. 'It will be good if the temple is a national monument. Babas and sadhus should not have free rein to do as they wish there. Only then Ayodhya will develop.'

Even the most religious have their reservations about Ayodhya's holy men.

20

Gaurav Tiwari 'Beeru'
Witness to the Worst

'Par tabhi yahaan magar, aisi kuchh hawaa chali, lut gayi kali kali ki ghut gayi gali gali,
aur ham lute lute, waqt se pite pite, saans ki sharaab kaa khumaar dekhate rahe,
kaaravaan guzar gaya gubaar dekhte rahe.'

(But just then there blew such a gust of wind here, every bud was violated, every lane was stifled.

And we, looted, beaten down by time, watched the intoxication
of the liquor of breath.
The caravan went by, and we watched the dust it raised.)

—Gopal Das 'Neeraj'

To stand out in the towns of Faizabad and Ayodhya, it is enough to be tall. The average height of males in these parts is five feet five inches, and women are even shorter. So when you encounter someone of more than average height, he or she tends to stick in your memory. Gaurav 'Beeru' Tiwari is a tall political activist who is also the quintessential neighbourhood boy. A Congress worker who has been associated with various campaigns for the development of Ayodhya, Beeru has widespread recognition and enjoys goodwill across the social spectrum – a definite asset for a political aspirant.

Beeru was born in Gonda, a small town about 40 km from Ayodhya, on 4 January 1974. His father was a supply inspector which meant that the family spent time in several towns across UP. However, in 1980, by the time Beeru was six, his family had come to live permanently in Ayodhya. Like many other boys of his generation, Beeru travelled the well-worn path of Awadh Vidya Mandir, Maharaja Inter-College and Saket Degree College. The only distinguishing feature of this trajectory was the fact that it coincided with the tumultous events triggered by the VHP during the late 80s and early 90s. From the time he was a teenager to his development as an articulate and politically aware youth, Beeru has borne witness to the calendar of shila pujans, shilanyas and other such VHP-sponsored functions, culminating with the demolition of the masjid. Following this, he has also played a part in building a popular resistance to the VHP and the Sangh.

Talking to Beeru is like reliving those years of recent history that tested India's strength and resilience as a democracy.

'The VHP and the RSS had a very well-thought out strategy for Ayodhya,' he says. 'What you have to understand is that as youths, we received no guidance from any source. No one was around to give us any perspective on what was going on. We had always lived in a religious atmosphere, growing up in Ayodhya. Suddenly we were faced with slogan-shouting crowds arriving from all over the country. Their passion and zeal attracted us. We began to feel, if they can be so passionate about Rama, then surely we must be too, as citizens of his birthplace.'

So was this the VHP success story then, I ask him. That they succeeded in creating such passion? *'Haan, unmaad ka ek vatavaran banane mein safal hue. Isi mein log behte chale gaye. Par iske peechhe unka koi zameeni kaam nahin tha* (yes, they were successful in building an atmosphere of fevered passion. People were carried away by the tide. But there was no actual work on the ground behind all this hype),' he says.

An interesting point that Beeru makes here is that the media played a very important role in this atmosphere building of the RSS, VHP, BJP and other Sangh outfits. 'The *Ramayana* serial on TV had made a big impact some years before the kar-sevaks began arriving here,' he says. 'It was being aired for a long time, and being seen in every village. People dropped whatever they were doing to see each episode. The character of Hanuman saying, "Jai Sri Rama!" and leaping into action had caught the imagination of everyone who watched, man, woman or child. In addition, the press reports of all the activities of the VHP and kar-sevaks, at least in the regional newspapers that we read here, used the vocabulary of heroism and exaggeration. For instance, they would write,

"*Shaheedon ke khoon se Ayodhya ki sadken laal ho gayin* (the streets of Ayodhya grew red with the blood of martyrs)" to describe a lathi charge on kar-sevaks in which a few may have got injured. I remember a particular picture had got printed in a paper, just showing slippers in a heap near Sarayu Pul. The caption interpreted this as a mass murder by unknown persons or the police, saying that hundreds of people were being killed and their bodies were being thrown into the river. But the truth is that you can find such a heap of chappals anywhere in Ayodhya, when people have gone for a darshan. Just a shot of this kind means nothing. The media definitely played a very negative role and created an atmosphere of hysteria.'

As if this were not enough, the rumour mills of the Sangh were very active, feeding a public already agitated by such public images with all kinds of new allegations everyday. '*Sangh ka afwah tantra bahut sashakt hai* (the rumour apparatus of the Sangh is very powerful),' says Beeru. But could such rumours and reports have created havoc if there hadn't been a collusion of some kind across all sections of society? When I ask Beeru this, he is very clear about what made the rumours of the Sangh penetrate the larger consciousness.

'In that period, no political party offered any effective protest here in Ayodhya to serve as a roadblock to the VHP and Sangh,' says Beeru. 'This is because all political parties had silent sympathizers in their ranks who secretly endorsed and believed in the agenda of the VHP. Apart from this, young people had been so misled by all the hype around the Rama Mandir that they had forgotten about their own career goals and aspirations. So they provided a large pool of slogan-shouting members to the mandir promoters. And most importantly, even the secular groups ended up strengthening the VHP in that time.'

'How did that happen?' I can't help asking.

'I remember, in 1991, the group SAHMAT from Delhi had organised a big programme at "Rama ki Pairi" that had attracted local crowds. They put up street plays, had a poster exhibition, music, speeches, all adding up to a unique experience for Ayodhya's people. Unfortunately, for reasons best known to them, at this programme, they announced that Rama and Sita were brother and sister, something that was completely baffling and very hurtful to the people who were present. Whatever they were trying to prove, this was not the way to do it. That used to make us think, *"Aap logon ne apni secularism ki dukaan chamkane ke liye Ayodhya mein karyakram kar liya, par yeh nahin socha ki iska kitna bura prabhav pad sakta hai* (you people came here to sell secularism to Ayodhya, but didn't care about what effects it could have in this town),"' says Beeru.

Beeru was in Ayodhya on both the seminal occasions in Ayodhya's recent history – the firing on 30 October and 2 November 1990, and the demolition of the Babri Masjid on 6 December 1992. Of October 1990, he remembers, 'I was fifteen or sixteen years old. There was curfew everywhere in Ayodhya except from Nirmohi Bazaar and along the sadhu belt towards Mani Ram Chhavani, Vasudev Ghat and beyond, where it was ineffective. Families and householders in Ayodhya did not wish to get affected by all the trouble, so we had been told not to go outside. We were playing marbles on a clear plot behind my house. There was the constant sound of slogan-shouting in the streets around us. We heard the firing of shots, and suddenly, the plot on which we had been playing was full of people who were running away from the shooting, some of them bleeding from cuts and injuries. Where we had been playing innocently just a few minutes earlier, we were now helping the hurt and wounded.'

Providing a direct experience of the exaggeration and rumour-mongering which was then at its peak, Beeru goes on to describe a scene shortly after the firing. 'From a vantage point on our street, we saw a PAC truck make its way along the street, going towards the station. It was carrying away two or three bodies, clearly visible to us from the top. However, a few minutes after this truck had passed, a sadhu came riding a cycle down the road from the same direction as the truck had come. He was shouting, "Hundreds of people have been killed in police firing!" To us, watching from above, this seemed like an exaggerated description. But who could counter these shouts, by yelling out the facts in turn?'

The firing in October and November actually represented an important success for the VHP. 'They succeeded in making martyrs. Although Mulayam Singh Yadav was doing the right thing by upholding the law and Constitution, his choice of words was unfortunate, and made people sympathize with the kar-sevaks.' The worst impact of the firing was on the families of those who died. 'There was one Rajendra Dharkar of Ayodhya who was killed. His family earns a living by making handmade cane baskets and *soop* (winnowing trays). I met his mother a couple of years ago, trying hard to have her BPL card made. She was in a pitiable condition, since he had been the main bread-earner. Those who were responsible for Rajendra Dharkar's death are nowhere to be seen today.'

Since he lives on a road connecting Ayodhya station to the town and marketplace, parallel to the main Ayodhya road, Beeru used to watch thousands of people going down the street almost daily all through 1991 and 1992. 'These angry, violent crowds, wearing headbands and armed with swords and trishuls, raising slogans like *"Jab katue kaate jayenge, tab Rama Rama chillayenge* (when the

Muslims are slaughtered they will shout Rama Rama)," used to make us uneasy and afraid. None of us liked it, but we did not know what to do about it. The relentless crowds arriving from all over the country upset the rhythm of life here in Ayodhya.'

And so life continued till the fateful day of 6 December 1992 when Beeru, along with friends like Rakesh Ojha and Anil Sonkar, had gone to spend the day playing cards at a room near the Barahdari Bangla Mandir (*see* Chapter 4 on Ram Sharan Das). Closeted indoors, the boys could hear the distant howl of the crowds all around the area. When it seemed to get extremely loud, they came out to understand what was happening, out of curiosity. They had moved only a few steps in the direction of the disputed site, when a man from their neighbourhood came running towards them, saying, 'Don't go there! Trouble has started.'

Of course, this only served to increase the boys' curiosity. They ventured in the direction of the noise, till they reached the disputed site and saw crowds entering the Babri Masjid. 'We saw Uma Bharati going around with a small mike in her hand. First, she was asking people to retreat. Then, some time later, seeing that the crowds were totally out of control and that no one was listening, she started saying, "*Ek dhakka aur do, Babri Masjid tod do* (one more push, and topple over the mosque)!" The sequence of events was this – controlled crowds, then uncontrolled masses, then controlled crowds once again.'

The group of curious local youth managed to tear through the crowds and reach the gate of the masjid. Here there was a stone embedded in the ground, with some ancient inscriptions. A man with a *bindi* was asking people to uproot this first, before they entered the mosque. 'We were scared to go forward. People were already on the domes, and somehow, they had implements with which to begin breaking the building. We went to the back of the masjid. There we saw around a hundred or a hundred and fifty CRPF men and women on alert, with their weapons. Then we went to the side of the masjid that adjoined the Tedhi Bazaar. We stayed within the compound on that side, watching. The domes started falling in front of our eyes.'

What Beeru saw during the course of that day was capped by something that finally turned Beeru into a committed opponent of the VHP, RSS, BJP and every other Sangh organization. 'The third dome fell at around 5.30 p.m. By around 4.45, we had already begun to see fire and smoke emanating from the Tedhi Bazaar side.' This area, directly behind and around the Rama Janmabhoomi police station today, is a predominantly Muslim area. The fire meant Muslim homes had been torched.

'It was evening, and the masjid had fallen. We began to make our way home. On the way, we heard that some people had got injured, and were in Sri Ram hospital. So we changed direction once again, and turned back towards Tedhi Bazaar. We wanted to see what we could do to help. At the Hanuman Garhi chauraha, a man came running, saying, "Muslims are shooting at Hindus!" We also began running and reached the Tedhi Bazaar area to find all Muslim homes insecure, under attack. The mosque near Hashim Ansari's house, which is a little way away, was also attacked then, and a Hanuman calendar had been put in it, with the words "Bajrangi Masjid" scrawled on it.'

The day of horrors was not yet done for Beeru and his friends. 'We stood at one spot, uncertain about what to do. I saw a Muslim man being burnt alive with a blazing tyre around his torso in front of a house. Someone from inside the house threw water on him, and the mob, under the leadership of a then Shiv Sena legislator, noticed this. "Search that place!" were the grim instructions from the legislator. We entered the house with the mob. My friends and I saw a girl, and before the mob could notice her, pushed her into a room and locked it. However, a second later, when the mob came there and began questioning us, my friend blurted out where she was. They opened the door and pulled her out. As she struggled with the mob, I didn't know what to do so I began to yell, "Run, run, Rai Sa'ab is coming!" referring to D.B. Rai, our then SSP. These words had a magical effect. The mob began to disperse, and in fact, the police did arrive there in a few minutes. I could not wait to make sure, but I presume the girl must have been saved.'

Making his way to the relative safety of his own home, Beeru sat on the terrace, in a state of shock and depression. 'After that, I kept thinking, okay, so the masjid fell, it was no big deal. I could live with that. But what about the Muslims who were getting killed? By the next day, we had a count of seventeen dead. Why did they have to be attacked? What was their fault? These were people we encountered on our streets, just like any ordinary Ayodhya-*wasi*. This, more than anything else, made me think – this is not a matter of faith, of a temple for Sri Rama. If it was, they would have been satisfied with the mosque falling. They wouldn't have randomly attacked and killed Muslims.'

This disillusionment was an important moment in the development of Beeru's own consciousness. In 1991, attracted by the zeal of those people who were coming to Ayodhya to court arrest at various functions organized by the VHP, he also participated in one such function. 'I responded to one of their calls to Maharaja College students to court arrest. We students were in school uniform and arrested at Amava Mandir, then released after a few hours. Now, in retrospect, I wonder why the school authorities didn't take any disciplinary action against us, going to a VHP function in school uniform. Something was seriously wrong then. When I was in Saket, we had a principal, Y.R. Tripathi, who asked his students and teachers to do kar-seva. Fortunately, at the time of the demolition, we had a Muslim chairman of the student council, elected to the post for the first time, and under his leadership, students rejected the demand. But thinking back, I wonder at the very nature of this – how could educational institutions be in the grip of this fever?'

The years following the demolition saw Beeru completing his graduation, then his MA, and being faced with the question of employment. 'Things are so bleak for young people looking for jobs in Ayodhya – there are no industries, no worthy educational institutions; this is such a difficult place to earn a living if you are not in the business of religion. When I was repeatedly encountering these kinds of difficulties, I understood how the mandir agitation and the demolition itself had wrecked Ayodhya's chances of economic recovery. By 1998, I decided to actively begin opposing those communal forces who had turned Ayodhya into an isolated, over-policed garrison.'

Beeru joined the Congress party on Republic Day, 1999, and soon began mobilizing local support against the VHP. 'First, we had a Sadbhavana Daud (Communal Harmony Race) from Naya Ghat to Raj Sadan. Then a group of us organized many smaller programmes without any noticeable support or encouragement from our political mentors. Once when the VHP was distributing trishuls and *talwars*, we distributed the Bhagavad Gita, pens, exercise books and pencils for thirteen days. By then, people in Ayodhya had themselves become fed up of these people, and supported our efforts. I used to go alone, sometimes with one or two others, with a letter to the District Magistrate, asking him to stop the programmes of the VHP from being staged.'

In the 2010-11 scenario, Beeru sees renewed attention on his town, its future, and progress. 'People have seen through the designs of the Sangh completely,' he says. 'In the name of our town and development, the Sangh leaders reached Lucknow and Delhi, and what did we get? We want good roads, hospitals, colleges. *Is vivaad ki kaali chhaya se ubarkar parampara ka nirvahan karte hue adhunikta mein pravesh karen* (we should enter a more modern era after casting off the dark cloud of this dispute, and staying true to our traditions).'

About the peace that prevailed in the wake of the Lucknow High Court judgement on the Ayodhya title suit on 30 September 2010, Beeru says, 'The administration and political parties cannot take credit for this. All credit goes to the ordinary people.'

Indeed, it is with these ordinary people of Ayodhya that Gaurav Tiwari 'Beeru' walks and lives.

21

Sri Krishna Madhukar
'Neta' News-vendor

Kitnau ahir pingal padhai, taba teen gun heen,
Uthna baithna bolna, leen vidhaata chheen.

(However learned an *ahir* becomes, he still lacks three qualities: the appropriate way of sitting, standing, speaking – the Lord deprived him of these.)

—Casteist rural proverb heard around Ayodhya
for ahirs (backward castes).

Opposite the Birla Dharamshala in Ayodhya is a shed housing PAC personnel. It is a beehive of activity in the early hours of the morning. This is from where bundles of newspapers are dispatched to homes all around Ayodhya. Once the cycle-borne delivery boys have left on their rounds, Sri Krishna Madhukar sits at a table with the newspapers displayed in front of him for retail sale. The spot becomes a meeting place for all kinds of regulars. People come for a cup of tea and greet 'Netaji', the man wearing all white khadi clothes, right up to his white turban; he has been a part of their lives for years. 'Ayodhya is unique. There is no other place like it on this earth,' says a smiling Netaji Madhukar. 'People know each other, they help each other.'

The eldest of four brothers and two sisters, Madhukar was born in Ayodhya on 20 November 1961 to his parents, the late Sitaram, and his wife Munni Devi. His father was a mason bricklayer, an office bearer of the Jan Sangh. One of those sitting next to us as we talk, describes him as having been 'an expert in *dharmik raajneeti* (religious politics).'

'When I was growing up, the population of Ayodhya was tiny. Any person was able to satisfy his immediate needs with ease,' recalls Madhukar. In those days, the Jan Sangh had a strong base in Ayodhya. Madhukar's father was associated with Bhagatji, or Ram Lakhan Sharan, who used to arrange kirtans at Rama Janmabhoomi, Mahant Ram Surat Sharan, and Harihar Das, then pujari of the *janmasthan* or the disputed site temple.

During the construction of the Manas Bhavan, very close to the Rama Janmabhoomi, Sitaram's views clashed with his friends' views. Money was being received from Marwaris for the construction. One Radhey Shyam Agrawal of Faizabad had put Sitaram in charge of construction. When he noticed a diversion of construction material to build a smaller temple elsewhere, he asked to be removed from his post. But the financing *seths* told him he could not leave.

Meanwhile, this caused resentment to build up against him among some people in the Sangh. In 1968, a group of them beat Sitaram up with lathis, and he was admitted to hospital. While he lay helpless, a pamphlet was distributed, purportedly from him, but actually written by a man named Laxman Das Shastri whose cunning and trouble-causing ways had earned him the nickname 'Naradji'. This pamphlet slandered a whole lot of people including Paramhans Ramachandra Das. The infuriated members of the lobby that had been slandered hatched a conspiracy to have Sitaram's arm amputated when he was still in hospital.

In this charged atmosphere, when Sitaram felt isolated and vulnerable, he received unexpected help and support from Mata Prasad Singh, Harishchandra Srivastava, and the young firebrand, Mitrasen Yadav, then a committed Marxist. The Communists offered protection to Sitaram and hailed him as a dalit (kori) standing up to the might of the mahants. For the next ten years, he was under the influence of the Marxists. Sri Krishna Madhukar's childhood was thus influenced by the two poles of traditional religiosity and atheist Marxism. 'I have imbibed deeply the egalitarian principles of Leftism,' he says. 'That will never leave me. These principles strengthen me in times of struggle.'

In 1968, Madhukar's father's arm injury prevented him from continuing his work as a mason. He began selling *Aaj* and *Gandiva*, two popular newspapers. 'In those days, few people knew how to read. People didn't go for individual copies of papers. Instead, there would be a *vachanalaya* (library) at various street corners, with blackboards announcing headlines. People wished each other at these corners, then exchanged their views about these headlines. Amrit Surmawale had a radio playing which was much in demand, as people used to get the most important news during emergencies from the radio.'

Madhukar's father's guru was a mercurial personality named Brahmachari Vasudevacharya, the editor of *Virakt* and the gurubhai of Paramhans Ramachandra Das. The paper had a strong presence in Ayodhya, representing the interests of the sadhu community. 'Earlier the ratio was three sadhus to one *grihastha* or householder in Ayodhya. Now the ratio has changed. Today there are definitely more families than ascetics. The aspirations of these men with families will define the future of this place,' says Madhukar.

Madhukar was soon to follow his father's footsteps. After completing school at Ramkot, and Katra ('at a time when the teachers were kind and good; they coached even the weak students without charging any extra fees'), he attended college at Saket. This signalled a coming of age. Madhukar was close to his teachers – Janardhan Upadhyay, Dr Radhika Prasad Tripathi, Dr Rama Shankar Tiwari, and the famous Marxist poet, Dr Swaminath Pandey of the Sanskrit department. However, he did not get involved directly with student politics. 'It was already dirty by then,' he says.

Instead, Madhukar started distributing newspapers, much like his father, while he was still a student. He went on to complete his MA in history, another in Hindi, and a BEd, but never stopped the newspaper business.

Madhukar's father died in 1998. He had studied only till class three. 'Even though it was very difficult for dalits to get an education in 1970-75, we are all educated,' says Madhukar. 'Both my sisters are teachers. One brother has been appointed as a lecturer. My father just said to us, "study", never "what are you doing with an education?" It was this support that prompted us all to get degrees.'

Since he has had the twin influences of tradition and modernity in terms of the Sangh and Leftism, where do his own personal inclinations lie? 'My personal influences make me spiritual,' says Madhukar. 'I have had experiences that reinforce my belief. I used to go to pour water over the Shiva linga at Kuber Tila. Once, past midnight on a full moon night, I was about to put my foot on the last step when I saw huge black scorpions walking in a line just below my foot. I closed my eyes for an instant in prayer. When I opened them again, there was no sign of the scorpions anywhere. Similarly, I go everyday, without fail for years now, to Kanak Bhavan and Chhoti Dev Kali temples. Once, again after midnight, there was a girl in a red skirt and *chunni* (stole) walking just ahead of me when I was doing parikrama (circumambulation) around the Devi temple. At the time, I didn't give it much thought, although there were only two of us in the temple, and it is a very unusual time for a girl to be alone. By the time I came out to look for her, she was nowhere to be seen. All this makes me feel that what we pray to is never very far away.'

About the movement for a Rama temple that has thrown Ayodhya into turmoil on repeated occasions, Madhukar says, 'In the Janmabhoomi agitation, a few things were overlooked. There was a Sufi saint who advised Mir Baqi – "This is a very holy place." I feel that Mir Baqi just built a grand house for the saint to live in. Then both faiths could go there and pray. In fact, the Sufi saint is still venerated on Thursdays near here. His *mazar* (final resting place) has the same black pillars as were there in the masjid.' Madhukar's belief has several factors in its favour, not least of which was the presence of at least eighty Sufi shrines around these parts at one time, many of which have been destroyed, or have seen their followers dwindle over time.

Madhukar remembers the days of the first kar-seva when the firing had taken place. 'On 30 October 1990, there was a huge demand for newspapers, but the PAC had forbidden us from selling newspapers on the streets. I used to be inside the ticket window at the old bus stand. The first bullets were fired on a seated crowd chanting "Sita Rama". This was at Lal Kothi where the two Kothari brothers from Kolkata died. The news spread like wild fire all over town. *Mulayam ke kaam ne Hindu jan manas ko andolit kiya* (Mulayam's actions caused the Hindu psyche to turn revolutionary),' Madhukar says.

'Then, on 2 November, he ordered firing on parikrama devotees, creating a lot more hatred in Ayodhya. It was unheard of for anyone to harm those who come for parikrama.' Were you politically involved in the resistance to Mulayam, I ask him. 'I was a Jan Sangh member from 1975, which later became the BJP. I have also been a young messenger for underground Sanghis in the Emergency,' he says with a grin.

So what do you feel then about the popular disenchantment with the VHP, I ask him. 'I support their stance against conversions, and their desire to protect the Hindu faith,' he says. 'The media is giving the Ajmer blasts and Sadhvi (Malegaon) cases undue prominence. I believe in the slogan, "*Hindu ghata toh desh bantaa* (if Hindus dwindle in numbers, the country gets divided)." There are many positive initiatives that the VHP is taking for the upliftment of Hindus in Ayodhya. For instance, they have a six-month training programme in "Ramkatha" for tribal girls and boys, from places which are very vulnerable to conversion. These youth are returned to their homes with a stipend. They are also doing a lot for education.'

But what about the Sangh's support for the caste system? Haven't you felt its ill effects as a dalit, I ask him. 'It's true, the Sangh and its organizations have never opposed the caste system,' he admits.

'But within the Sangh, caste names are not used. And after all, what is wrong? I say, let the caste system flourish, but let the harmful psychological effect of it be removed.'

Easier said than done, I cannot help muttering. 'See, I am called "netaji" because 90 per cent of people know me by face, some by name. I have held many party posts, but for my own community, I set up the Sant Ravidas Vansh Utthan Seva Samiti in January 2006. My aim was to remove social evils from the dalit community. I oppose child marriage through the Samiti, and have made the youth join in my fight against it. I oppose the serving of liquor and meat on all occasions, and today, this has stopped completely at social functions. I have motivated people – the money they save on liquor and meat can be used to send their child to school instead.'

Sri Krishna Madhukar formed the Ayodhya Vyapar Mandal in 1995 and leads it even today. It serves to improve the morale of traders. Once, when shopkeepers around the Hanuman Garhi temple were facing trouble from Mahant Gyandas, who had threatened to have their establishments closed down, he interceded on the behalf of the shopkeepers. 'Mahant Gyandas was talking to Sant Ram Das of the Ujjaini Patti,' recalls Madhukar. 'Sant Ramji recognized me and greeted me. This was enough for Gyandas to recognize that I had once opposed the "Heritage City" scheme for Ayodhya (a short-lived government scheme to which the Hanuman Garhi mahant had taken exception) and he asked me if I was the same person. When I answered in the affirmative, he was very friendly and I came to view him as a *kaka* . When he finally asked me why I was there, I told him, "Kaka, the shopkeepers are very unhappy with your move against them." He saw my point. He stopped his crusade. His tenant shopkeepers were very enthused by this meeting of ours. They considered it a major victory.'

One of the few people I have met who feels that the Rama Janmabhoomi agitation actually brought economic benefit to Ayodhya, Madhukar is convinced that a temple will contribute to Ayodhya's development. Then echoing the sentiments of many others, he says, 'Rama Janmabhoomi should be a national trust, not part of any individual matt or mandir. It should be announced as a national asset, maintained as national wealth.'

But can any such thing happen without the dispute being settled, I ask him. What is his opinion of attempts to solve the problem through dialogue? 'Individual attempts at solving the dispute are futile,' says Madhukar, obviously referring to the Gyandas-Hashim Ansari efforts. 'Dialogue is now meaningless. What's the point when the court itself has now accepted that there was no masjid there?'

This contrary personality who has survived in the politics of the Sangh despite being a dalit reiterates his attachment to Ayodhya. 'I don't give importance to money, only to social standing. That I have a lot of in Ayodhya. *Hum jaise aadmi ko itna prem mila. Dhanya hai Ayodhya! Hamaare jeevan ki sabse badi uplabdhi* (a man like me could gather so much affection. Blessed is Ayodhya! It has given me my life's greatest achievements).'

As we walk away from the Birla Dharamshala, more people gather to greet this man with respect and affection, as if underlining his recent words.

⎯⎯⎦⎧⎦⎧⎦⎯⎯

22

Asad Ahmad
Necessary Stoicism

Yaaron kisi qatil se kabhi pyaar na mango
Apne hi gale ke liye talwaar na mango.

(Friends, do not ask for love from a killer. Do not ask for a sword
to be placed on your own neck.)

—Qateel Shifai's ghazal sung by Mehdi Hassan

The mangled remains of the jeep used in the July 2005 terrorist attack on the makeshift temple at Rama Janmabhoomi is visible as we turn the corner from Tedhi Bazaar towards the home of Asad Ahmad. This ghost jeep, used by heavily armed Lashkar-e-Toiba terrorists to storm the barricaded Babri Masjid-Rama Janmabhoomi complex in July 2005, stands alongside the compound wall of the Rama Janmabhoomi police station, an important police station behind which lies the largely Muslim-dominated locality where Ahmad lives. He has been a municipal corporator since 1995, and is even today, a Samajwadi Party backed member of Ayodhya's municipality.

Asad Ahmad was born on 20 January 1964 in Ayodhya, into a zamindar's family. The members of the household had distinguished themselves by regularly going for Haj, the pilgrimage to the holy destinations of Mecca and Medina, which in years past, used to be so perilous, that Hajis bid farewell to their families before each trip, not knowing when and if they would return. 'At the time when my family first began going for Haj, things were not like they are now, with every possible convenience in travel and stay. My grandfather, Haji Feku, was a very pious man and went for Haj many times. It is because of him that our family earned the title "Haji" that came to be used before all our names. He was a well-respected man who looked after the day-to-day arrangements for worship at the Tedhi Bazaar Masjid, the place where we pray even today.'

Ahmad remembers a childhood free of religious controversy, or any sense of discord between the Hindu and Muslim communities. 'There had never been communal riots in Ayodhya in living memory, when we were children. It was regarded and remembered as a peaceful place.' In fact, the shrine to 'Badi Bua' between

Faizabad and Ayodhya, captures a particular quality of this place. Badi Bua, sister of Hazrat Khwaja Nasiruddin, the successor of Hazrat Khwaja Nizammudin, was a strikingly beautiful woman, who chose to serve God by serving the poor. When faced with opposition from the then clergy, she is supposed to have declared the area around Ayodhya, '*Na aalim rahega, na zalim* (this place shall harbour neither cleric nor oppressor).'

'The idols had been kept in the masjid in my grandfather's time,' says Asad Ahmad. 'But there was no problem between communities. We walked past the masjid daily on our way to school, and played games in the open grounds around it. It was only from 1982-83 that the seeds of communal hatered began to get planted.'

So when the visible signs of such communal tension could be seen and felt in Ayodhya, didn't the Muslim community also organize itself, or register any protest, I ask him. 'There was no sense in us organizing ourselves to deal with this,' says Asad Ahmad. 'The poison of communal hatred was percolating into every layer of society, sparing no one. People, once close, were growing suspicious of one another, without a word being said. If we had protested at that point, it would have worsened matters. People from our community talked at street corners, worried for our survival. We did not know whose help to take.'

By 1989-90, Asad Ahmad had climbed the first rungs of a political career, joining the Janata Dal. 'Under the local leadership of Jai Shankar Pande, we organized meetings and rallies at which we raised slogans for communal harmony. But ordinary people were almost completely enamoured with the ideas and policies of the Sangh. Within our political party, we were afraid to oppose them, for fear of being viewed as social outcasts in our own families and neighbourhoods.' He stresses the bafflement of his own community once again, when he says, 'People were clueless in those days. Just didn't know what to do. The administration meant nothing.'

In 1990, Asad Ahmad was witness to the leadership of Mulayam Singh Yadav, a leader whom he is committed to as a Samajwadi Party member for the past fifteen years or more. 'He had a difficult choice before him in 1990,' Ahmad says, speaking for the Samajwadi leader. 'Either believe in law and order and uphold it, or accept jungle raj in UP and other parts of the country. Mulayamji chose to uphold law and order, no matter how difficult it was. The worst part is, leaders are always secure in any agitation. It is the innocents who are exploited and made to face the bullets of the police. This is what happened with the VHP. But I am not saying that the firing should not have happened, or could have been avoided. The circumstances of that time were compelling, to say the least.'

Then what about the rejection of Mulayam by the people in the days following the 30 October and 2 November firing in Ayodhya, I ask him. How did he and other Samajwadi Party workers face that? 'See, as for that, it is a fact of life in *raajneeti*. We faced the difficult circumstances of Mulayam's rejection with stoicism, knowing that people would return.'

On 6 December 1992, Asad Ahmad was at home. 'The whole area was jam-packed with kar-sevaks. Till the 5th, we had been moving around freely. But on that day, there was no question of our leaving our house. We gathered on our terrace, and witnessed the fall of the domes from there. Following this, chaos erupted all around us, with many homes being burnt. I remember, five people were burnt in our very neighbourhood – one in Mohd.

Aslam's house, a boy named Salman, then Mohd. Sabir and Nazir, and Shaukat Ali and his son, Tony. On 7 December, the FIR in these matters was filed by my uncle, Haji Mehboob.'

With a bitterness that is inevitable in the circumstances, Asad Ahmad says of the Rama Mandir agitation, 'They wanted to use Ayodhya as a project, an experiment with which to do a whole lot more in different parts of the country. But it is easy to destroy something, much more difficult to build anything. See, even today, they have not been able to build the temple with which they fooled so many for so long.'

In 1995, Asad Ahmad contested and won municipal elections for the first time, and has since been working to address Ayodhya's municipal issues as a corporator. 'The most difficult task before us has to do with calm and peaceful arrangements for the four melas in Ayodhya's annual calendar,' he says, echoing Municipal Chairman Mithilesh Pande's sentiments. 'Apart from there not being separate budgetary provisions for these events, the bureaucratic control over their administration is stifling,' he says. 'If the CMO, or the DM is in charge of mela arrangements, whom can the public approach for redressal of their grievances? The officers come and go from meeting to meeting, having tea and biscuits, but it is the municipality workers who do the actual work, and who have to face the ire of the public.'

In an Ayodhya dominated by religion, Asad Ahmad rues the lack of proper education and employment. '*Dharm adharit Ayodhya mein shiksha aur rozgar ka abhav hai* (in this town controlled by religious fervour, there's no hope for education and employment),' he says. 'This has always been a place where many faiths have co-existed, people are helpful, everyone will stop to show you the way when you ask for directions. But now people have to move out of Ayodhya to get a proper job, for their own development and that of their family.'

In a grim reminder of the actual costs being paid by the nation everyday, Ahmad says, 'The dispute is the biggest obstacle in Ayodhya's development. When you think of the money being spent on security everyday – twenty-five lakh rupees, you can imagine what a wonderful place Ayodhya could have been if these resources were instead spent on creating better facilities and services here. No one can think of doing business in Ayodhya. Even the price of vegetables is affected by the huge numbers of PAC and police contingents permanently parked here. In our neighbourhood, we suffer the added indignity of having to explain our presence daily to police and para-military personnel. It is a living nightmare.'

So is there no hope of moving past the events of 1992? Asad Ahmad replies with wry candour, 'For the children born after 1992, all this talk of mandir-masjid is of no interest whatsoever. They do not have any idea of all this; they do not even want to know. In our own homes, if they come in from playing and find us talking about the issue, they immediately run out again! I think it is they who will finally make a difference – restore justice and hope where we seem to have lost it.'

In 2011, more than eighteen years after the tragic events of December 1992, it is hard not to wish, with a fierce and fervent devotion, that Asad Ahmad's prophecy about the children of Ayodhya comes true, that India and the idea of India are taken forward by citizens untainted by the collective madness we succumbed to in those unhappy days.

23

Raj Kishor Maurya
Grassroots Journalism

Jo namazi bhi nahin, jo pujari bhi nahin,
Mandir masjid ke liye ghamdeen rehte hain.
Hum hain Ayodhya ke, Ayodhya hai hamaari,
Lekin surkhiyon mein Singhal aur Shahabuddin rehte hain.

(Those who neither offer *namaaz*, nor do any puja are most concerned and worried for a temple or a masjid. We belong to Ayodhya, and Ayodhya to us, yet it is Singhal and Shabuddin who remain in the headlines.)

—Popular lines from the secular resistance to
the VHP in Ayodhya.

On the main road leading to Naya Ghat in Ayodhya, where the bridge over the Sarayu is a departure point for Basti, Gonda, Gorakhpur and beyond, is a little shop indistinguishable from the others around it. It holds children's toys and the little knick-knacks that tourists are likely to buy. Hand-held video games, little torches and batteries, key chains and the tiny locks used to make handbags and suitcases safe from the nimble fingers of roaming thieves – all these make a colourful display in the midst of which sits a small, dark, slightly-built man.

He could be just any other ordinary shopkeeper, except that people keep stopping to ask him things, or just say hello, without buying anything. The three-wheeler Vikram tempo, the all-weather symbol of transport between Faizabad and Ayodhya, also stops outside the shop. A driver peers out and greets the shopkeeper. He returns the greeting and gives a small folded piece of paper to the driver's assistant, who has stepped out of the vehicle to pick it up. Then the tempo roars off.

Raj Kishor Maurya, the shop keeper-journalist, has just sent off his latest Ayodhya report to the Lucknow bureau of *Swatantra Bharat*.

As a rural journalist, Raj Kishor is intrinsically tied to the people around him and represents their problems with authority; he highlights the flaws of a system that fails to deliver justice. While we talk, he keeps getting calls from various people about the location of a particular DSO responsible for kerosene supply under the public distribution system. He has promised to meet and speak to this man about issues regarding the sale of kerosene, and his friends keep him informed about where the DSO is, so that he can catch him at a particular spot.

'I have been the UP state secretary of the Rashtriya Journalist

Association for the last two years,' says Maurya, who is also the Ayodhya chief of *Dainik Bharatiya,* a paper brought out from Basti, and contributes to another paper, the *Awadh Comment Week*. His unorthodox style of filing reports is typical of a man who has lived his life struggling for survival, something he has in common with millions in rural and small-town India. This frail-looking scribe has not lived anywhere but in Ayodhya.

Born in Ayodhya on 30 November 1953, Raj Kishor recalls the Ayodhya of his childhood. 'I was always conscious of Ayodhya being a religious place and people of all religions visiting.' Ayodhya is a very important pilgrimage centre for Jains too, since five of their twenty-four Tirthankars were born here – Rishabh Dev, Ajit Nath, Abhinandan Swami, Sumati Nath and Anant Nath. 'There is a large Digambari Jain temple at Raiganj,' says Raj Kishor Maurya. 'As children, we used to see nude Jain *munis* come here and make offerings during their festival. We used to steal the dry fruits they had left as contributions to the temple!

'At other times, we used to exuberantly participate in the Urs celebrations for Syed Shah Ibrahim. There were always good sweets to be had. When the Bale Miyan mela happened at Bahraich, we used to have a corresponding Gudada mela in the Gola bazaar area. This was great fun too. Then there have always been the four melas of Ayodhya in different seasons, with *nautanki* and Ramlila performances, plenty of shops and pilgrims for us to gape at. Ayodhya was always celebrating some religion!'

Raj Kishor went to the government school at Katra from class one to six, before moving to the Maharaja Inter-College to complete school. He was one of two brothers, and had a sister. Life would have followed an even course, like the lives of many friends and neighbours, if it had not been for Maurya's father's propensity to fuel an extravagant lifestyle with loans. 'My father had been a pampered only son. He enjoyed the good things in life, eating well, living well. But he never developed the ability to earn enough money for this. Instead, he took loans that dragged us all down. We had hell facing debt-collectors and doing without many things so that he could keep paying back his loans.'

What was most injurious to the young Raj Kishor's spirit was the way he was compelled to drop out of his degree due to the family being completely broke. 'I was studying at Motilal Manoharlal Inter-College in Faizabad. I was determined to graduate, and even liked to study. For my first three exams, I got a lift with a friend. For the fourth paper, I had no money to reach the exam centre. Somehow, this was just too much for me to take at that point, even though it does not seem like much now.' Raj Kishor had been arranging for money to study by selling vegetables on his head in a basket, or on a cart in the street; the prospect of having to walk to his exam centre and perhaps risk reaching after the exam was over, was the last straw.

Another period of intense struggle stretched on for eighteen years, as Raj Kishor strove to win back two rooms belonging to his family which had been sealed after a raid by the Central Excise Department. 'We had sold tobacco to Haji Mehboob, who collected it from our door. There was a tax to be paid on the load, which he assured us he was paying. But when the raid took place, they told us that the tax had not been paid and slapped a case on us that took nearly two decades to resolve,' says Maurya, without a trace of anger or bitterness.

In the manner of that time in Ayodhya (the sixties), Raj Kishor was married when he was ten-years-old to his wife, then a girl from a village in Faizabad district. However, the *gauna* (her departure from her parental home) happened some years later. Still, by the time he was in class eight, Raj Kishor Maurya was a married youth with responsibilities towards a wife as well as parents. The couple has four sons – Skanda Maurya, Shakya Singh Maurya, Kishan Kumar Maurya and Awadh Kishor Maurya. We have heard of the first one in Chapters 1 and 3 on Vineet Maurya and Yugal Kishor Sharan Shastri.

When Raj Kishor first began seeing the bands of kar-sevaks descend on Ayodhya, he thought, '*Is desh ki janta bhramit hui hai* (the people of this country have been misled).' He says he felt unease and fear, and wondered, 'Who are the people who have brainwashed these hordes?' Describing the build-up to the actual demolition in 1992, he says, 'When the VHP first gave a call to Hindus to come and demolish the disputed structure, people here were worried. After all, so many basic issues of survival remained unsolved for them – drinking water, for instance, or clean and adequate latrines for visitors and pilgrims. In fact, even proper latrines and toilets in their own homes have remained a luxury for many in Ayodhya up to the present day. So people were worried about how their lives would be affected by any large-scale agitation. And among them, the Muslims became especially fearful; Hindus at least, did not fear for their lives. In Ayodhya people have always known how to live together. It's the outsiders who have caused trouble.'

By the time the structure was demolished in December 1992, locals had become completely fed up of the daily and weekly scenes of slogan shouting VHP activists, the rituals of shila-pujan and the fund-raising efforts of the VHP and Bajrang Dal. On the day of the demolition, Raj Kishor Maurya went to the site and watched, along with thousands of fellow Ayodhya citizens, while the mobs went berserk. 'I did not regret the masjid falling,' he says, 'not because I wanted to destroy another man's place of worship, but because, for me, it had become a symbol of the trouble we were facing in our daily lives. I felt that as long as it remained standing, it would cause even more pain and fighting.'

Unfortunately, this estimation of Maurya's turned out to be an erroneous one. While the mobs of kar-sevaks were left without an immediate target after the demolition, the pain and fighting did not stop with the effacing of the masjid. In fact, it deepened and left an indelible scar on the soul of modern India. Displaying the first sign of bitterness, Raj Kishor Maurya says, 'After the demolition, Ayodhya has become a place that is not fit to visit, leave alone pray in. Events here have caused the country so much anguish. What the madmen who are fighting for either mandir or masjid don't seem to understand is, if there won't be any country, what is the use of either mandir or masjid?'

In a town that receives crores of rupees annually by way of temple offerings, Raj Kishor is critical of the religious power structure. 'Offerings in temples are not used for the upliftment of Ayodhya, but the lifestyle and expenses of mahants and sadhus. If a rule is invoked that says pilgrims shall worship without paying money in the form of offerings, mahants will begin to close down their temples!' he says. 'If a sadhu has a bank balance and every luxury, he is not a true sadhu,' he continues. *Jiske paas sadhana nahin hai, wah kaisa sadhu hai?* (If a man shows complete disregard for the austerities demanded of a spiritual life, how can he be called a sadhu?)'

Having perceived the VHP as opportunists who would prove to be disastrous for Ayodhya, Raj Kishor Maurya has been a part of various initiatives for secularism in the temple town, including

Ayodhya ki Awaz. He impressed me on my first visit here in 2005 with a particularly balanced and articulate account of how hate-mongers had to retreat from Ayodhya with their tails between their legs following a complete rejection by the people. He was also associated for some time with Yugal Kishor Sharan Shastri. But this association was permanently strained when Raj Kishor's eldest son, Skanda Maurya, spent three months in jail with Shastri and others following the infamous episode of a portrait of Sri Rama being garlanded with chappals (*see* Chapters 1 and 3).

'I was very hurt by the episode of garlanding Rama with chappals,' he says. 'Just because I love or worship one god, it gives me no right to insult another. Besides, how did this help the secular cause? I had to run around for three months trying to get my son out of jail. People who loved and respected me, who had known me for years, used to stop by my shop and say, "We never expected this of you and your family." It was deeply shaming, and completely unnecessary.'

Raj Kishor Maurya has regained his following due to the efforts he undertakes on behalf of so many. When I ask how he perceives himself in the small town of Ayodhya, he smiles. 'It is true that Ayodhya is a small place where people know each other. It is also such a small place that it has entered the hearts and minds of people all over the world!' he says with obvious pride. 'I feel I have made some progress,' he continues, musingly. 'But I still consider myself an ordinary man.'

Unlike Singhal and Shahabuddin, Raj Kishor Maurya may have missed being in the headlines, but his story and spirit reflect the ground realities of a hurting, wounded Ayodhya.

⟨ᴑᴊᴑ⟩

24

Dr Swaminath Pandey
Lyrical Marxist

Neta
+ afsar
+ seth
+ lekhak
+ patrakaar
+ desh ki chinta
= coffee house

(Politician + official + businessman + writer + journalist + worry about the country = coffee house.)

—From the collection of poems, *Khel*,
by Dr Swaminath Pandey

Dr Swaminath Pandey, like so many personalities from around Ayodhya, has imbibed different streams of thought and crafted his own unique identity. Poet, Marxist, teacher of Sanskrit classics and authority on Goswami Tulsidas, this now retired professor of Sanskrit at the Saket Degree College, the most prominent educational landmark between Faizabad and Ayodhya, is fondly remembered by students as a man who always had time to stop and talk for a few moments.

'One could set out to buy vegetables and meet him on the street,' says Srikrishna Madhukar. 'And a conversation would begin and time would fly. Several other people would gather. Then, much later, if one folded one's hands and said, "Got to be getting along Sir, have to buy vegetables," Sir would gather himself too, and exclaim, "Hey you are right! I too have to get mine." Then he would be off. There was always plenty to learn from him, because he had a unique perspective on things.'

Until recently, such impromptu gatherings at various places around Ayodhya with friends, fellow lecturers and students tended to be the norm for Dr Pandey. However these days, he has not been venturing out much, following a blackout during which he had a fall at home. 'I miss my long talkathons with people on the street. When I lost my guru (Dr Ramaranjan Mukherjee, former VC of Rabindra Bharati and Chancellor of Tirupati University), I came to know about it a month later from the Bangla papers – I couldn't sleep properly for many weeks. The blackout I suffered was because of this.'

Dr Pandey arrived in Ayodhya in 1971 after a long spell in Kolkata. He lived in Howrah and completed his MA and Ph.D from Jadavpur University, before teaching there on a temporary assignment for three years. Spending such time in Bengal as a young man ensured that he would be committed to Marxist thought, develop a passion for football, and proficiency in Bengali literature and writing.

When I land up at his house after fixing an appointment with his nephew, he is as delighted at the prospect of having an extra cup of tea with a visitor, as with the possibility of conversation! The tea is excellent, and occasionally, I see members of his brother's family, who have shared a house with him for many years. Dr Pandey has remained a bachelor; he is the quintessential man of ideas and letters, happy to be surrounded by his books, and now, a large colour television on which to watch football. In his quiet scholarship and enjoyment of company, one sees that he is free from over-ambition. Dr Swaminath Pandey has remained true to Ayodhya's character – *masti* and *phakkad*ness – also seen in other Ayodhya legends. Leading simple lives, and staying immersed in their own individual passions has been the way for these men.

'Some great personalities lived in Ayodhya not so very long ago,' he says in a reflective tone. 'Of course, there was Pagal Dasji, whose musical genius enthralled people during Ramlila and at solo concerts. Then there was Ram Kumar Dasji Ramayani of Mani Parbat. In his time, there was a grand library here, which would have put even universities to shame. Paramhansji – *vani mein nipun, tark mein bejod* (wonderful speaker, unparallelled in his assertions). Lakshman Qiladhishji – few have such a mastery over the scriptures, or such charisma. Sanskrit scholarship has seen wonderful personalities from Ayodhya: Panini, who died a decade ago, Pandit Rudra Prasadji Awasthi, a great grammarian who taught at the Rajagopal Vidyalaya, his student Acharya Baijnath Dwivedi who was himself an excellent grammarian. Kamalakant Jha, a famous astrologer – the list can go on.'

Dr Pandey is alternatively lyrical and satirical, spouting doggerel that can make biting social comments, or poems that make one yearn with nostalgia for a lost, less harsh and disturbing world. '*Chhoot gaya palkon se sapnon ka gaanv* (the village of dreams is lost to the lashes),' he declares in one poem, while in another, he can rattle off the conversation of middle-class men, '*Suit kitne mein silaaya? Joota kitne mein pada? Scooter kitne mein aaya?* (How much did the tailor charge for the suit? What did you pay for these shoes? How much for the scooter?)' His collections of poems include *Path Haara* – mostly lyrical poetry, *Jhaanwa* – satirical and topical poems, *Ajaayabghar* – a collection of satirical essays, *Khel* – poems that make social comments, *Tulsi Sudha Bindu Shatakam* – the selected poems of Goswami Tulsidas translated into Sanskrit, *Goswami Tulsidas: His Life and Works*, and *Hanuman Bahu*, again translated into Sanskrit.

Having had rich experiences on campus over three decades, Dr Pandey turns nostalgic as he speaks of the years in Saket. 'In the beginning, there was an atmosphere conducive to good education,' he says, referring to the 1970s. 'Teachers were good and capable, students were interested in learning. They were socially and politically conscious.' What happened later, I ask him. His wry expression and the shake of his head convey deep sorrow. Clearly, standards steadily fell across campuses in UP in the 80s, when goons and a *goonda raj* became the norm rather than exceptions on campus. 'The later years were less enjoyable,' he admits.

Saket Degree College did not stay untouched during the height of the VHP's campaign for a Rama temple in Ayodhya. As we have seen from Gaurav Tiwari Beeru's account (*see* Chapter 20), the principal himself had appealed to the students to participate in kar-seva activities. Dr Pandey recalls this with regret. 'Kar-sevaks had taken over the town, and the Saket campus was not spared either. People were forced to offer hospitality.' Differing from the general outrage over the actions of Mulayam's police in the two incidents of firing in 1990, Dr Swaminath Pandey says, 'The firing in 1990 happened in difficult circumstances. The administration had their hand forced by angry mobs.'

Dr Pandey's views are ratified by the account of Suman Gupta, senior journalist with *Jan Morcha*, whose struggles with the mob on 6 December 1992 have been described elsewhere in this book (*see* Chapter 3). Suman speaks of her unease with the way things have changed in Ayodhya after 1984. She describes the conditions in 1990 thus: 'Advani's rath yatra and the restrictions imposed by the administration on the parikrama at Ayodhya – both these things bothered me a lot. Traditionally, the parikrama is attended by rural pilgrims from places near Ayodhya. So this need not have got the administration into such a tizzy. But the fact was that only hard-core people had arrived for the parikrama that year. The regulars hadn't come in such numbers. About eighteen to twenty thousand people of the BJP-VHP had reached on the parikrama days. At the time, we had a DM called Ram Sharan Srivastava who was rumoured to be close to the VHP. He later wrote a book called *Rama Janmabhoomi-Babri Masjid: Ek Drishtikon* (Rama Janmabhoomi-Babri Masjid: A Viewpoint). The administration had made tight arrangements. The local people arriving for the parikrama faced road blocks. We had no newsprint stock to print the paper. People's resentment against the government was visible on the streets.'

Suman Gupta says that the accounts of the police firing wantonly on people chanting 'Sitaram' only tell part of the story, at best.

'The hard-core people who had arrived on the parikrama dates were not only mentally trained, but were physically trained too. Shipra Das of PTI, and myself, we saw a plan unfold. First, women left their homes, beating *thalis*, creating an atmosphere of protest. We had gone to Ayodhya in the morning with Janata Dal legislator, Sant Sriram Dwivedi. From 7.30 a.m. we began seeing angry, slogan-shouting crowds arrive. A bus was hijacked in front of our eyes and driven to Manas Bhavan, breaking all barricades. Shirish Chandra Dixit, ex-DGP of police, and Ashok Singhal arrived on the scene. There was huge crowd pressure. People quickly scaled the masjid and put up flags.' Volunteers who quickly scale buildings have obviously been physically trained.

'Meanwhile, at Dasharath Mahal or the Bada Sthan, police posts had been constructed. These were brought down by kar-sevaks with the policemen still inside them. We were blinded by tear gas. I had a small handkerchief, which I kept dipping in water, trying to counter the effects of the gas. Shipra Das arrived with *chuna* (whitewash) on her face. She had got this from the kar-sevaks who had also told her that chuna lessens the effect of tear gas! Water was being thrown on the kar-sevaks from rooftops all along the Raj Sadan-Hanuman Garhi route. How could this have been done unless it was a well-planned strategy? Members of the press were sitting shocked and huddled, trying to estimate the numbers killed by the shots fired. Ram Sharan Srivastava began to cry and appealed to Shitla Singh, "Please speak to the CM". A lot of the police force had crumbled under the might of the committed crowds of the VHP. A few policemen like Subhash Joshi and Madhukar Gupta stood firm. Even in 1990, people climbed the dome, but because it had been repaired in 1965, it did not break immediately.' About the disparity in figures of those killed in the police firing, Suman says that kar-sevaks went especially searching for BBC and *Jan Morcha* reporters the next day to seek revenge for publishing the 'wrong' figures.

It is Dr Pandey's assertion that the administration had its hand forced by angry mobs in 1990, and the description of chaos in the previous paragraphs certainly reinforces this.

As for the events of 6 December 1992, Dr Swaminath Pandey escaped being involved, because he was at Meerut. 'All of Ayodhya was poisoned by what happened that day,' he says. 'Before this happened, people had not imagined that things could get this bad. There was no turning back after those awful hours.'

Accustomed to being part of many *kavi-sammelans* and seminars in the fairly rich and well-populated intellectual calendar of Ayodhya and Faizabad in times gone by, Dr Swaminath Pandey says, 'The falling of the structure put paid to everything.'

He does not see anything in the near future that will bring a resolution of the conflict, either. 'Only time will heal,' he says. 'What can we do? It has become a problem for the whole country.'

Time has consistently emerged as the single factor that inspires faith. Everything else has been found lacking.

25

Tarunjeet Varma
Inherited Involvement

Kaabu mein majdhar usi ke, haathon mein patwaar usi ke,
Teri haar bhi nahin hai teri haar, udaasi man kahe tu dare?

(He controls the river mid-stream, and the oars too are in His hands. Even your defeat is not actually a loss, so why do you fear, O sad heart?)

—Lines from the popular bhajan,
Tera Ramji Karenge Beda Paar

Tarunjeet Varma practises law at the high court in Lucknow, which means he is there several days a week. But he arranges it in such a way as to reach his home in Ayodhya after each day of work. 'I sleep properly only when I am back home,' he says. For this young man brought up in Ayodhya, even the 133 kilometre distance to Lucknow seems like too much from his beloved hometown.

In the weeks preceding the judgement in the Ayodhya title suit by the Lucknow bench of the Allahabad High Court on 30 September 2010, Tarunjeet didn't know if he was in Ayodhya or Lucknow, asleep or awake. 'The tension was unbearable. Everyone was trying to gauge which way the judgement would go. At one point it seemed definite that the Muslim claim would be given priority over the land. My heart sank, I became extremely depressed. I thought, "We won't be able to show our faces in Ayodhya if this happens!"'

Tarunjeet Varma is the third generation of his family to be involved in the Ayodhya title suit. His grandfather, Sarabjit Varma, who had taken up legal practice in 1933, had first formed a bond with the sadhus of the Nirmohi Akhara in 1934. These sadhus became his clients when they filed their claim in the Ayodhya title suit on 17 December 1959. 'My grandfather was a politically conscious lawyer who worked mainly for freedom fighters during the pre-Independence period,' says Tarunjeet. 'In 1934, there had been an incident of cow slaughter at Shahjahanpur, one of the villages near Ayodhya, during the Rama Navami mela. This sparked off communal riots in Ayodhya and the surrounding areas, during which the masjid at Rama Janmabhoomi was attacked. Some Nirmohi Akhara sadhus had FIRs registered against them at that time, and my grandfather represented them. That is how they turned to him when they needed to file their case.' When Tarunjeet's father Ranjit Lal Varma took up legal practice in 1961, he cut his teeth on the Ayodhya title suit, and has been involved ever since on behalf of the Nirmohi Akhara.

Tarunjeet was born in Ayodhya on 1 December 1972, and travelled the well-worn path of Maharaja Inter-college and Saket University, before becoming a lawyer. He had completed school, when the events of 1989-90 unfolded. 'We were just teenagers and were prevented from going out by our parents. We were told there was trouble outside. But somehow, the charged atmosphere was hard to stay away from. I went for kar-seva and even got arrested for a few hours on one occasion.'

I then speak to him of the problem of law and order in 1990. Perhaps Mulayam had his hand forced? What could he have done in the face of unruly crowds? But Tarunjeet shakes his head emphatically. 'I may have been a young boy then, but I was old enough to understand that Mulayam Singh could have prevented the firing if he had wanted to. The firing was only about appeasing his Muslim vote bank. Every ordinary, poor, illiterate person understood that at the time. Why would they have called him "Mulla Mulayam" otherwise?'

An interesting point that emerges in our conversations that go tangentially back and forth is that the stronghold of sadhus on Ayodhya in the past really meant living in an atmosphere of fear. Everyone was terrified of the orange and white robed figures. It reminds me of what has been told to me by so many of those I have interviewed, and especially by the family of Hari Dayal Mishra (*see* Chapter 2), living in the vicinity of Hanuman Garhi. 'The decade between the 80s and the 90s was dominated by panic, apprehension amongst householders about the sadhus in Ayodhya,' says Tarunjeet. 'In fact, things have improved a lot after 1992, with the massive presence of the police around us. It has neutralized the sadhus. Even the criminals among them cannot afford to operate in the open now.'

When I begin to talk to Tarunjeet about the Ayodhya title suit, he reminds me that the Nirmohi Akhara has the oldest claim on the site. In fact, many, including Hashim Ansari, mentioned this in the 1880s – that the Nirmohi Akhara had filed a claim on the property, and this was actually the first case disputing the ownership of the land around the masjid.

'The first case filed by the akhara was in itself regarding permission to build a temple. It had been filed because the Faizabad deputy commissioner had refused to let Mahant Raghubar Das of the Nirmohi Akhara build a temple on land adjoining the disputed structure. Mahantji then filed a title suit in a Faizabad court, seeking permission to build a temple on the chabutara on the outer courtyard of the disputed structure,' says Tarunjeet.

'But this case was dismissed,' I say.

'Yes, but it forms the basis of the Nirmohi Akhara's claim,' says Tarunjeet. 'You see, our assertion is based on the historical division of territory for worship and control, decided among the three akharas – the Nirvani, Nirmohi and Digambari Akharas. There is documentary evidence, dating back to the fourteenth and fifteenth centuries, speaking about the seven villages of Ayodhya, which are today eighteen villages. These had been divided among the three akharas in this manner – the Nirvani Akhara was to control the Ramanandi Vaishnav puja and other arrangements at Ganga Sagar and Hanuman Garhi, the Digambari Akhara controlled this at Tirupati and their own akhara premises in Ayodhya, and the Nirmohi had been granted rights at the Rama Janmabhoomi and at Ramghat in Ayodhya. So according to this evidence, there must have been portions of the Janmabhoomi that were clearly the property of the Nirmohi Akhara. Which are these portions?

'The Rama Chabutara, Sita Rasoi, Bhandar Griha and Sant Nivas used to be under the possession of the Nirmohi Akhara till 1982. Then the court attached these portions. But in the 30 September 2010 judgement, they again made references to these portions as part of the Nirmohi claim. Somewhere along the way, Baba Dharamdas also took control of portions of this land and destroyed evidence.' This is when Tarunjeet pales and says, 'You know him? Oh he is a very bad man . . .'

Tarunjeet's family's representation of the Nirmohi Akhara is definitely one of the oldest links to the beginning of the Ayodhya title suit. But there is a corresponding political game plan that increased the significance of the milestones in the case. When Mahant Raghubar Das' claim seeking to build a temple was dismissed by the Faizabad court in the 1880s it seemed to be an example of great judicial good sense. Following the placing of the idols in the mosque in December 1949, the structure was attached and placed in the custody of receiver Priya Dutt Ram, appointed by the Faizabad additional city magistrate. The court authorities arrived at a scheme for administering the property. A pujari was appointed for puja to be continued at the site.

By January 1950, two additional cases had been filed in this matter and the idols remained in place, where, from 26 April 1955, pilgrims began getting free entry for puja and darshan at the site. This is when the Nirmohi Akhara entered the fray a second time, filing a suit on 17 December 1959 against the receiver. The UP government staked its own claim over the property. Two years later, on 18 December 1961, the Sunni Central Wakf Board filed their own suit for the structure to be declared a mosque, for the plot surrounding it to be handed over to it, and for the removal of idols and other articles.

From 1964, when all four cases were combined into one titile suit, everything stayed dormant for years. The only activity linked to the Janmabhoomi was the resonance of *kirtans*, described by Peter Van der Weer in *God Must Be Liberated! A Hindu Liberation Movement in Ayodhya*. He writes, 'From 1950 the members of the Rama Janmabhumi Seva Committee obtained permission to worship Ram's idol once a year on the night of 22 to 23 December. Besides that, the committee organized a so-called uninterrupted devotional singing (*akhand kirtan*) in front of the mosque, as long as the birthplace was not liberated. The execution of this activity was given into the hands of a sadhu Ram Lakhan Saran, who was succeeded by Ram Dayal Saran in the sixties.' The kirtan was a fund-raising activity, and the celebrations around the Prakatya Divas (Day of the Appearance) on 22-23 December every year were spectacular, with an elephant and procession being led through Ayodhya's streets. This has been described to me by some Ayodhya old-timers like Ram Sharan Das and Sri Krishna Madhukar.

Still, all this was just part of Ayodhya's day-to-day existence, where property disputes mark every family's history, and Sri Rama is worshipped on multiple dates in an annual calendar. The people of a nation did not have to be roused to raise blood-curdling slogans or spill hate on the streets, to continue with these activities.

The legal and political history of Ayodhya began to converge in a frightening manner from 1984. Van der Weer describes the initial meeting of the VHP on the banks of the Sarayu on 7 October 1984 thus. '. . . a platform had been erected on a stretch of wasteland near the river. On the side of the platform facing the audience, a large painting was fixed representing a fight between Muslims with swords and sadhus without weapons. On the platform, a rather large group of sadhus took their places, while between the platform and the audience some room was left for the press. As far as I could see, only some five to seven thousand people had come to listen to the speeches. This seemed a disappointing number, since Ayodhya is a pilgrimage centre which attracts regularly thousands of pilgrims; and, on festivals, even hundreds of thousands. The Hindu press was not taken aback by this number, however, and inflated it to fifty thousand and in some papers even to a hundred thousand, numbers which were taken over by the national press.' While we can take Van der Weer's 'Hindu press' to mean the regional Hindi papers which had earlier been accused of peddling hugely exaggerated accounts by Beeru (*see* Chapter 20), what is of more interest is his description of those who were on the stage, and spoke at the meeting.

Van der Weer continues, 'The office-bearers of the VHP who spoke at the meeting were an abbot of the Gorakhnath jogis from Gorakhpur, Mahant Avaidyanath, and a former Congress (I) minister of Uttar Pradesh, D. Khanna. They spoke about the disgrace that although India had become independent in 1947, Hindus were still second-rate citizens, who did not even have access to their most sacred places. After them a few sadhus from Ayodhya came forward. The most powerful speech was delivered by Paramhans Ramachandra Das, the active abbot of the Digambar Akhara of the Ramanandi order. He asked loudly: "Where are the Ramanandis of Ayodhya? Does it not interest them that their god is in a Muslim jail?" . . . The sadhus of Ayodhya were succeeded by a seemingly unending row of religious leaders, belonging to various religious orders, and coming from regions as far apart as

Panjab and Kerala. Their speeches all amounted to the same message, but one recurring theme has to be mentioned here. The audience was asked repeatedly to give their vote only to those parties which explicitly promised to give the Hindus their sacred places back. We have to realize that all this happened before the murder of Mrs Gandhi, who had announced that general elections were to be held in the beginning of 1985. The liberation movement was, therefore, perfectly timed for putting pressure on the politicians.'

If the politicization of the Ayodhya title suit from 1984 have become common knowledge, we still need to know – how and where did it all begin? A long and detailed conversation I had recorded on video in 2005 with Shitla Singh brought many startling facts to light.

Communalism reared its head around the Ayodhya issue from the 1948 by-election for the Faizabad-Ayodhya assembly seat, according to Shitla Singh. 'There was no Jan Sangh or VHP then. In 1948, the Congress Socialist Party split from the Congress, and 18 MLAs resigned from the UP Assembly. One of them was Acharya Narendra Dev from Faizabad, and another was Sarabjit Lal (Tarunjeet Varma's grandfather). When Acharya Narendra Dev decided to contest the by-election again, the Congress put up Baba Raghav Das, a sadhu from Gorakhpur, as their candidate from Ayodhya. The belief behind this was that the strengthening of Hindu roots would be good for the Congress in Ayodhya. By positioning a religious man against a popular leader like Acharya Narendra Dev, who had been at various times an atheist, a Marxist, and a Buddhist, the Congress was playing the communal card. Besides, the assertion of their candidate Baba Raghav Das was, "We should avoid Gandhian secularism." Jawaharlal Nehru refused to come to Ayodhya to campaign for Baba Raghav Das, ostensibly because he was supposed to have said that the candidate was strong enough, and did not require his intervention. Then in 1949, we actually have a letter dated 10 July 1949, from Kehar Singh, then joint secretary in the UP government, to K.K. Nayar, the Faizabad DM, saying, "Sir, please send us the plan of where you want the temple to be built", to which we also have Nayar replying, "It is nazul land. There is no problem except that there is a masjid at the spot." Subsequently, nothing is heard of this plan, but there was an appointment of one Sadiq as DM, and he is said to have asked to see the plan. He may have shot it down.'

If Shitla Singh points to the Congress as being the first to bring religion into the political arena at Ayodhya, many (including Van der Weer) have also made mention of Daudayal Khanna, a Congress minister in the UP government, who later became very close to the VHP. Sharad Sharma described the circumstances of his joining the saffron camp; it revolved around having beef thrown at him when he had organized a camp to serve food and water to ordinary devotees at some religious mela. The irony was that he was serving Muslims when this happened. After the incident, he turned bitter.

The VHP leadership in turn had reason to be very upset after the death of Mrs Gandhi in 1984. The resultant sympathy wave swept every other party out of electoral reckoning in the elections that followed. According to Shitla Singh, frustration crept into the VHP's ranks. 'There was a meeting of the VHP in 1986 at Paramhans' house, at which Avaidyanath appealed to me,' reveals Shitla Singh. 'He said, "*Baccha, ee logan ka kewal vote aur note chahi* (son, these people only want notes and votes). You help to get this temple built."'

Shitla Singh recalls saying he would, there was no problem. 'The Muslims are ready. The temple can come up on the Rama

Chabutara and the acquired land, as long as the masjid remains intact, I told them,' he says. 'Deoki Nandan Agrawal (Rama Lalla's friend in the 1989 title suit) was also at that meeting. So was DGP Sirishchandra Dikshit, Daudayal Khanna and Nritya Gopal Das. I said, let there be a temple trust made up only of people from Ayodhya. I have spoken to Shahabuddin and the Muslim leaders, and they have no objection. On 26 December 1986, two of the publications of the Sangh – the *Organiser* and *Panchjanya* – published this news as a lead story, saying, "*Rama ki jai hui!* (Rama emerged victorious)" and mentioned that Shri Shitla Singh, close confidante of the CM, was going to be the secretary of the trust. Soon after this, there was pressure on me from various quarters to have members from outside Ayodhya in the trust.'

But the culmination of the story is chilling. Apparently, a mere week after the publication of the article in the *Organiser* and *Panchajanya* lauding Singh's initiative, the meek figure of Ashok Singhal stood before Shri Balasaheb Deoras at Keshav Sadan in Jhandewalan. 'I had actually been speaking to Bhausaheb Deoras, through a mutual friend, Nirmala Deshpandeji,' says Shitla Singh. 'But the announcement of the trust and temple being built with mutual efforts did not go down well with Balasaheb Deoras. He is said to have scolded Singhal and reminded him, "There are crores of temples to Sri Rama in this country! We don't really need another one. What we need is to be in power. How is it that you haven't understood this so far?" Ashok Singhal crept out, chastised, and communicated a new message to his peers and subordinates within the organization immediately. The same *Organiser* and *Panchjanya*, which had praised my efforts, began to adopt a much shriller tone immediately after, and indulged in their sabre-rattling,' says Shitla Singh. '*Sampradayikta inki rajnaitik avashyakta rahi hai* (communalism has been a political necessity for them).'

Tarunjeet Varma says that what Shitla Singh has described must undoubtedly have taken place, but his role as the leading light for the solution of the mandir-masjid crisis would have been in jeopardy anyway in due course. 'It is all a matter of perception,' he says. 'Shitlaji is considered a man with Leftist leanings. Sooner or later the religious groups would have had a problem with him.'

So how can a solution be found today? Is there any hope for this matter, I ask the lawyer. 'It may take a decade more, but the issue will get solved,' says Tarunjeet. 'A higher authority may have to step in and involve local players. People have become more educated and aware. Muslims have also become more educated and their approach has changed to all this. Privately, many admit that they are reconciled to the idea of a temple at the spot.'

About his immediate strategy, Varma has no specific targets, except that he has joined all the other concerned parties in appealing against the 30 September 2010 judgement in the Ayodhya title suit in the Supreme Court. 'This was an absolute necessity only because the order given is impossible to execute. The kind of three-way division recommended by the court will be practically impossible to carry out.'

'But you will remain open to a solution in the larger interests of the nation?' I ask him. 'Just because you have been fighting over the land, you will not forget what this judgement means to the country, no?' 'Of course, I'll remember,' he replies. 'Why talk about India? Ayodhya's own soul has been entrapped since 1992.'

Finding a solution to the Ayodhya crisis also means proving that the soul of the town and this country are really no different. What hurts and imprisons one must necessarily hurt and imprison the other.

Epilogue

Towards the end of this book, I went as an ordinary visitor to the Rama Janmabhoomi. This sprawling, heavily barricaded complex illustrates the failure of the Indian state like no other place. It is not in some remote border area, but in India's most populous and mainstream state. It does not have the vaguest resemblance to a place of worship, but looks, and is, a fortified battle zone, where any suspicious action can have you shot in seconds.

At one of the many points where one is frisked and relieved of belongings – pens, belts, or something equally commonplace – I asked to see Manas Bhavan. A burly policeman in mufti immediately pricked up his ears. 'Where have you come from?' he asked. 'Faizabad,' I replied. 'And you have come for a darshan?' he asked, looking thunderstruck. 'Yes,' I said again. He shook his head, looking unconvinced. The thought that anyone local could actually come to the Janmabhoomi to seek a darshan seemed incredible to him. And it's true. Local people avoid going to the Janmabhoomi, unless they are accompanying curious or devout visitors and guests.

In March 2011, more than five months after the 30 September 2010 Lucknow High Court judgement in the Ayodhya title suit, Ayodhya has returned to the national news – this time because the CBI has sought a review of the cases in the Supreme Court against leaders like L.K. Advani and Bal Thackeray for their role in the events leading up to the demolition of the Babri Masjid. A baffled bench, angry about the long gap between the May 2010 order of the high court upholding the dropping of the charges of conspiracy against the leaders, and the application by the CBI of quashing this order, reportedly asked the CBI lawyers, 'With what face are you coming to us now?'

But that is the way it is in our country, where justice is often deliberately delayed or denied by powerful vested interests. The judicial process is used more to cover up the omissions and commissions of the executive rather than sharpen its policies. If the Ayodhya issue has remained a problem for so many decades, it is because there has been no attempt to solve this issue through actual dialogue and affirmative action. The title suit has been left to fester in court. The national drama of shilanyas, shila pujan and such other orchestrated events, designed for maximum emotional impact, were allowed to continue until they had done lasting damage to the fabric of the nation.

Following the September 2010 judgement, two parties attempted a dialogue of sorts – the initiatives of Mahant Gyandas and Hashim Ansari. But this has also not achieved lasting results because it has stayed isolated – there has been virtually no official approval of their ideas; nobody from the state or Central government has acknowledged their work. Only the local Hindi papers regularly report their attempts.

In January and February 2011, three meetings took place between industrialist Sanjay Dalmia and the main parties who have been engaged in fighting the title suit, besides some other prominent citizens of Ayodhya and officers, at Delhi, Lucknow and Ayodhya. This private attempt was backed by an offer from Mr Dalmia to spend the crores necessary to build a multi-faith centre at the spot. However, local parties have termed this a 'fast-food' solution that will not be acceptable to any of the parties. Since Dalmia was making this offer in his personal capacity, and was not backed by any mature communicator who could have presented things differently, this initiative too does not seem as if it will achieve its objective.

At present, things remain stagnant in Ayodhya, with all the parties – the Nirmohi Akhara, Sunni Wakf Board and the friends of Rama Lalla having approached the Supreme Court to appeal against the September 2010 verdict.

Meanwhile, on a different level, a secular initiative has taken shape in Ayodhya in recent months. This is the setting up of the Sarva Dharma Sadbhav Kendra (Multi-faith Harmony Centre) a trust registered in August 2011, of which Yugal Kishor Sharan Shastri is the Managing Trustee, with Zafar Saifullah, former cabinet secretary to the Government of India, and Dr Sandeep Pandey being guiding spirits and fellow trustees. Designs for this centre are being sought from different architects for a resource centre, library, and meditation hall. One of the designs visualized a seven-storey building, with a floor for each of the major faiths of the country, including one for atheists! While the physical structure of this centre may take some time to shape up, it has already begun conducting regular programmes such as workshops and inter-faith seminars. So what of this book? It would have served its purpose if, reading it, people are able to ask themselves any of the following questions, that push towards a solution:

Will a more just and inclusive model of development prevent the creation of more Ayodhyas?

Do the answers to the temple issue lie in the development of the town itself?

Have we learnt our lessons from the years preceding 6 December 1992?

Will we again permit politics to use emotional triggers like 'faith', 'national pride' and 'identity' to amass followers? Or will we work hard to enforce accountability from our leaders? Is the long-standing problem in Ayodhya also partly a failure of the secular, educated, privileged classes to communicate with their fellow citizens?

And if so, does a deeply religious society like India need a new model of secularism to communicate the ideals of truth, justice, honesty and kindness to all?

Only time will tell.

SCHARADA DUBEY
Faizabad, March 2011

Glossary

Akhara: Used to denote a wrestling arena, this word also describes the group to which a sadhu belongs. There are Shaivite (worshippers of Shiva) and Vaishnav (worshippers of Vishnu) akharas among sadhus. The 'Juna' akhara referred to during Kumbh melas is a Shaivite akhara, while the akharas referred to in this book are Ramanandi Vaishnav sects. 'Ani' is a term referring to the military aspect of the akhara.

Chela: Follower or disciple. This term is loosely used in Ayodhya even to describe admirers and hangers on.

Chadhaava: The offerings in cash and kind that pilgrims make at various temples. Some believe that the fight for a Rama Janmabhoomi temple is an attempt to wrest control of such offerings from Hanuman Garhi and Mani Ram ki Chhavani, presently receiving the lion's share. Whether or not this is true, the economics of temple affairs definitely plays a part in the power equations of this town.

Gaddinashin: The figurative head of the Hanuman Garhi temple. The name is a Persian expression meaning 'one who occupies the throne'. It is in Persian because the temple's bye-laws are in this language. Nawab Safdarjang gave land to Abhay Ram Das, of the Nirvani Akhara, for building a temple on 'Hanuman Garhi' or Hanuman's hill. Asaf-ud-Daulah's diwan, Tikait Rai, helped build the fortress-like temple on this land.

Gurubhai: A 'gurubhai' is someone with whom one has shared a guru. In the tradition of Hinduism, this is a special bond, since it implies being like a sibling within the family one has adopted after becoming a renunciate, that is, the guru as parent, and the others as one's peers, to be held in affection and loyalty.

Bhandaara: Large community feast, literally referring to an abundance, in the form of 'bhandaar' or a storehouse. This is the main form of canvassing for public support by the matts and mandirs of Ayodhya. There are people who go from one bhandaara to another, eating what they can. Sadhus subsist on bhandaaras, and visiting pilgrims are also given food by certain temples.

Jhaanki: A richly decorated, resplendent glimpse of a deity. The specially decorated figures of Rama-Sita-Lakshman, completely decked in flowers, are a special annual draw at the Kanak Behari temple. The Awadh tradition of the Ramlila emphasizes this tableaux in its presentation.

Mela: Large gathering, usually a fair or carnival. Ayodhya has four well-defined melas – the Saawan ka mela in July-August, the Parikrama mela in October-November, the Chait Rama Navami mela in March-April and the Rama Vivaah mela in December-January.

Mahant: A senior priest, of some years' standing, who is in charge of a mandir (temple) or matt.

Mandir, matt: A mandir is a temple. If a temple is well-established and has the resources to house several pujaris and other dependents, it becomes a matt.

Panda: The guides who will take you anywhere in town, as well as help you to perform certain pujas in temples. A panda is part of a well-oiled network that works with hotel owners, tour operators, priests and pujaris to give you the complete Ayodhya experience. Many have a rudimentary knowledge of several Indian languages.

Parikrama: The circumambulation of a deity or divine location. The Chaudah Kosi parikrama, which is roughly forty-two kilometres long, and the Panch Kosi of around fourteen kilometres are very important annual events in Ayodhya. Lakhs of pilgrims arrive from rural areas like Gonda, Basti, Bahraich, Sitapur, Hardoi, Gorakhpur and elsewhere, to participate in these every year in October-November. Parikrama dates are announced according to the Hindu lunar calendar.

Sadhu: An ascetic who has received diksha or initiation by a guru and leads a life of renunciation from ordinary domesticity. A sadhu is distinct from a pujari, who can be a married man performing temple duties, although both may look similar in appearance, with long beards and foreheads adorned with tilaks (devotional markings worn on the forehead).

Bibliography

Veer, Peter van der, 'Taming the Ascetic: Devotionalism in a Hindu Monastic Order', *Man, New Series*, Vol. 22, No. 4 (Dec., 1987), Royal Anthropological Institute of Great Britain and Ireland, UK, pp. 680-95
    Stable URL: http://www.jstor.org/stable/2803358

Veer, Peter van der, *God Must Be Liberated! A Hindu Liberation Movement in Ayodhya*
    Stable URL: http://igitur-archive.library.uu.nl/UC/2005-0622-191327/4858.pdf

Agrawal, Purushottam, 'In Search of Ramanand—The Guru of Kabir and Others', *Pratilipi*, March to June 2010.

Nandy, Ashis, Shikha Trivedy, Shail Mayaram, Achyut Yagnik, *Creating a Nationality: The Ramjanmabhumi Movement and Fear of the Self*, Oxford India Paperbacks, 2005.